JOININGS

Compound Words in Old English Literature

Joinings

Compound Words in Old English Literature

JONATHAN DAVIS-SECORD

UNIVERSITY OF TORONTO PRESS
Toronto Buffalo London

Toronto Buffalo London
www.utppublishing.com

ISBN 978-1-4426-3739-9

Library and Archives Canada Cataloguing in Publication

Davis-Secord, Jonathan, author
Joinings : compound words in Old English literature / Jonathan Davis-Secord.

(Toronto Anglo-Saxon series)
Includes bibliographical references and index.
ISBN 978-1-4426-3739-9 (bound)

1. English language – Old English, ca. 450–1100 – Compound words.
2. English literature – Old English, ca. 450–1100 – History and criticism.
3. English language – Old English, ca. 450–1100 – Style. 4. English language – Old English, ca. 450–1100 – Grammar. 5. Language and culture – England – To 1500. I. Title. II. Series: Toronto Anglo-Saxon series

PR173.D385 2016 829′.09 C2015-908296-X

This book was published with the generous assistance of the Book Subvention Award from the Medieval Academy of America.

University of Toronto Press acknowledges the financial assistance to its publishing program of the Canada Council for the Arts and the Ontario Arts Council, an agency of the Government of Ontario.

Canada Council for the Arts Conseil des Arts du Canada

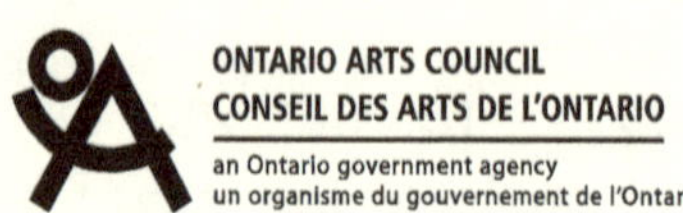

Funded by the Government of Canada Financé par le gouvernement du Canada

Canada

To SCDS, both of you

Contents

Acknowledgments

I have benefitted tremendously from the training, advice, and support of many people and institutions in writing this book. This network in fact took form before I even imagined this book, beginning with the excellent instruction and inspiration provided by my professors at Brandeis University, especially Joan Maling, who first taught me linguistics and Old English, and Mary Baine Campbell, who first taught me how to write and how to be a medievalist. I subsequently benefitted from the friendship and encouragement of the amazing community of faculty, graduate students, and their spouses at the University of Notre Dame, especially Scott Smith and Renée Trilling, both of whom generously read and commented on parts of this book, and Calvin Bower and Brian Krostenko, both of whom gave generously of their time to train me in elements fundamental to but often hidden in this book. I continue to benefit greatly from my current colleagues at the University of New Mexico, especially Helen Damico, Timothy Graham, and Anita Obermeier. At the University of Toronto Press, I frequently tested the patience of and relied on the expertise of Suzanne Rancourt and Barb Porter. Institutionally, I have received important support from Notre Dame's Medieval Institute, the Dolores Zohrab Liebmann Fund, the English Department at the University of New Mexico, the British Library, Oxford's Bodleian Library, and the Medieval Academy of America. Without this network, this book would not be half of what it is now, although all mistakes remain my own.

Several people deserve special thanks for their enduring and uplifting support. My family on all sides has provided inspiration and motivation throughout and in the most difficult moments, especially my parents-in-law, Terry and Catherine Davis, and my parents, William and Linda Secord, whose unflagging encouragement allowed me to begin this journey in the first place. My dissertation co-directors, Michael Lapidge and Katherine O'Brien O'Keeffe, were instrumental not only in teaching and advising me but also in further kindling my love for Anglo-Saxon studies. They guided me expertly, and I am particularly grateful for their support over the past several years as I transitioned onto the tenure track. Without these people, this book would not exist.

Finally, I am more grateful than I can express for the love and support of my wife, Sarah, and my daughter, Sage. You enrich my life beyond measure and make me a better person. Without you, this book would mean nothing.

Abbreviations

ASE	*Anglo-Saxon England*
ASPR	Anglo-Saxon Poetic Records
BT	Joseph Bosworth, *An Anglo-Saxon Dictionary*, ed. and enlarged by T. Northcote Toller (1898; Oxford: Oxford University Press, 1973)
CCSL	Corpus Christianorum, Series Latina
CH I	Peter Clemoes, ed., *Ælfric's Catholic Homilies: The First Series, Text*, EETS s.s. 17 (Oxford: Oxford University Press, 1997)
CH II	Malcolm Godden, ed. *Ælfric's Catholic Homilies: The Second Series, Text*, EETS s.s. 5 (London: Oxford University Press, 1979)
CSASE	Cambridge Studies in Anglo-Saxon England
DOE	*Dictionary of Old English: A to G*, ed. Angus Cameron, Ashley Crandell Amos, and Antonette diPaolo Healey (Toronto: University of Toronto Press, 2007)
DOEC	*Dictionary of Old English Corpus on the World Wide Web*, compiled by Antonette diPaolo Healey with John Price Wilkin and Xin Xiang (Toronto: Dictionary of Old English Project, 2009)
EETS	Early English Text Society
JEGP	*Journal of English and Germanic Philology*
Lewis and Short	Charleton T. Lewis and Charles Short, *A Latin Dictionary* (1879; Oxford: Clarendon Press, 1989)
LS	Ælfric, *Lives of Saints*
NM	*Neuphilologische Mitteilungen*

JOININGS

1 Connecting Grammar, Style, and Culture

Ælfric prefaces his treatise on grammar and rhetoric with the following explanation of its motivation: "stæfcræft is seo cæg, ðe ðæra boca andgit unlicð" [grammar is the key that unlocks the meaning of those books].[1] This seemingly obvious statement actually expresses a complicated, fundamental paradigm for Anglo-Saxon linguistic art that hides several important assumptions and itself serves as a key to understanding Old English literature. Ælfric does not simply claim that grammar reveals the meaning of a sentence by organizing its syntax. Rather, *stæfcræft* construes Latin *grammatica*, which connotes a vastly larger set of meanings and relationships than the modern sense of "grammar." *Grammatica* became a foundation of medieval culture, producing the literacy that alone allowed comprehension of the Christian literary canon and membership in an international community linked and defined by Latin.[2] *Andgit*, which *stæfcræft* unlocks in Ælfric's formulation, has more complicated connotations as well, going beyond "meaning" in any restricted sense to become an intrinsic part of Christian faith in Ælfric's homilies.[3] The specific locks opened by *stæfcræft* thus give access to those homilies as collections of Christian knowledge and faith. This *cæg*, then, is in fact a combination – a joining – of multiple

1 Zupitza, *Ælfrics Grammatik*, 2. See the discussions of this sentence in Menzer, "Ælfric's *Grammar*," 642–4; Hill, "Learning Latin," 7–8; and Menzer, "Ælfric's English *Grammar*," 124. Unless otherwise noted, all translations of Old English and Latin are my own, and all editorial and diacritical marks are omitted.

2 Irvine, *The Making of Textual Culture*, 1. See also Copeland, *Rhetoric, Hermeneutics, and Translation*, 9, and Hill, "Learning Latin," 7–8.

3 Menzer, "Ælfric's *Grammar*," 645.

levels of language and meaning, from basic grammar through rhetorical style to forms of knowledge within a Christian cultural framework. It is this subtle but fundamental joining of grammar, style, and culture that concerns this book, which investigates the relationships between minute linguistic details and their larger contexts of style and culture.

Compound words specifically effect this intersection of grammar, style, and culture most completely in Old English. As the joining of two words, each compound involves fundamental processes of grammar and semantics, while simultaneously forming an essential stylistic feature of Old English literature that produces meanings in culturally specific ways. No other Old English linguistic feature bridges the supposed divides between basic word formation, rhetorical traditions, and cultural practices. *Joinings: Compound Words in Old English Literature* focuses therefore on the different uses of compound words in a variety of texts from several different moments in Old English literary history to uncover several important joinings: word with word, grammar with rhetoric, and style with culture. Informed by this paradigm of joining, the following chapters examine the fundamental role of compound words in Old English literature and thereby present a new understanding of the vernacular literature of the Anglo-Saxons and their theories of language and literature.

This paradigm of joining, unfortunately, never overtly appears in any Anglo-Saxon text. Indeed, no Anglo-Saxon treatise on the vernacular survives, and any account of a vernacular theory of language and literature ultimately requires reconstruction from indirect sources.[4] Ælfric's comments regarding *stæfcræft* seem to apply to his Old English homilies, and his bilingual *Grammar* may extend the Latin grammatical tradition to the vernacular, but his treatise nonetheless applies the paradigm explicitly only to Latin. Even if Ælfric was indeed "the first writer to commend and practice the study of English grammar and style by the methods applicable to Latin," how did Anglo-Saxons conceive of vernacular linguistic art before him?[5]

4 See the discussions in Robinson, "Two Aspects of Variation," 125; Gneuss, "The Study of Language," 82; and Law, *Grammar and Grammarians*, 200.

5 Sisam, "The Order of Ælfric's Early Books," 301; see also Menzer, "Ælfric's *Grammar*," 645, and Gretsch, "Ælfric, Language and Winchester," 119. Law, *Grammar and Grammarians*, 212–13, dissents, maintaining a conservative view that Ælfric's *Grammar* functions solely to explain Latin grammar. At the very least, Ælfric's treatise exposes the reality that Old English can to some extent be analysed with the same terms and systems as Latin, which may have been a revelation to some Anglo-Saxons. Dumitrescu, "Bede's

Comments on "vulgar" poets or poetry suggest rare snippets of insight but generally fail to fulfil their promises, as with Bede's description of rhythmic verse:

> Videtur autem rithmus metris esse consimilis, quae est uerborum modulata conpositio, non metrica ratione, sed numero syllabarum ad iudicium aurium examinata, ut sunt carmina uulgarium poetarum.[6]
>
> Now rhythmic verse seems entirely similar to quantitative metrical verse, in that it is the measured arrangement of words scanned not in the manner of quantitative metre but by the number of syllables according to the judgment of the ears, as are the songs of "vulgar" poets.

Bede here compares Latin rhythmical poetry, which relies on natural rhythm and the number of syllables rather than the quantitative weight of syllables, to what he terms "vulgar" poetry. This characterization suggests an awareness of vernacular poetics, but Bede goes on to cite examples of rhythmic verse in Latin only, since his concern remains composition in Latin. The applicability of his comments to the vernacular, then, remains tangential at best, and *vulgar* may not denote the vernacular at all in this instance.[7] Ælfric's exhortation to read for spiritual meaning, discussed in detail below, perhaps provides something close to an expression of the process of composition and interpretation in the vernacular. His comments, however, draw very clearly on a patristic, Latin conception of interpreta-

Liberation Philology," 45, claims that Bede (indirectly) posited "that spoken English has a discernible grammatical structure and can thus be acquired through the same pedagogical processes as written Latin." This claim, however, is based on her interpretation of the miracle giving speech to a mute boy in Book 5, chapter 2, of the *Historia ecclesiastica* and not on any clear statements by Bede. Thornbury, *Becoming a Poet*, discusses Anglo-Saxons' conceptions of poets from a cultural standpoint, but not their conceptions of poetry in technical, stylistic terms.

6 Kendall, *De arte metrica*, in *Bedae Venerabilis Opera, Pars I*, 138.

7 Kendall, *Libri II De arte metrica*, 161, translates *vulgar* as "common," adding in 161n92 that "[t]empting as it is to assume that Bede is here referring to poets writing in their native Anglo-Saxon tongue, it is more likely that he has in mind composers of crudely isosyllabic, non-quantitative Latin poems." For more on the meaning of *rithmus*, see Crocker, "*Musica rhythmica*"; Stevens, *Words and Music*; and Fassler, "Accent, Meter, and Rhythm." For a discussion of this issue with regard to Old English poetry, see Cable, *Meter and Melody*, and Cable, "Meter and Musical Implications."

tion and epistemology, and they, like Bede's, focus on understanding the Latin text of the Bible, not an Old English text.[8]

Bede's account of Cædmon of course touches on vernacular composition, but again only tangentially, giving a Latin translation of the *Hymn* and noting the difficulty of translating from one language to another with little comment on the original.[9] The rest of Cædmon's story and other descriptions of vernacular performers give tantalizing hints, but no actual details on theories of vernacular linguistic art. For example, the characterization of the thane celebrating Beowulf's victory over Grendel provides just the barest of information:

Hwilum cyninges þegn,
guma gilphlæden, gidda gemyndig,
se ðe eal fela ealdgesegena
worn gemunde, word oþer fand
soðe gebunden; secg eft ongan
sið Beowulfes snyttrum styrian
ond on sped wrecan spel gerade,
wordum wrixlan;[10]

Every so often, the king's thane, a man heaped with glorious words and mindful of songs, who remembered a great quantity of old tales, found other words bound in truth; the man began again wisely to recite Beowulf's achievement and skillfully to recount a fitting tale, to exchange his words.

This description is remarkably imprecise. The mentions of memory and variation can be taken as indications of an oral-traditional poet, but

8 For discussions of this tradition as it informs Old English literature, see Horner, "Spiritual Truth and Sexual Violence," 662–70; Horner, "The Violence of Exegesis"; and Horner, *The Discourse of Enclosure*, 134–6.

9 Colgrave and Mynors, *Bede's Ecclesiastical History*, IV, c. xxiv, concentrates on the different order of words ("ordo ipse verborum") as the main issue with no comment on the reason for the difference.

10 Fulk, Bjork, and Niles, *Klaeber's Beowulf*, lines 867b–874a. See the discussions of this passage in Nolan and Bloomfield, "*Beotword*, *Gilpcwidas*, and the *Gilphlæden* Scop of *Beowulf*," and Niles, "*Beowulf*," 37–9.

they remain vague.[11] The exact meanings of the terms for what the thane remembers – *gidda* and *ealdgesegena* – are also unclear.[12] The description of the poet varying his words seems more securely informative, but the penchant for *word* to refer to large discourse units rather than single words or phrases muddies the waters again.[13] While the passage itself seems to exemplify the concept of variation, that correspondence may simply be wishful thinking, given the terseness and lack of detail of the phrase "wordum wrixlan."[14] Moreover, these characterizations may simply be traditional and not representative of actual practice.[15] Unfortunately, the passage's utility as a self-conscious reflection on poetic process wavers upon detailed investigation. As a result of such wavering, investigations of Anglo-Saxon vernacular poetics rely on comparison and analogy.[16] That statement is by no means a condemnation but simply a recognition of the nature of the evidence that we have.

Ultimately, we are left with no direct expression of an Anglo-Saxon theory of vernacular language and literature, with even the most promising commentary failing to provide rigorous and reliable detail. The following discussion therefore triangulates from three different angles to elucidate the issue. The Latin grammatical tradition, so robustly represented in Anglo-Saxon England, provides the first point of reference. At least for literate Anglo-Saxons, that tradition must have informed their conceptions of the vernacular as well. Along with the common features of the Anglo-Latin treatises, the following discussion of the Latin tradition relies heavily on Ælfric's *Grammar*, which comes the closest to porting the Latin

11 See Opland, "*Beowulf* on the Poet"; Amodio, *Writing the Oral Tradition*, 40–2; Amodio, "Res(is)ting the Singer"; and Griffith, "Old English Poetic Diction."

12 See the discussion on genre below.

13 See BT, s.v. *word*, sense II, and the discussion of *wordhord* in Mize, "The Representation of the Mind," 69–71.

14 See Greenfield, *The Interpretation of Old English Poems*, 63–4.

15 See Amodio, "Res(is)ting the Singer"; Frank, "The Search for the Anglo-Saxon Oral Poet"; Niles, "The Myth of the Anglo-Saxon Oral Poet"; and Thornbury, *Becoming a Poet*, 11–36.

16 For example, Opland, *Anglo-Saxon Oral Poetry*, relies on comparing Old English poetry to the oral traditions of the Xhosa and Zulu. Of course, Oral Theory, which is discussed in greater detail below, began as a comparative endeavour; see Parry, *The Making of Homeric Verse*.

methodology to Old English. The contiguous tradition of Old Icelandic treatises on Old Norse language and poetics forms the second point of reference and supplies an important vernacular parallel to the Latin tradition. Although the actual Icelandic texts date later than the Anglo-Saxon period, Anglo-Saxons must have known early elements of that tradition through their various contacts with Old Norse speakers. The final point of reference comes from modern theoretical perspectives, including Oral Theory and linguistic reevaluations of Old English stylistic patterns. Medieval sources provide important direct testimony, but many features of vernacular verbal art remain unexpressed in the primary sources, even the Icelandic treatises. Modern frameworks reveal important elements that complement and fill in the gaps of the two medieval treatise traditions. Triangulating from these three points of reference, this introduction lays the foundation of Anglo-Saxon theories of vernacular verbal art. It also lays out the reasons that compound words are the most completely representative distillation of those theories, motivating the contextualized analyses of compound words in the following chapters.

Although there are no extant treatises on Old English vernacular verbal art, Anglo-Saxon England boasts a tradition of native-written handbooks on Latin grammar and style.[17] Derived from classical theories and models, their characterizations of composition ultimately hinge on a fundamental concept most clearly expressed in the term *figura*, which recurs multiple times in the treatises.[18] Rather than denoting solely typological interpretation, the term *figura* in these treatises links the seemingly disparate arenas of grammar, rhetoric, and biblical exegesis, referring at various points to the different types of letters, to a word's compound status, to figures of speech, and to structures of meaning in Christian culture. This repetition of *figura* in different contexts may initially seem accidental or simply an artefact of the sources, but the concept behind each occurrence of the

---

17 Treatises survive on spelling, grammar, metrics, and rhetoric by Aldhelm, Bede, Tatwine, Boniface, Alcuin, Byrhtferth, and Ælfric. See Law, *The Insular Latin Grammarians*, 53–80; Lapidge, "Anglo-Latin Literature," 2; and Irvine, *The Making of Textual Culture*, 272.

18 For discussions of the grammatical tradition and the classical and late-antique sources for Anglo-Saxon grammatical and rhetorical treatises, see Law, *The Insular Latin Grammarians*; Knappe, *Traditionen der klassischen Rhetorik*; Law, *Grammar and Grammarians*; Knappe, "Classical Rhetoric"; Knappe, "Rhetorical Aspect"; and Steen, *Verse and Virtuosity*, 7–20.

term reveals a single understanding of language and meaning operating at multiple levels. Indeed, for Anglo-Saxons, rhetoric and grammar were not mutually exclusive domains of language: grammar was the foundation and vehicle for learning rhetoric, which then became an outgrowth of grammar.[19] Rhetoric, furthermore, was not an end unto itself but rather a means through which to understand the text fundamental to Christian culture, the Bible. *Figura*, then, while morphing to specify different individual elements at each level of language and meaning, maintains the single paradigm of joining that links all those levels, just as does Ælfric's *cæg*.

Derived from *fingo* [to fashion], the definition of which encompasses linguistic expression as well as the plastic arts, *figura* captures the senses both of creating and of adorning.[20] Furthermore, the basic sense of "to touch" expressed by *fingo* implies intervention, an intentional alteration of some medium, whether language or clay.[21] It is this open range of meaning that allows the term *figura* to play so many roles in the grammatical treatises, beginning with the basic elements of language. For example, in the discussion of the alphabet that begins Ælfric's grammatical treatise, *figura* indicates the types of letters in terms of how they are *gesceapen* [formed] in speech as vowels or various kinds of consonants.[22] This collocation of *figura* and *gesceapen*, with its basic senses of "shaping" and "creating," overtly signals the presence of intervention even at this most basic level of language. Indeed, sound itself becomes intelligible (*andgytfullic*) only through striking (*geslean*) the air and separating it so that it is no longer confused (*gemenged*).[23] This sense of meaning as the product of intervention appears again when Ælfric characterizes the process of compounding

19 Knappe, "Rhetorical Aspect," 20–1, and Gneuss, "The Study of Language," 99–100.

20 For the development and various meanings of *figura*, see Eric Auerbach, "Figura"; the essay begins with a history of the term's development from literal "plastic signification" (15) to its applications in grammar and rhetoric (11–28) before engaging with its use in typological interpretation. For discussion of *figura* in relation to Anglo-Saxon usage, see Chapman, "Composing and Joining," 45–7.

21 Accordingly, occurrences of *fingo* in Anglo-Saxon glosses refer to casting pottery and planting trees in addition to grammatical connotations; see Chapman, "Composing and Joining," 45.

22 Zupitza, *Ælfrics Grammatik*, 5. For fuller discussions of Ælfric's Old English grammatical terms, see Shook, "Aelfric's *Latin Grammar*"; Williams, "Ælfric's Grammatical Terminology"; Pàroli, "Indice della terminologia grammaticale de Aelfric"; Law, *Grammar and Grammarians*, 214–15; and Chapman, "Uterque Lingua / Ægðer Gereord."

23 Zupitza, *Ælfrics Grammatik*, 4.

words as another type of intervention by translating *composita* with *gefeged* [joined] and *figura* itself with *gefegednes* [a joining].[24] Thus, Ælfric explains the most basic elements of language, such as phonology and word formation, in terms of fashioning and intervention. Bede employs similar language regarding not phonology but rhetoric: "Quod grammatici Grece 'schema' vocant, nos habitum vel formam vel figuram recte nominamus, quia per hoc quodam modo vestitur et ornatur oratio" [What grammarians call "schema" in Greek, we rightly name "appearance" or "form" or "figure," because through it, in some way, speech is clothed and adorned].[25] Here *figura* denotes not phonological features or word formation as it does for Ælfric's treatise but rather rhetorical adornment. The sense of clothing or adorning speech through rhetoric nonetheless still activates the basic definition of *fingo*, applying the same sense of intervention to rhetoric that Ælfric's treatise applies to grammar. The base materials of words and syntax become the medium that human intervention fashions into an appealing, adorned product.

These occurrences of *figura* in different contexts are not accidental: for Bede and Ælfric, language fundamentals and rhetoric are linked. For example, although his treatises on metre and rhetoric are superficially separate, Bede considered them connected and unified, providing together a cohesive handbook.[26] Ælfric's treatise also ultimately builds a connection between grammar and rhetoric in the appendix that briefly describes the thirty divisions of grammar: with no sense of discontinuity, the appendix begins with *vox* [sound] and *littera* [letter] and moves through schemes and tropes.[27] The connection between grammar and rhetoric in Anglo-Saxon England is also clear from the standpoint of transmission: grammatical treatises are the most likely sources for Anglo-Saxon knowledge of Greek and Roman rhetorical theories.[28] The move from grammar to rhetoric in this context of transmission required not a transformation but an evolution and "extension" of functions of

24 Zupitza, *Ælfrics Grammatik*, 87, line 9 (for *composita*) and 217, line 10 and 223, line 13 (for *figura*); see Chapman, "Composing and Joining," 45–7.

25 Kendall, *De schematibus et tropis*, in *Bedae Venerabilis Opera, Pars I*, 142.

26 Kendall, *De arte metrica*, 141.

27 Zupitza, *Ælfrics Grammatik*, 289–96; for a brief discussion, see Gneuss, "The Study of Language," 88.

28 Knappe, "Rhetorical Aspect," 19–20; Knappe, "Classical Rhetoric"; and Steen, *Verse and Virtuosity*, 7–20.

language shared by both grammar and rhetoric, and this joining is distilled in the recurrences of *figura*.[29] These various uses of *figura* thus express the otherwise silent assumption in the treatises that grammar and rhetoric are in fact different expressions of the same paradigm of joining.

Anglo-Saxons pursued this extension of grammar into rhetoric not to study classical literature but rather to understand the Bible: knowledge of grammar, metre, and rhetorical style were essential tools for the full comprehension of Christian literature, especially scripture.[30] Early Christians had found scripture lacking in rhetorical sophistication, and they had disdained the study of rhetoric and even grammar as a result, associating them with pagan activities.[31] Latin came to Britain, on the other hand, inextricably bound up with Christianity: Anglo-Saxons had to study Latin grammar in order to gain even basic access to the textual culture of their new religion.[32] Bede discusses the Roman alphabet and the letters that it borrowed from Greek as overtly Christian, demonstrating that Christianity permeated every aspect of his culture, even the most fundamental elements of language.[33] Ælfric considers even vowel length to be connected to religious meaning, for example, pressing for *pater* to be pronounced with a long *ā* when referring to God the Father in prose rather than the correct short *ă* in order to give greater prominence to God.[34] Grammar and its extension, rhetoric, thus became important elements of Anglo-Saxon Christian culture, and Bede and others

29 Knappe, "Rhetorical Aspect," 20–1, and Gneuss, "The Study of Language," 99–100.

30 See Curtius, *European Literature*, 46, and Irvine, *The Making of Textual Culture*, 14. Gneuss, "The Study of Language," 86, briefly suggests that Ælfric "was conversant with the debate on the relationship between grammar and the language of the scriptures"; see also Grundy, "Ælfric's Grammatical Theology." Bede's view of the exegetical function of grammar has been discussed extensively; for recent overviews, see Luhtala, "Linguistics and Theology," and Franklin, "Grammar and Exegesis."

31 Law, *Grammar and Grammarians*, 74.

32 Law, "Irish Symptoms," 82; Law, *Grammar and Grammarians*, 92; and Gneuss, "The Study of Language," 80.

33 Kendall, *De arte metrica*, 82; cited and discussed by Heikkinen, "The Christianisation of Latin Metre," 10.

34 Zupitza, *Ælfrics Grammatik*, 2, lines 9–11; cited and discussed in Gneuss, "The Study of Language," 86.

Christianized them, continuing the work begun in the late fourth and early fifth centuries.[35]

Figura also plays a major role in the larger systems of meaning in Christian culture. Bede and Ælfric both emphasize spiritual interpretations as essential to the true meaning of scripture. For them, the (Christianized) rhetorical level contains or concretely links to the historical reality and spiritual meaning of Christian culture.[36] As noted above, Ælfric exhorts his audience to find the spiritual meaning hidden within the text through the vehicle of language basics, since "stæfcræft is seo cæg, ðe ðæra boca andgit unlicð" [grammar is the key that unlocks the meaning of those books].[37] He writes in greater detail in his homily on Midlent Sunday discussing the miracle of the loaves and fish:

> Ðis wundor is swiðe micel 7 deop on getacnungum; oft gehwa gesihð fægere stafas awritene. þonne herað he ðone writere 7 þa stafas 7 nat hwæt hi mænað; Se ðe cann þæra stafa gescead. he herað heora fægernysse. 7 ræt þa stafas. 7 understent hwæt hi gemænað; on oðre wisan we scawiað metinge. 7 on oðre wisan stafas. ne gæð na mare to metinge buton þ[æt] ðu hit geseo. 7 herige; Nis na genoh þ[æt] ðu stafas scawie. buton þu hi eac ræde. 7 þ[æt] andgit understande;[38]

> This miracle is very great and profound in its meanings.[39] Often, someone sees beautiful letters written and then praises the writer and the letters without knowing what they mean. The person who has accurate knowledge of the letters, he praises their beauty and reads the letters and understands what

35 Lapidge, "Anglo-Latin Literature," 15; Law, *Grammar and Grammarians*, 74; and Heikkinen, "The Christianisation of Latin Metre," 2–4.

36 Irvine, *The Making of Textual Culture*, 293–7, and Knappe, "Classical Rhetoric," 17. See also the application of this paradigm in O'Brien O'Keeffe, *Stealing Obedience*, 112.

37 Zupitza, *Ælfrics Grammatik*, 2. On Ælfric's interest in spiritual interpretation, see Clemoes, "Ælfric," and Horner, "The Violence of Exegesis."

38 *Dominica in Media Quadragesima* (*CH* I.12) in Clemoes, *Ælfric's Catholic Homilies*, 277, lines 64–70.

39 While "meaning" alone is an adequate translation for *getacnung*, BT also gives "sign, signification, token, type," and the latter two of those options, along with the exemplary quotations provided in the entry, suggest the possible presence of typological or figural allegory specifically.

> they mean. We look at paintings in one way, but at letters in a different way. A painting needs nothing more than that you see and praise it; it is not enough for you to look at the letters unless you also read them and understand the meaning.

This passage stresses the linked importance both of figural interpretation and of fundamental grammatical learning. For Ælfric, the audience must work to reveal the hidden meanings of the miracle, and those meanings will remain inaccessible without the "accurate knowledge of the letters." An alternative translation of the phrase *cunnan gescead* ("to have accurate knowledge" in my translation) renders the phrase as "to be able to distinguish between." This sense of producing meaning through distinguishing between the letters aligns well with Ælfric's interest in explaining the Roman alphabet in his *Grammar*: the first step towards understanding meaning must be learning the distinctions between the letters. Moreover, Ælfric often uses *andgit* to denote Christian belief;[40] in that sense, grammar unlocks not just meaning, but faith. Ælfric thus links linguistic fundamentals to higher meanings and belief in the same manner as is implied by the repetitions of *figura*.

Bede influentially dissects allegory and divides it into verbal allegory and factual allegory, with a further subdivision into historical and spiritual allegory.[41] Through this system, he delineates the different types of allegory but also demonstrates their shared method of signification. Verbal allegory involves interpreting words with no real referent in the world as signs expressing something other than what is literally denoted, such as the image of a branching, fruit-bearing tree signifying the birth of Jesus to Mary in the line of David.[42] The other types of allegory – typological, tropological, and anagogical – have real referents in the world, but those referents link to another reality, such as signifying the ages of the world with the six days of creation or the beauty of divinely instilled virtues with Joseph's coat

40 Menzer, "Ælfric's *Grammar*," 645.

41 See Irvine, *The Making of Textual Culture*, 262–5 and 293–6, and Copeland and Sluiter, *Medieval Grammar and Rhetoric*, 260. On the lasting influence of Bede's subdivision of allegory, see Copeland, "Rhetoric and the Politics," and Strubel, "'Allegoria in factis' et 'allegoria in verbis.'"

42 Kendall, *De schematibus et tropis*, 165; see the discussion in Irvine, *The Making of Textual Culture*, 294–5.

of many colours.[43] Thus, in Bede's scheme, allegories are realized in one of two main spheres: rhetoric or reality, whether that reality be historical or spiritual.[44] Nonetheless, although verbal and factual allegory produce meaning through different paths, they can both reach the same end meaning,[45] and they do so through a shared hermeneutic structure. In each case, a sign and a previously unconnected signified are joined, either through linguistic means or through an interpretation of historical events. As Martin Irvine explains, "History itself can be a trope, a polysemous sign, since the structure of history is divinely ordained."[46] Importantly, Bede's allegorical signification proceeds *figurate* [figuratively],[47] bringing *figura* again into the discussion, and this understanding of allegory as an umbrella for both the rhetorical and the real expresses again the paradigm of joining seen elsewhere in the repetitions of *figura*. Bede conceives of allegory – even the historical and spiritual kinds – as an element of grammar and rhetoric, a fact further demonstrated by the inclusion of his lengthy and influential discussion of allegory in *De schematibus et tropis* along with other rhetorical devices.[48] *Figura* as allegory is a *figura* in the rhetorical sense, which is to be understood through learning the *figurae* of basic grammar. Thus, for Anglo-Saxons from Bede to Ælfric, a sense of joining characterizes and links meaning, style, lexicon, and even sound in Latin, for all those different pieces were wholly Christian and fundamentally similar.

This discussion of the Latin grammatical tradition relies on a connection between Latin and Old English, or at least an applicability of Latin language theory to Old English. This assumption reflects another, nearly ubiquitous joining: the vast majority of Old English works are either overtly related to Latin or were produced in a milieu in which the two languages mixed.[49] To cite only a few of the English-Latin intersections,

43 Kendall, *De schematibus et tropis*, 166–7; see the discussion in Irvine, *The Making of Textual Culture*, 295–6.

44 For full accounts of allegory in medieval hermeneutics, see de Lubac, *Exégèse médiévale*, and Irvine, *The Making of Textual Culture*, 244–71 and 293–6.

45 Kendall, *De schematibus et tropis*, 165; see Irvine, *The Making of Textual Culture*, 295.

46 Irvine, *The Making of Textual Culture*, 296.

47 Kendall, *De schematibus et tropis*, 166, line 239.

48 See Irvine, *The Making of Textual Culture*, 293, 295, and 296.

49 A great deal of scholarship addresses the connections between Latin and Old English; see, among others, Gneuss, "*Anglicae linguae interpretatio*"; Stanton, *The Culture of Translation*; and Timofeeva, "Anglo-Latin Bilingualism before 1066."

Aldhelm composed Latin verse employing elements of vernacular style,[50] the Alfredian translation program promoted both English and the cultural capital of Latin,[51] Cynewulf translated Latin sources into Old English poetry,[52] and Wulfstan wrote homilies in both Latin and Old English.[53] There remains, however, the challenge of fully bridging the gap between the Anglo-Saxon theory we have available, which directly addresses only Latin, and Anglo-Saxon conceptions of linguistic art composed specifically in Old English. Byrhtferth's bilingual *Enchiridion* contains sections in Old English explaining elements of grammar and style, but it again focuses on Latin texts, not vernacular.[54] Ælfric's *Grammar* gives some sense of how Anglo-Saxons might have applied one language theory to both Latin and the vernacular, but it too provides little pragmatic information for contemporary understandings of style and composition specifically in Old English.[55] His *Grammar* may suggest an otherwise unrecorded approach to grammatical studies at Winchester in the 960s and 970s, but that approach remains just a suggestion.[56] Again, we lack any significant, overt discussion of the vernacular specifically.

A second avenue to approach theories of Old English linguistic art is through Old Norse treatises on grammar and poetics. While this avenue also provides only indirect access to Anglo-Saxon conceptions of vernacular literature, it does at least yield evidence specifically on the vernacular. Literature in Old Norse certainly differs significantly from that in Old English, but the two corpora share several basic characteristics. Most fundamentally, both languages are Germanic, which allows for a less complicated set of comparisons than does Latin, an Italic language. While all three languages in question belong to the Indo-European language family and thus share some elements, the commonalities within the Germanic

50 Orchard, *The Poetic Art of Aldhelm.*

51 Discenza, *The King's English.*

52 Steen, *Verse and Virtuosity*, 110–38.

53 Hall, "Wulfstan's Latin Sermons."

54 Baker and Lapidge, *Byrhtferth's Enchiridion*, 88–93 and 162–9.

55 Menzer, "Ælfric's *Grammar*," and Menzer, "Ælfric's English *Grammar*," argue that Ælfric indeed intended his treatise to apply to English; on the other hand, Law, "Anglo-Saxon England," argues that the treatise focuses solely on Latin.

56 Gretsch, "Ælfric, Language and Winchester," 121. Gretsch notes that the grammatical terms in the Old English translation of the *Rule of Chrodegang* may support this view of the Winchester approach to grammar, citing Gneuss, "The Study of Language," 87.

branch are much more pronounced than those between branches. Of particular interest for this discussion is that Old English and Old Norse share to some extent an inherited Germanic poetic tradition, including, for example, a system of alliterative verse.[57] Anglo-Saxons had direct contact with speakers of Old Norse and, at least in a few instances, adopted elements of the Norse genre of skaldic praise poems.[58] This degree of interface consequently suggests a common understanding of vernacular poetics and literature, or at least a common awareness of the patterns. With the appropriate caveats, then, ideas concerning Old Norse vernacular poetics should prove useful for reconstructing those concerning Old English. One major caveat must be that the Old Norse treatises hail from a period later than the Anglo-Saxon period, and one must extend those theories backward in time only with great care. The importance of tradition in the treatises, however, suggests that, although they were composed after the Anglo-Saxon period, the vernacular paradigm must have endured for perhaps centuries beforehand.[59] Moreover, the early composition of the source texts employed in the treatises and the cross-linguistic influence evident

57 One of the most important and influential works on shared Germanic literary traditions is Heusler, *Die altgermanische Dichtung*. Harris, "Older Germanic Poetry," provides an excellent overview of scholarship on this issue and states that "when we find that a single basic poetics is shared across all the earliest Germanic peoples where verse is in evidence, it is reasonable to believe that the roots of this poetics follow the trail of the dialects back to the common proto-language" (255). For treatments of Germanic metre, see Lehmann, *The Development of Germanic Verse Form*; Russom, *"Beowulf" and Old Germanic Metre*; and Dance, "The Old English Language."

58 On skaldic poetry and influence in Anglo-Saxon England, see Opland, *Anglo-Saxon Oral Poetry*, 172–7; Frank, "Did Anglo-Saxon Audiences Have a Skaldic Tooth?"; Townend, "Pre-Cnut Praise-Poetry"; Townend, "Norse Poets and English Kings"; Townend, "Contextualizing the *Knútsdrápur*"; and Thornbury, *Becoming a Poet*, especially 90–1. For Anglo-Saxon interactions with Danes, see Pons Sanz, *Analysis of the Scandinavian Loanwords*; Townend, "Viking Age England as a Bilingual Society"; Hadley, "Viking and Native"; Townend, *Language and History*; Frank, "Terminally Hip and Incredibly Cool"; Pons-Sanz, *Norse-Derived Vocabulary*; Abrams, "King Edgar and the Men of the Danelaw"; and Pons-Sanz, *The Lexical Effects*.

59 Discussing the views on vernacular poetics of Snorri Sturluson, Anthony Faulkes, *Poetical Inspiration in Old Norse and Old English Poetry*, 4, posits that, "although he was writing towards the end of the period when oral skaldic poetry was cultivated in the North, it is likely that his views about poetry would have been shared by many poets and their audiences in his time and earlier."

during the Anglo-Saxon period support the application of the theories in these treatises to the earlier period.

Medieval Icelanders produced several grammatical treatises, the most significant of which was Snorri Sturluson's *Skáldskaparmál*, a portion of his *Edda*.[60] The *Edda* and the other treatises sometimes adopt the framework of Latin models but address the vernacular without reference or comparison to Latin and often provide commentary unique to vernacular composition.[61] For example, Snorri provides in-depth discussions of alliteration and rhyme that are independent of any Latin tradition and demonstrate an interest in "native poetics" specifically.[62] The *Edda* thus constitutes a "free and original treatise" on vernacular poetry,[63] and the *Third Grammatical Treatise*, by Óláfr Þórðarson, presents a "fusion" that adapts the Latin model (but not content) to explain fundamentally vernacular diction.[64] These two works, with occasional recourse to the other treatises, offer the best opportunity for gaining indirect insight into Anglo-Saxon concepts of vernacular linguistic art.

Most importantly, as in the models of the Latin tradition, the concept of intentional joining forms a fundamental connection between grammar and style in Old Norse texts. Indeed, Icelanders often present linguistic composition in much the same terms as the original connotations of *fingo*, with poets commonly describing themselves as plying a craft, analogous to metalwork or woodworking.[65] The anonymous author of the *First Grammatical Treatise* makes the comparison clearly: "Poets are the authorities in all matters of the art of speech (*rýnni*) or distinction of language (*málsgrein*), just as craftsmen [are of their craft] or lawyers of the laws" (Skáld eru hǫfundar allrar rýnni eða málsgreinar sem smíðir

60 Clunies Ross, *Skáldskaparmál*, 25–6; Nordal, *Tools of Literacy*, 206; and Clunies Ross, *Old Norse Poetry and Poetics*, 170.

61 Clunies Ross, *Skáldskaparmál*, 25, 29, and 91; Clunies Ross, *Old Norse Poetry and Poetics*, 150–1; Faulkes, *Edda: Skáldskaparmál 1*, xxxvi; and Faulkes, *Edda: Prologue and Gylfaginning*, xx–xxi. See also Tranter, *Clavis metrica*, 113–18; Faulkes, *Edda: Háttatal*, xii–xvi and 77–91; and Pálsson and Faulkes, *The Uppsala Edda*, cxv.

62 Clunies Ross, *Old Norse Poetry and Poetics*, 166; see also Tranter, *Clavis metrica*, 97.

63 Clunies Ross, *Old Norse Poetry and Poetics*, 152.

64 Nordal, *Tools of Literacy*, 206. Clunies Ross, *Skáldskaparmál*, 24, points out that both Bede and Óláfr take Donatus's *Ars maior* as the basis for their treatises, but Óláfr's text clearly departs from its source, as in the description of alliteration quoted below, while Bede's remains very faithful.

65 Clunies Ross, *Old Norse Poetry and Poetics*, 1–2, 34–9, and 84–91.

[smíðar] eða løgmenn laga).[66] Just as *figura* secondarily connotes material art in the Anglo-Saxon treatises, craftsmanship informs the First Grammarian's conception of poets. The First Grammarian's decision to employ examples of skaldic verse in his treatise on phonetics and orthography also reveals a connection between grammar and style, just as in the Anglo-Saxon treatises. Specifically, he uses passages from Old Norse poetry to create "minimal pairs" for illustrating phonemic differences.[67] Such a discussion of phonemic details clearly belongs to the grammatical aspect of medieval language theory, and skaldic poetry just as clearly involves rhetoric and stylization, but the First Grammarian considered it appropriate and perhaps even necessary to merge those two linguistic levels.

This paradigm also informs Óláfr Þórðarson's description of alliteration in terms of ship building in the *Third Grammatical Treatise*:

> Þessi figura er mjǫk hǫfð í málssnildar list, er rethorica heitir, ok er hon upphaf til kveðandi þeirrar, er saman heldr norrœnum skáldskap, svá sem naglar halda skipi saman, er smiðr gerir, ok ferr sundrlaust ella borð frá borði. Svá heldr ok þessi figura saman kveðandi í skáldskap með stǫfum þeim er stuðlar heita ok hǫfuðstafir.

> This figure is much used in the art of eloquent speech, which is called rhetoric, and it is the foundation of that poetical effect that holds together Norse poetry, just as nails hold a ship together, which a [ship]wright makes, and [which] goes in loose order or plank from plank. So too this figure holds together the poetical effect in poetry by means of those staves which are called *stuðlar* ["props, supports," alliterating letters in odd lines] and *hǫfuðstafir* [chief alliterating staves, in even lines].[68]

Alliteration holds together the poetry through a process of joining, linking discrete pieces into one whole. Notably, Óláfr employs the

66 Benediktsson, *The First Grammatical Treatise*, 224–7; quoted, normalized, and translated with bracketed and parenthetical comments by Clunies Ross, *Old Norse Poetry and Poetics*, 154.

67 Clunies Ross, *Old Norse Poetry and Poetics*, 154–5.

68 Magnússon Ólsen, *Den Tredje og Fjærde Grammatiske Afhandling i Snorres Edda*, 96–7; quoted, normalized, and translated by Clunies Ross, *Old Norse Poetry and Poetics*, 87.

term *figura* here, revealing his debt to the structure and terminology of Latin treatises. Nonetheless, his topic and comments in this instance are decidedly vernacular, given the conception of alliteration as a fundamental aspect of poetry rather than an adornment of speech, which is its category in the Latin tradition. The overt characterization of poets as shipwrights accords well with the implied senses of intervention and art connoted by *figura*, marking another important consonance between vernacular and Latin treatments of composition. Conceiving of a *figura* as a "foundation" is especially telling. On one hand, as noted above, figures of speech are generally presented as linguistic ornaments; indeed, the traditional title for Óláfr's discussion of figures of speech is "Knowledge of the Ornaments of Diction" (*Málskrúðsfræði*).[69] On the other hand, alliteration for Óláfr is clearly not an adornment but a necessity in poetry. Employing the term *figura* for a necessary, intrinsic feature thus makes the same connection between fundamental elements of linguistic structure and aspects of style as discussed above, with a single paradigm of human intervention and arrangement applying at all levels of form and style.

For Snorri and Óláfr, another fundamental aspect of Norse poetry consists of the kenning.[70] A kenning is a deeply allusive simile compressed into a single compound word or phrase that often approximates a riddle in its semantics. A classic example in Old English is *merehengest*, which literally means "sea horse" but actually signifies "ship" through the implication that a ship sails on water like a horse gallops on land. Snorri specifies kennings as one of the most important features of Old Norse poetry, and their centrality to Norse poetics is further illustrated by the large portions of Snorri's and Óláfr's treatises dedicated to carefully dissecting their structure, types, and application.[71] For both authors, kennings prove to be inextricable from other aspects of the language and poetry, including orthography, phonology, metrical form, and figurative language.[72]

69 Translation of the title *Málskrúðsfræði* by Clunies Ross, *Skáldskaparmál*, 26; see also Clunies Ross, *Old Norse Poetry and Poetics*, 236.

70 Nordal, *Tools of Literacy*, 205; Clunies Ross, *Old Norse Poetry and Poetics*, 105–6 and 236.

71 Clunies Ross, *Skáldskaparmál*, 39.

72 Nordal, *Tools of Literacy*, 206. For example, discussions of kennings appear in both the *Háttatal*, which is focused on verse forms, and the *Skáldskaparmál*, which is focused on diction (Clunies Ross, *Old Norse Poetry and Poetics*, 168–72).

Kennings thus involve the same overlap and intersection of spheres of language that *figura* implies in the Anglo-Saxon treatises and their sources: they are a major *figura* for skaldic poetry in rhetorical, stylistic terms, and their complex structure marks them as *gefeged* – Ælfric's translation for compound *figura* – at the grammatical level.[73]

For the Norse vernacular tradition, the connection of these language fundamentals to the systems of cultural meaning, whether Christian or non-Christian, becomes evident in the content of the *Edda*, with its inclusion of Norse mythology in the *Skáldskaparmál* section and of the entire *Gylfaginning* section, which is dedicated to a lengthy recounting of the myths. Indeed, Snorri considered the cultural context of Norse poetics so necessary for understanding the literature itself that he begins his treatise with the *Gylfaginning*.[74] Even in a Christianized society, Snorri and the other grammarians found a way to retain the non-Christian myths by interpreting them typologically. Ultimately, the approach of figural allegory underlies Snorri's presentation of the myths as not necessarily literally true but rather allegorical prefigurements of Christian history.[75] This reinterpretation became necessary in response to Christianization and was thus at least a partial departure from a theoretically "pure" vernacular paradigm of composition due to the introduction of the Latin tradition's conception of metaphorical language as technically "improper."[76] The retention of the non-Christian material in the face of these changes demonstrates the indissoluble connection between the literature and Norse cultural traditions. Snorri prefers a historicized source of meaning for kennings, that is, a source in the cultural context of the myths.[77] Without those myths, argues Snorri, the "ancient kennings" would disappear from the poetry.[78]

In multiple facets, then, the vernacular theory of language and literature expressed in the Icelandic treatises agrees with the Latin tradition found in Anglo-Saxon England: both traditions subtly – at times almost silently –

73 Knappe, "Rhetorical Aspect," 12, discusses the overlap of kennings with multiple figures of Latin rhetoric.

74 Faulkes, *Gylfaginning*, xix.

75 Clunies Ross, *Old Norse Poetry and Poetics*, 123–4.

76 Clunies Ross, *Old Norse Poetry and Poetics*, 236.

77 Faulkes, *Skáldskaparmál*, xxxi.

78 Sturluson, *Edda*, 64–5; cited and discussed in Clunies Ross, *Old Norse Poetry and Poetics*, 124.

posit a fundamental link between grammar, style, and culture. Kennings and *figura* each appear in the areas both of grammar and of style, and their resonances are often dependent on or inextricable from their cultural contexts. It seems therefore entirely possible that the adoption of the Latin grammatical and rhetorical tradition by Anglo-Saxon scholars proceeded with little difficulty because it was consonant with the vernacular language theory already held by the Anglo-Saxons and later articulated in the Icelandic treatises. At the very least, Anglo-Saxons could easily have known of the Norse tradition that must have preceded and underpinned Snorri's early-thirteenth-century work. The praise poems of the *Anglo-Saxon Chronicle*, for example, reveal knowledge of skaldic poetry in tenth-century Anglo-Saxon England; Wulfstan of course interacted and worked with Danes; and there must have been earlier influences as well. It seems entirely possible that the Anglo-Saxons could have produced independent Old English treatises on vernacular linguistic art matching those of the Icelanders that have simply not survived. Perhaps, had the influx of Norman cultural paradigms after 1066 not interrupted the continuity of Anglo-Saxon scholarly culture, those treatises might well have been extant today.

The main consonance between the Icelandic and the Anglo-Saxon, Latin-based theories of language, then, hinges on the joining of grammar, style, and culture that is most clearly expressed in Icelandic by kennings and in Latin by the repetition of the term *figura*. In Old English, these connections are best exemplified by compound words. Beyond the fact that the majority of Old English kennings are compounds,[79] all compound words, including non-kennings, generate several joinings that correspond to those in the Latin and Old Norse traditions. They display a type of linguistic complexity that combines lexical storage with syntactic and semantic processing,[80] just like kennings. Anglo-Saxons express that complexity

79 Gardner, "The Old English Kenning," 115. Clunies Ross, *Old Norse Poetry and Poetics*, 24, points out that Eddic rather than skaldic poetry is a much closer analogue to Old English poetry, due to, among other elements, the comparatively smaller amount of kennings in Eddic poetry, which is relatively proportional to the amount in Old English poetry. Gardner, "The Old English Kenning," 117, concludes that kennings are characteristic only of "Old North Germanic poetical diction" and not other Germanic branches.

80 Libben, "Why Study Compound Processing?" 3; see also the following discussions in this chapter, chapter 2, and chapter 3 below.

with a term that connotes material as well as linguistic joining – *gefeged* in Ælfric's treatise. Old English *gefegan* [to join], the infinitive for *gefeged*, covers nearly the same semantic spheres of material and linguistic joining as Latin *fingo*, including the compounding of words, the function of conjunctions, poetic metre, the composition of poetry, and the building of a material structure. This breadth also matches with near perfection the analogy between poets and craftsmen in the Icelandic treatises. Moreover, compounds constitute a major feature of Old English style, just as kennings for Old Norse and the tropes known as *figura* for Latin.[81] Old English compounds, in sum, display the same linguistic complexity and were understood in nearly the same manner as *figura* in Latin grammar and as the kennings of Old Norse poets.

The connection between language and systems of cultural meaning is somewhat harder to assess directly for Old English than for the Latin and Icelandic traditions. Anglo-Saxons – Bede, for example – were clearly aware of a general connection between language and cultural identity, given the division of Britain's inhabitants into groups defined by language in the opening to the *Historia ecclesiastica*.[82] Further details, however, escape easy detection in extant primary sources that rarely ruminate self-reflectively on such connections to their contemporary culture in the ways found in the Latin and Old Norse treatises.[83] Oral Theory, the study of oral-traditional composition, performance, and reception, provides useful insight on this issue, since all verbal art constitutes cultural work in its paradigm.[84] Spoken language inherently generates social culture through linguistic interaction, and oral narrative – perhaps (but not necessarily) in an extreme view – can be considered "the chief basis of culture itself."[85]

81 See below for references for scholarship on compounds.

82 Colgrave and Mynors, *Bede's Ecclesiastical History*, I, c. i.

83 While poems such as *The Wanderer* and *The Seafarer*, for example, present moments of apparent deep self-reflection, their actual content cannot readily be taken as representative of Anglo-Saxon culture. Even the accuracy of King Alfred's preface to the Old English translation of the *Cura pastoralis* can be questioned; see Morrish, "King Alfred's Letter." Law, "Anglo-Saxon England," 48, states that Anglo-Saxons showed "little sign of linguistic introspection" regarding their vernacular.

84 For a recent and useful overview of the development and approach of Oral Theory, see Foley and Ramey, "Oral Theory and Medieval Literature."

85 Niles, *Homo Narrans*, 2 and 66–88.

This claim assumes that, without the interaction of language, cooperative society and therefore communal human culture would be impossible. With regard to artistic expression specifically, no audience can fully comprehend an oral work without knowledge of its cultural tradition.[86] An oral work produces meaning primarily by referencing the context of its tradition: individual traditional elements of the work resonate with and metonymically invoke the entirety of the tradition.[87] The negative, and incorrect, view of this relationship between a poet and the tradition is that the poet simply repeats old phrases unthinkingly. Rather, "[t]he expectation was that his inherited material would be reexpressed in newly chosen, although thoroughly traditional, terms."[88] That is, oral poets remain creative, but their materials – individual occurrences of words, phrases, images, etc. – recall all their other associated occurrences along with the traditional meanings ascribed to them. The creativity of oral poets, moreover, necessarily enmeshes grammar and style within cultural resonance: the fundamental units of oral-traditional composition, such as formulas, coalesce only on the basis of grammatical and prosodic repetition.[89] Traditional oral art thus also depends on the paradigm of joining grammar, style, and culture.

Particularly germane for the current discussion is the importance given to compound words in this approach to Old English verbal art.[90] Compounds are indispensible in that they allow traditional style to function adequately within the alliteration-based metre of Old English.[91] On the metrical level, compounds fit where simplices would not, individually filling verse half-lines in otherwise unattainable ways.[92] They also provide the ability to vary the initial sounds of words by employing

86 See Foley, *Immanent Art*, 1–60; Foley, *The Singer of Tales*, 1–59; and Tyler, *Old English Poetics*, 1–7.

87 Foley, *Immanent Art*, 7.

88 Clemoes, *Interactions of Thought and Language*, 170.

89 The scholarship on oral-traditional methods of composition is vast, and discussions of specific elements appear in the chapters below; for an overview and definitive account of the different types of repetition, see Foley, *Traditional Oral Epic*.

90 See Niles, "Compound Diction"; Mazo, "Compound Diction"; Clemoes, *Interactions of Thought and Language*; and Tyler, *Old English Poetics*.

91 Niles, "Compound Diction," 490–2.

92 Russom, *Old English Meter and Linguistic Theory*, 91–4, and Terasawa, *Nominal Compounds in Old English*, 2–4.

different first constituents and can thereby create alliteration on any sound needed.[93] Moreover, the second constituent of a compound need not vary along with alliteration, thereby simultaneously allowing the repetition so important to the formulaic character of traditional style. Complementarily, changing the first constituents of compounds also partially fuels the variation of diction expected of oral-traditional works, such as the seven different epithets for God in the nine lines of *Cædmon's Hymn*, four of which involve compounds.[94] Epithets and variation are by no means restricted to compound words, but there is an extensive overlap. These epithets are also a prime example of the traditional phraseology that invokes a work's entire tradition in each individual occurrence. For example, Beowulf's entire character becomes active and present each time the poem employs a traditional epithet – such as *feþecempa* [foot soldier] or *hordweard* [hoard guardian] – to refer to him, regardless of the details or placement of the specific scene at hand.[95] For an audience fully cognizant of the tradition behind the poem, Beowulf would, to repurpose a phrase, always already embody the different aspects of his character, at least when the audience is reminded of that fact through the appearance of traditional phraseology. Compounds are thus key to several of the most important aspects of traditional style: metre, alliteration, repetition, variation, epithets, and the linkage to the cultural context of the tradition.

The insights of this theoretical framework are not limited to purely oral works or even textual recordings of oral performances: fully literate compositions employing oral-traditional style still "expect" full familiarity with oral-traditional poetics.[96] Without that traditional frame of reference, the work as it stands could never have been composed in the

93 Brodeur, *The Art of "Beowulf,"* 16; Russom, *Old English Meter*, 92–7; and Russom, "Aesthetic Criteria," 71.

94 The compounds are *heofonrice*, *wuldorfæder*, *monncynn*, and *ælmihtig*. On variation, see chiefly Fry, "Variation and Economy in *Beowulf*," and Robinson, *Appositive Style*. For a discussion of the competing pressures of repetition and variety, see Russom, "Artful Avoidance of the Useful Phrase."

95 Foley, *Immanent Art*, 197. On epithets in *Beowulf*, see also Whallon, "Formulas for Heroes."

96 Foley, *How to Read an Oral Poem*, 38–52; cited and discussed in Foley and Ramey, "Oral Theory," 85. See also, among others, Finnegan, *Oral Poetry*; O'Brien O'Keeffe, *Visible Song*; Doane and Pasternack, *Vox Intexta*; Amodio, *Writing the Oral Tradition*; and Chinca and Young, *Orality and Literacy in the Middle Ages*.

first place, and no audience would be able to comprehend it fully, be it literate or oral. A literate yet traditional text still requires its cultural context to create meaning. Since a large proportion of Old English poetry and even prose falls into this category of literate composition in an oral-traditional style, the connections posited by Oral Theory easily apply generally to the corpus.[97] Thus, from the perspective of Oral Theory in addition to that of the medieval treatises, Old English literature – as a literate form of traditional verbal art – is inextricably bound up with its cultural contexts, with compounds comprising a primary element joining the grammar and style of a specific text with its cultural surroundings.

Compounds also effect a similar but not precisely equivalent set of joinings in modern linguistics; research on compounds, both theoretical and experimental, has grown quickly in recent years,[98] and compounds are now considered central to all fields of linguistics.[99] Current theoretical work in linguistics tries to specify exactly what compounding involves in universal terms, since the definitions seem to shift from one language to another.[100] Many recent experimental studies also concentrate on compounds, because they bridge supposedly discrete features of language, such as syntax and lexicon.[101] As a consequence of the interaction between syntax and entries in the mental lexicon, understanding the meaning of a compound, as opposed to a simple (monomorphemic) word, often requires extra-linguistic, contextual information in order to specify the intended relationship between the two constituents of the compound.[102] Compounds thus join lexical, syntactic, and contextual

97 On verse, see, for example, Benson, "Anglo-Saxon Formulaic Poetry"; Orchard, "Old English and Latin Poetic Traditions"; and Orchard, "The Word Made Flesh." On prose, see, for example, Orchard, "Crying Wolf"; Orchard, "Oral Tradition"; and VanderBilt, "Translation and Orality in the Old English *Orosius*."

98 According to Gagné, "Psycholinguistic Perspectives," 255, the amount of psycholinguistics research on compounds nearly doubled from 1986 to 2006.

99 Libben, "Why Study Compound Processing?" 2–3, and Scalise and Vogel, "Why Compounding?" 1.

100 See Dressler, "Compound Types," and Lieber and Štekauer, "Introduction: Status and Definition of Compounding."

101 See, for example, the discussion and citations in Ji, Gagné, and Spalding, "Benefits and Costs," 406–8.

102 See, for example, Jackendoff, "Compounding in the Parallel Architecture," 114–17.

(often cultural) information in a comprehensive manner that no other feature of language achieves. From the abstract perspective of modern linguistics, then, compounds comprise a unique linguistic feature, the study of which promises great insight into language and, therefore, linguistic art.[103]

Modern perspectives such as current linguistic approaches provide a solution to a significant obstacle of the preceding arguments, namely that poetry has been the main focus of the discussion. Oral Theory is generally restricted to poetry, and the Latin and Norse traditions of language theory almost entirely address poetry. However, the seemingly stable distinction between Old English prose and poetry, which some modern scholars often take as an essential given, is not entirely clear.[104] Anglo-Saxons focused primarily on metre as the essential difference between prose and verse in relation to Latin,[105] but the distinction between the two in Old English is difficult to discern. Old English genre terms that might point to an answer are fluid and difficult to pin down, and Anglo-Saxons clearly made little or no distinction between vernacular prose and poetry in terms of manuscript presentation.[106] The rigidity of the divide between prose and poetry softens further when one focuses on large-scale discursive patterns rather than metre, which

---

103 Specific linguistic issues will be explained and employed in the appropriate chapters that follow. This study – a work of literary criticism – proposes no new linguistic theories, but it may hopefully add to the various conversations, joining linguistics, literary studies, and medieval studies.

104 Most recently and most germanely, see Beechy, *Poetics of Old English*. See also Stanley, "Studies in the Prosaic Vocabulary of Old English Verse"; Griffith, "Poetic Language and the Paris Psalter"; Frank, "Poetic Words"; and Mitchell, "Old English Alliterative Verse and Ælfric's Alliterative Prose."

105 See also the discussion of Ælfric's labelling of Bede's prose *Vita Cuthberti* as "straightforward" and his verse *Vita* as "artful" in Frank, "Poetic Words," 88, and Beechy, *Poetics of Old English*, 31–2.

106 Possible Old English terms for literary genres are *gydd*, *sang*, *leoð*, *spell*, and *fitt*. For discussions of these terms, see Parker, "*Gyd*, *Leoð*, and *Sang* in Old English Poetry"; Reichl, "Old English *giedd* and Middle English *yedding* as Genre Terms"; Frank, "Poetic Words"; Niles, *Homo Narrans*, 26–30; and Beechy, *Poetics of Old English*, 31–8. Without addressing these specific genre terms, Foley, "How Genres Leak in Traditional Verse," discusses the lack of distinction between poetic genres.

reveals "poetic" elements in texts historically considered prose.[107] In his *Grammar*, Ælfric tersely defines *prosa* as "forðriht ledon buton leoðcræfte gelencged and gelogod" [direct Latin expanded and styled without the art of poetry] and straightaway presents *metrum* [metre] as the element distinguishing prose from *leoðcræft* [the art of poetry] in Latin.[108] According to this definition, prose lacks the features of poetry, but, importantly, it is not wholly bereft of adornment: it remains *gelogod* [styled], simply in different ways. *Gelogod*, moreover, is a close synonym for *gefeged*, Ælfric's gloss for *figura*, and it too involves many of the same connotations as *fingo*.[109] This semantic overlap suggests that, in Ælfric's view, (artistic) prose and poetry are indeed produced through the same fundamental process of joining, arranging, and styling but with different details for each. Rather than being divided, then, all artistic verbal expression more aptly coalesces as "functional speech of a highly wrought, privileged kind."[110] Within this paradigm, metre becomes a secondary consideration, which allows the style of Old English "prose" to be more effectively compared to that of "poetry" and supports the application of the paradigm of joining to all Old English literature, whether traditionally identified as verse or prose. Treating all linguistic art in Old English as a continuum of expression reveals the similarities between, say, Wulfstan's Old English homilies and *Beowulf*. While only one employs metre, they both display great attention to language and style, and, tellingly, both use compounds to achieve their ends within their respective cultural contexts. In other words, for Anglo-Saxons, the concept of joining is always at play in every piece of linguistic art: grammar, style, and culture are always interacting.

As I have already suggested at several points in various contexts, an examination of compound words and their roles in Old English texts

---

107 See Niles, *Homo Narrans*, 28–30, and Beechy, *Poetics of Old English*, 2–13, who specifically follows Roman Jakobson (along with Aristotle and Philip Sidney) in uncoupling poetics from metre for her examination of Old English prose. Bredehoft, *Early English Metre*, 81–90, identifies Ælfric's works as poetry, but he argues on the basis of a reevaluation of late Old English metrical patterns, not discursive patterns.

108 Zupitza, *Ælfrics Grammatik*, 295–6.

109 BT, s.v. *gelogian*.

110 Niles, *Homo Narrans*, 66.

most directly accesses that interaction, which was fundamental to Anglo-Saxon understandings of linguistic art. Most scholarship specifically on compounds has concentrated on their linguistic structure,[111] their cross-linguistic parallels,[112] their formal features in terms of alliteration or metre,[113] their marking of poetic diction,[114] their participation in literate originality,[115] or their participation in oral traditionality.[116] While much previous work does not deny "aesthetic" applications, rarely are the effects uniquely created by compounds examined within their cultural contexts.[117] In the following chapters, I do just that, mounting arguments that compounds perform all those functions already studied while also doing much more when considered in relation to their contexts and in light of the concept of joining that underlies Anglo-Saxon vernacular verbal art. I maintain that, without reference to extra-textual history, politics, traditions, literary culture, etc., the manners in which compounds work in any particular text cannot be fully clear. Compounds are certainly not the only important or even the only *gefeged* [joined] feature of Old English, but, according to the language theory of the Anglo-Saxons set out in this book, they are the best objects of study for evaluating Old English literature in the same manner that the

111 Storch, *Angelsächsische Nominalcomposita*; Carr, *Nominal Compounds*; Einarsson, "*Kyning-Wuldor* and *Mann-Skratti*"; Reibel, "A Grammatical Index to the Compound Nouns of Old English Verse"; Gardner, "Semantic Patterns in Old English Substantival Compounds"; Overholser, "A Comparative Study of the Compound Use of *Andreas* and *Beowulf*"; Sauer, *Nominalkomposita im Frühmittelenglischen*; Kastovsky, "Semantics and Vocabulary," 362–77; and Lass, *Old English*, 194–8.

112 Magoun, "Recurring First Elements"; Kock, "Old West Germanic and Old Norse"; and Hulbert, "A Note on Compounds in *Beowulf*."

113 Krackow, *Die Nominalcomposita*; Bryan, "Epithetic Compound Folk-Names in *Beowulf*"; Russom, *Old English Meter and Linguistic Theory*, 92–7; Terasawa, *Nominal Compounds in Old English*; and Russom, "Aesthetic Criteria," 71.

114 Krackow, *Die Nominalcomposita*; Koban, "Substantive Compounds in *Beowulf*"; Chapman, "Poetic Compounding"; Chapman and Christensen, "Noun-Adjective Compounds"; and Lapidge, "Old English Poetic Compounds."

115 Brodeur, *The Art of "Beowulf*," 7–38 and 254–71.

116 Niles, "Compound Diction"; Griffith, "Poetic Language"; Mazo, "Compound Diction"; Clemoes, *Interactions of Thought and Language*; and the discussion of Griffith's claims with regard to *Judith* in Hartman, "A Drawn-Out Beheading," 424n11.

117 Clemoes, *Interactions of Thought and Language*, is a notable exception to this trend. For an excellent overview of earlier work, see O'Brien O'Keeffe, "Diction, Variation, the Formula," 92–3.

Anglo-Saxons seem to have understood it: a joining of grammar, style, and culture.

The variety of features and effects made possible by compounds and their unique joinings requires a multifaceted lens for examining them. The paradigms normally applied in isolation to compounds, noted in the previous paragraph, are all valid and fruitful, but they fail individually to comprehend the full complexity of compound words within Old English literature and culture. *Joinings* therefore combines several different paradigms to produce a new and unique approach. Each chapter below explores a different aspect of the use of compounds, usually through different methods in each case, often combining several approaches that do not normally appear together. For example, the analyses below employ data from experimental linguistics in combination with Oral Theory, historical inquiry, the Jakobsonian theory of linguistic functions, theories of Old English metre, translation theory, Bakhtinian genre theory, modern rhetorical theories, and even film theory. This book does not fabricate a new method whole-cloth; rather each chapter successively adds new pieces and joins together previously unconnected approaches into a unique amalgamation, creating a new methodological joining in order to understand the joinings of compound words in Old English, a process that reaches full fruition in the conclusion.

Joinings thus presents an in-depth, contextualized examination of compounds as the major linguistic feature that Anglo-Saxons most likely saw as the fullest manifestation of the intersection of grammar, style, and culture in Old English, an intersection that was fundamental to their theory of language and artistic expression. Combining various lenses and approaches, this book explores the different uses to which compounds are put in Old English texts in a variety of genres and time periods in order to elucidate fully their artistic power and adaptability. Chapter 2 explores what would seem to be one of the most fundamental applications of compound words in Old English: translating Latin words. Given the inherent difficulty of conveying the full range of meanings and implications of a word in a different language, it would make sense that the semantic flexibility and precision allowed by compounding should well suit the process of translating. Compounds provide much more control over meaning than simple words, and they do some work as translation tools in texts such as Cynewulf's *Juliana* and *Elene* and the Old English *Boethius*. Nonetheless, those texts, which are representative of the translation practices of the larger corpus, employ compounds for that purpose infrequently at best. Rather, chapter 2 shows that compounds create patterns and emphases that generate or highlight aspects deemed most important for making the text acceptable to the audience. Compounds clearly perform important discursive work in these texts, but their utility in the translation process grows out of other, fundamental uses for and characteristics of compounds in Old English literature.

Chapter 3 analyses the linguistic source and basic application of the fundamental capacity of compounds for creating rhetorical emphasis. Modern linguistics and neuropsychology elucidate the utility of compounds by demonstrating that the nature of compound structures produces unique cognitive effects that create rhetorical weight simply through the presence of compound structures. For example, through careful deployment of compounds, *Beowulf* foregrounds war-gear and violence, especially at politically sensitive moments when they could produce egregious havoc. In shorter texts, the divergent interests of *The Wanderer* and *The Seafarer*, so alike in many ways, become powerfully clear through an examination of their compounds, with the mind as an enclosure fascinating one and the sea as an open metaphor the other. Compounds in Wulfstan's Old English homilies emphasize dangers to socio-political cohesion in the midst of the eleventh-century Danish attacks. In each case examined in chapter 3, the grammar of the compounds interfaces with and affects the style of the texts in ways that react to their cultural contexts, always dependent on the basic characteristics of compound structures.

Chapters 4 through 6 then explore different ways in which texts harness this fundamental cognitive and rhetorical weight of compound structures. Chapter 4 specifically analyses the different generic affiliations that compounds can invoke and the effects of those affiliations in Cynewulf's *Juliana* and the Old English *Boethius*. *Juliana* mixes quotidian, perhaps monastic language with the elevated diction of traditional Old English poetry; similarly, the prosimetric version of the Old English *Boethius* alternates between the vocabulary of standard prose and the same elevated, poetic diction. Features such as simple, monomorphemic vocabulary and the presence or absence of metre support the successful creation of these various discourses, but chapter 4 demonstrates that compound words perform the bulk of the work invoking them. These texts utilize the linguistic weight of compounds to do more than create emphasis on a concept or theme. Rather, the texts deploy compounds that have connections to specific speech genres and interlink with non-lexical features; those connections – this interlinking – produce expectations of particular vocabulary, styles, themes, and cultural contexts that accompany the compounds. The heteroglossic patterns of style produced by the compounds in the *Boethius* and *Juliana* mould the texts in ways that support the texts' themes and emphases in subtle and powerful ways unachievable through other means.

Chapters 5 and 6 both cover the effect clusters of compounds have on pace. Chapter 5 concentrates on pace in Wulfstan's Old English homilies, and chapter 6 on pace in *Beowulf*. While compounds that occur individually in Wulfstan's homilies are discussed in chapter 3, the majority of the compounds in his homilies occur in clusters, grouped together as rhetorical units, most often lists. The lists are essentially set pieces in that they are relatively independent within their homily as a whole. For example, they have their own internal organizations as series of doublets, and their content, while not incongruous, does not specifically advance the main argument of their homily. Given these large compound-laden passages, the presence of the compounds registers not just at the level of individual sentences but also at the larger discourse level of the entire homily, differentiating the set pieces from the rest of the text. Ultimately, these set pieces retard the pace of the homilies in which they appear, allowing Wulfstan to dwell on a particular point without having to produce any further explanation, argument, or narrative. Thus, the compound structures that make these set pieces of doublets and lists formally possible and coherent allow Wulfstan to control the pace of his prose and force his audience to concentrate on the points that he considers most important.

The pace of action in *Beowulf* often slows nearly to a standstill, with lines upon lines filling up with description or variation, but no development of the plot. This manipulation of pace comprises a pervasive and important feature of *Beowulf*. Variation plays a prominent role in this narrative slowing, and compound words constitute primary building blocks that allow variation to succeed by providing several degrees of freedom in manipulating initial sounds for alliteration, in repeating second elements, and in filling half-lines. Moreover, beyond even their utility in producing variation, the very structure of compounding creates a degree of linguistic weight that in and of itself slows the narrative. Chapter 6 explores how *Beowulf* uses this capacity to slow the narrative to stretch out moments of important violence, not to celebrate or savour them but to drain out their physicality and undercut the possibility of celebration.

This book concludes, in a sense, where it begins, with Ælfric. Ælfric's Old English homilies remarkably avoid compound words, seemingly challenging my interpretation of them as fundamentally important linguistic tools for Old English literature. That avoidance, however, in fact confirms my claim when analysed in light of Ælfric's interests in clarity and traditional, orthodox Christian faith. Compound words were too closely tied to specifically Anglo-Saxon cultural contexts, not by their individual meanings but by the importance of their abstract structure and value in Old English literary culture. Ælfric's homilies eschew compounds in pursuit of knowledge and culture that transcends Anglo-Saxon England, thus proving my claim that compounds inextricably connect grammar with style within specific cultural contexts. In strategically employing compounds, the other texts discussed in this book manipulate basic elements of grammar in order to mould their styles in ways that create meaning within each one's specific milieu. Ælfric, on the other hand, sought to transcend his milieu and join the supposedly decontextualized traditions of Christendom writ large. The absence of compounds in his homilies, therefore, confirms their primary importance as representatives of and participants in a specifically Anglo-Saxon conception of vernacular verbal art.

Through these analyses of representative texts, *Joinings* explores in greater detail than any previous study the specific effects produced by the presence of compound words in Old English literature. From the minute details of their grammar, through their influence on style, to their interaction with extratextual contexts, compounds are complicated and adaptable pieces of Old English language and literature. Understanding compound words in these three areas with nuance and depth provides for modern scholars a deep understanding of Old English literature. Ultimately, understanding compounds in these ways also allows us to understand Anglo-Saxon theories of language and verbal art: to put it most succinctly, they considered grammar and style to be parts of culture in much more powerful ways than we have recognized before. Grammar was culture for the Anglo-Saxons, for they saw the universal Christianity to which they aspired suffusing every element of language, from the largest systems of cultural meaning to the smallest pieces of sound and syntax. Compound words present the clearest distillation of this concept both in theory and in practice, and it is no surprise then that compounds are such prominent and important elements of Old English literature.

A Definition of "Compound Word"

Although this book does not focus primarily on the linguistic issues of compounding, in order to appreciate the characteristics and utility of compounds, a definition of their fundamental nature and structure is necessary. Of primary importance is that this study covers compound nouns and adjectives, but not verbs, a distinction that led previous studies of these same words to employ the term *nominal compound*. To simplify and streamline this book's discussions, I omit the word *nominal* most of the time, but readers should keep in mind that I refer to nouns and adjectives (and not verbs) when I employ the terms *compound* and *compound word*. Those terms unfortunately are not perfectly clear or well defined universally, nor even is *nominal compound*. Each study of Old English compounds formulates its definition – and therefore its data set – somewhat differently, and even the basic notion of compounding has not gone unchallenged.[118] The essential point of the various definitions is that a compound is a single word composed of two or more other words, but the details remain variable, thus requiring an overt statement of definition. Beyond issues of definition lie the challenges of characterizing the relationships between the constituents of compounds.[119] The different types of relationships between constituents, however, interest me less than the simple presence of some type of relationship, and I therefore do not enter into those debates.

My working definition of "compound word," then, is as follows: a compound word is a single noun or adjective consisting of two or more independently occurring words which combine to become the constituents of the compound. In Old English the final constituent of the compound takes morphological inflection whereas non-final constituents normally do not, usually allowing reliable identification of compounds. Some general "behavioural" traits of compounds subsequently become clear: the meaning of a compound and the relationship between its constituents are not predetermined by the individual constituents but are negotiated in the creation and/or interpretation of the compound. In other words, although there are general trends of compound formation, no one constituent necessarily locks its compound into any one relational class due to its preformation specifications.

Definitional issues arise most frequently around the status of affixes (prefixes and suffixes) and the issue of classifying as compounds those words formed through affixation. For the most part, affixes do not occur as independent words, and for this reason many studies of compounds

118 Levi, *Syntax and Semantics*, 38–48, challenges the existence of compounds as a distinct and well-defined linguistic category based only on compounds in Modern English.

119 For example, the earliest classification scheme for compounds originated in Sanskrit philology and divided compounds into five groups named in Sanskrit: *Dvandva*, *Tatpuruša*, *Karmadhâraya*, *Dvigu*, and *Bahuvrihi*. For discussion of this system, see Carr, *Nominal Compounds*.

omit words formed through affixation. Some studies, however, admit complex words formed in this fashion into their data sets, making no distinction based on affixation.[120] This book is interested in the complexity created by the joinings involved in compounding, and affixation does not create semantic or syntactic complexity in the same way. Derivational suffixes in particular affect little in the way of the general semantic content of the words to which they attach, often simply acting to change the syntactic category. For example, in Old English the suffix *-nes* changes the syntactic category of a word from adjective to noun, such as from *clæne* [clean] to *clænnes* [cleanness, purity]. In a technical sense, words like *clænnes* are complex words since they are composed of two morphemes, or lexical units, but this type of suffix never occurs independently and itself carries little semantic content. Moreover, certain metrical constraints of Old English poetry apply to "true" compound words that do not apply to derived words. For example, the second constituents of complex words formed of independent morphemes – i.e., not derivational suffixes – must alliterate and are therefore precluded from b-lines, in which double alliteration is not allowed.[121] Words incorporating derivational suffixes, on the other hand, freely occur in second half-lines, demonstrating that they do not fall under the same constraint. This disparity in metrically controlled positioning cannot arise from an inconsistently applied rule. Rather, from both the semantic and metrical points of view, words formed through the addition of derivational suffixes belong to a class separate from compounds. Derived words are therefore omitted from most studies of compounds, and I follow this trend and do not include complex words formed only through derivational suffixation in my data sets. I do, however, include words with derivational suffixes when the bases to which those suffixes attach are themselves already compounds, such as *eadmodnes* [humility]. Words formed through prefixation are also often omitted in studies of compounds, again because the prefixes do not occur

120 For example, Chapman, "Stylistic Use," 31, includes complex words formed through prefixation, claiming that Wulfstan perceived them as compounds and not simply complex, prefixed words. Carr, *Nominal Compounds*, xxiii, questions the modern ability to classify derivational affixes since the historical development of this class of morpheme is not perfectly clear, a concept also suggested in Kiparsky, "Dvandvas, Blocking, and the Associative."

121 Fulk, *Old English Meter*, §§195–6, and Campbell, *Old English Grammar*, §§88–9. See also the discussion in chapter 2 below, which covers additional metrical restrictions on compounds.

independently and are therefore subject to different semantic and metrical rules than "true" compounds. Although prefixes often carry important semantic information, nevertheless they are not independent words and do not create the multifarious complexity that interests this study, and I again follow the majority of previous studies on compounds and omit words formed through prefixation.

Complicating this treatment of affixes are those lexical units which seem to function as suffixes but also appear as independent words. Due to the apparently liminal status of these words, scholars have variously termed them "compositional suffixes," "semi-suffixes," or "suffixoids." For example, the word *had* [rank, order, condition, state] also appears as the suffix *–had*, such as in *mægðhad* [virginity, the condition of being a maiden]. In both occurrences (independent word and constituent of a complex word), *had* provides essentially the same meaning and so seems to be the same word. The behaviour of *–had* as a second constituent of complex words, however, reveals that it is not exactly the same as *had* the independent morpheme. In particular, *–had* only attaches to nouns, meaning that it has a prerequisite for affixation, just as *–nes* only attaches to adjectives. Constituents of true compounds have no such prerequisites, but affixes must have individual rule sets to determine the words to which they can attach. The independent word *had* carries with it no word formation rules, but the fact that *–had* does filter out certain syntactic categories of words prior to attachment shows that it and other so-called suffixoids, which behave the same way, are indeed simply suffixes. The complex words which they form are thus not compounds in the sense that interests this book and are therefore omitted.

Verbally derived compound constituents also present some difficulty: words such as *reordberend* [speech-bearer, i.e., human] and *daroðhæbbende* [holding a spear] function substantivally or adjectivally, but their second constituents are derived forms of verbs. Initially, it would seem that any compound clearly derived from a verb should be omitted from this study since the focus is not on verbs. Nonetheless, these verbally derived compounds perform the same functions as other compounds, and, moreover, they behave more like nominal compounds than verbal compounds. In general, compound verbs are not as productive as compound nouns or adjectives, mainly being limited to formation through prefixation with constituents such as *ut-*, *for-*, *be-*, etc.[122] Verbally derived constituents of

122 Chapman, "Stylistic Use," 33.

nominal compounds are not limited in this manner; they combine with other nouns and adjectives just as easily as non-verbally derived constituents and are not restricted to compounding only through affixation. In a sense, the transition from verb to adjective or noun takes place before the compounding process itself, and so the verbally derived constituent behaves just as any other noun or adjective would. Compounds such as *reordberend* involve an internal complexity of relationship in the same manner as any other nominal compound, and I thus include them in my study.

2 Compounds as Translation Tools

Given the inherent difficulty of conveying the full range of meanings and implications of a word in a different language, it is no wonder that Anglo-Saxon glossators frequently employed several words and even full sentences to gloss a single Latin lemma.[1] Recreating the depth and variability of possible meanings expressed by a source word is often an impossible task to achieve with a single word in the target language; in other words, there is no "one-to-one" correspondence between any two languages.[2] Compound words, with the semantic complexity that they offer, seem well suited to provide translations that are both compact and possibly more

1 Lendinara, *Anglo-Saxon Glosses and Glossaries*, 72, gives the following example of multiple (Latin) glosses for a single lemma: "Cicatrices: plagae, scis<s>urae et in vestimento et in corpore" [Scars: wounds, cuts both in clothing and on the body]; the gloss originally appeared in Lindsay, *The Corpus Glossary*, 39, gloss C 413. For different strategies of glossing, see Sauer, "Language and Culture."

2 The lack of one-to-one correspondence is a basic tenet of translation theory, which essentially denies the very existence of a perfectly adequate translation – i.e., a translation that with perfect accuracy retains the vocabulary, modes of speech, ideas, etc. of the original text. The other axis employed in translation theory is acceptability, which measures the degree to which a translation conforms with the usages of the target culture, that is, the degree to which a translation employs the linguistic constructions, patterns of argument, etc. that would be expected by its new audience. See Toury, *Descriptive Translation Studies and Beyond*, 56–7 and 70–4, and Malmkjær, *Linguistics and the Language of Translation*, 13–15. For discussions of this issue with relation to Anglo-Saxon works, see Discenza, *The King's English*, and Thijs, "Early Old English Translation."

accurate to the original than simplices.[3] The underlying morphological and semantic structures of compounds – possibly providing at times a complexity equivalent to that of a full sentence – should allow the flexibility that glossators found in sentence-length glosses, but in a compressed form. Perhaps unintuitively, regardless of these possible advantages, compounds were in fact not universally adopted as translation tools across the corpus of Old English. Some texts display a level of consistency in using compounds for construing words from their Latin original, while others do not.[4] On one level, there seem to have been two "camps" on this issue, with one group of texts using roughly one quarter of their compounds to construe Latin words directly,[5] and a second group using only about one tenth of their compounds for direct construal.[6] The two versions of the Old English *Boethius* fall into the first camp, and Cynewulf's *Juliana* and *Elene* the second, and this chapter concentrates on those four as representative texts. Ultimately, an in-depth analysis of these representative texts shows that the strategies of the two camps, although superficially

3 For a discussion of compounds in relation to glosses, see Krackow, *Die Nominalcomposita*, 49–59.

4 For purposes of precision, I maintain a distinction between the terms *translate* and *construe*. I use *translate* to refer to the larger process of converting a text from one language to another, but *construe* for individual instances of rendering one word or phrase from the original as one word or phrase in the target language. I reserve *gloss* for direct translation of an individual word or phrase outside of a full-scale translation, i.e. interlinearly or in a glossary.

5 The texts that I have assessed in this regard that represent this first camp are *The Whale*, *Azarias*, the first portions of *The Phoenix* (verse and prose), and the prose sections of the Old English *Boethius*. *The Whale* employs approximately 23 per cent of its compounds as translation tools, *Azarias* approximately 23 per cent, the first one hundred lines of *The Phoenix* approximately 28 per cent, the equivalent section of the prose *Phoenix* 25 per cent, and the *Boethius* just under 30 per cent (236 of 796 occurrences of compounds).

6 The texts that I have assessed in this regard that represent this second camp are *Juliana*, *Elene*, and *The Panther*. In *Juliana*, only roughly 12 per cent (31 of 254 occurrences) of the compound words directly construe a word or phrase in the Latin source, along with roughly 10 per cent (51 of 489) in *Elene* and 11 per cent in *The Panther*. Interestingly, although they were both supposedly composed by the same author, *The Panther* and *The Whale* differ from each other as far as employing compounds for direct construal, showing the possible variability of translation strategy available. Statistics, of course, can be misleading, especially when, as is the case here with *The Panther* and *The Whale*, the numbers stem from a rather small sample.

divergent, are in fact fundamentally the same. The apparent difference is only one of degree and the product not of different theories of translation but rather of different cultural situations. As this chapter demonstrates, this conclusion necessarily implies that compounds were valuable not for their content, but for their form.

King Alfred's famous formulation of the poles of translation – word for word against sense for sense[7] – is in fact an inheritance from classical tradition that grew out of a framework of the interaction of grammar and rhetoric.[8] The basic issue was interpretation: translation was more than simply making the text available in a different language; it was a process of interpretation and explanation.[9] The cultural contexts of a source text are absent from, and of little help for, a far-removed target culture in understanding the text, leading to "transformations" as part of the translation process in order to create sense within the new cultural context.[10] These transformations, or translation strategies, necessarily differ from text to text, depending on what audience the text targets. The features that seem to divide Old English texts into camps, however, are in reality different tactics employed in the pursuit of the same strategic goal of porting a text into Anglo-Saxon culture. The Old English *Boethius* and Cynewulf's poems have different target audiences and different literary goals on one level, but fundamentally they all seek to interpret their sources and fit them into Anglo-Saxon culture.

Unfortunately, just as with the paradigm of joinings discussed in the introduction, no Anglo-Saxon text overtly discusses the role of compounds in the translation process nor even – in anything other than snippets in grammatical treatises – the concept that compounds are substantively different than simple words.[11] Attributing utility to compounds in Old English translations, however, requires proof of

7 "hwilum word be worde, hwilum andgit of andgi[e]te," in Sweet, *King Alfred's West-Saxon Version of Gregory's Pastoral Care*, 1:7, lines 19–20.

8 See Copeland, *Rhetoric, Hermeneutics, and Translation*, 9.

9 Copeland, *Rhetoric, Hermeneutics, and Translation*, 37.

10 See Thijs, "Early Old English Translation," 151 and 163. See also Bately, *The Literary Prose of King Alfred's Reign*; Stanton, *The Culture of Translation*, 74; and Discenza, *The King's English*, especially 87–122.

11 See Thijs, "Early Old English Translation," 157. Thijs also points out that the Alfredian prefaces imply that translation methodology was indeed examined, although no overt theory is ever presented (157 and 159).

an awareness on the part of Anglo-Saxons of the status of compound words qua compounds, rather than simply as "big words," as it were. Ælfric's *Grammar* shows that literate Anglo-Saxons certainly had such awareness at an abstract level, attending to a word's complexity (*anfeald* [simple] or *gefeged* [joined]) along with its case, number, and gender.[12] Newly coined and perhaps even rare compounds would surely have been recognized and processed as complex words. An awareness of "compoundedness," however, may not have been present at all times or for all compounds. The ability to break down a compound into its constituents would not necessarily have been applied to commonly occurring compounds, such as *mancynn* [humanity] or *middangeard* [earth]. Moreover, an awareness of compounds in written Latin, with which Ælfric's comments are at least superficially concerned, should be quite different from such an awareness with relation to Old English and certainly spoken Old English. Without substantial, direct discussion of compounds in this manner, indirect evidence from Old English metrical patterns and modern linguistics studies provides the only access to Anglo-Saxon conceptions of compounds.

Several different metrical restrictions on the placement of different types of words suggest Anglo-Saxons' possibly common awareness of compound status in Old English specifically. In one restriction, complex words formed through derivation or affixation, such as *wisdom* [wisdom] and *wærfæst* [faithful], can appear in metrical positions that are illegal for "true" compounds. Specifically, affixes like *–dom* and *–fæst* may appear in the second drop of a verse, but the second constituent of a compound may not do so, because they carry different levels of stress.[13] In another restriction, compounds with a particular metrical pattern are barred from poetry, although syntactic phrases with identical scansion nonetheless appear: for example, **hildewiga* [battle warrior] is not attested, but *deofla hryre* [destruction of devils] is.[14] A third type of metrical restriction

12 Zupitza, *Ælfrics Grammatik*, 87; *gefeged* in this context refers to both compounds and to words produced through affixation. See also Chapman, "Composing and Joining."

13 Fulk, *Old English Meter*, §§195–6, and Campbell, *Old English Grammar*, §§88–9.

14 Terasawa, *Nominal Compounds in Old English*, 73; the pattern is long stressed syllable-unstressed syllable-short stressed syllable-unstressed syllable.

involves the participation of compounds in alliteration: compounds almost always participate in alliteration, and sometimes their second constituents do as well.[15] *Beowulf* lines 176 ("wigweorþunga, wordum bædon") and 394 ("heardhicgende hider wilcuman") are good examples of these tendencies, with the a-verse of both lines consisting entirely of a compound with both constituents participating in double alliteration.[16] Importantly, compounds that create double alliteration in this manner may appear only in the a-verse, since double alliteration is disallowed in the b-verse.[17] Moreover, the general restriction of type D verses, which commonly contain compounds and commonly involve double alliteration, to the a-verse seems to be a product of the alliterative tendencies of compounds as well.[18] A compound may not appear in a type D verse in the b-verse, however, because it would either create double alliteration, which, again, is disallowed in the b-verse, or violate the general rule of double alliteration for compounds in type D verses.[19] Complex words created through affixation, on the other hand, can appear in type D verses in the b-verse, since they do not carry the same alliterative tendencies as compounds.[20] These restrictions illustrate that at least Anglo-Saxon poets recognized that compounds have special metrical rules as a different type of word than simplices and even affixed words.

Recent linguistic experiments and the resulting theoretical developments offer additional insights that can be indirectly applied to Old English. The main, seemingly conflicting theories on the mental processing of compounds present two options. First, a compound may be broken down into its constituents, the individual entries for which are then activated in the mental lexicon before an evaluation of the semantic or syntactic

15 See Kendall, "The Prefix *un–*"; Kendall, *Metrical Grammar*, 159–74; and Stewart, "The Mind and Spirit of Old English *mōd* and *fer(h)ð*."

16 See Fulk, *Old English Meter*, §195, for a discussion involving these two lines.

17 Fulk, *Old English Meter*, §195; Hoover, "Evidence for Primacy of Alliteration"; and Hoover, *Old English Meter*.

18 Terasawa, *Old English Meter*, §3.3 and §4.3.

19 Fulk, *Old English Meter*, §195, and Bliss, *The Metre of "Beowulf,"* §§61–2.

20 Fulk, *Old English Meter*, §66 and §195, and Kendall, *Metrical Grammar*, 175–99.

relationship between them.[21] Alternatively, once learned and encountered frequently enough, a compound may be stored as a whole, single word in the mental lexicon (i.e., lexicalized) and then accessed in exactly the same manner as any simple word.[22] Early work presumed that common compounds would lexicalize, leaving only very rare or "novel" (newly coined) compounds to be recognized and treated as complex words in mental processing.[23] However, according to recent experiments gauging eye-fixation times, lexical decision tasks, naming tasks, and other criteria, the brain processes even seemingly lexicalized compounds by decomposing them into constituents.[24] Subsequent experiments have shown that compounds in fact never fully lexicalize, insofar as the brain only ever activating the whole-word entry for a compound.[25] Rather, processing any compound involves both retrieving the lexical entries of the individual constituents (and constructing the relationship between them) as

21 For recent discussions of the theoretical frameworks of constituent computation versus whole-word storage, see chiefly Libben, "Why Study Compound Processing?"; Semenza and Mondini, "The Neuropsychology of Compound Words"; Heyvaert, "Compounding in Cognitive Linguistics"; and Gagné, "Psycholinguistic Perspectives."

22 Lipka, "Lexicalization and Institutionalization," 2165, defines "lexicalization" as follows: "the process by which complex lexemes tend to become a single unit, with a specific content, through frequent use." For more recent discussions of defining "lexicalization," see Lipka, Handl, and Falkner, "Lexicalization and Institutionalization," and Bell and Plag, "Informativeness is a Determinant of Compound Stress in English," 494–6.

23 For example, Brekle, "Reflections on the Conditions," and Butterworth, "Lexical Representation." For an experimental perspective attempting to distinguish lexicalized compounds from "novel" compounds, see Coolen, van Jaarsveld, and Schreuder, "The Interpretation of Isolated Novel Nominal Compounds."

24 See, among others, Juhasz, Starr, Inhoff, and Placke, "The Effects of Morphology on the Processing of Compound Words," 239–40; McCormick, Brysbaert, and Rastle, "Is Morphological Decomposition Limited to Low-Frequency Words?"; and Marelli, Aggujaro, Molteni, and Luzzatti, "The Multiple-Lemma Representation of Italian Compound Nouns," 856 and 860. For an excellent overview of early theories of lexical access, see Isel, Gunter, and Friederici, "Prosody-Assisted Head-Driven Access to Spoken German Compounds," 277–8.

25 This statement applies only to compounds that remain "functional," that is, compounds that can still be analysed as the combination of two separate constituents that could appear individually as stand-alone words. Words that had been compounds etymologically in earlier forms of Germanic but did not functionally remain so in Old English must have been largely lexicalized. For example, on *hlaford* being fully lexicalized, see Hartman, "Stressed and Spaced Out," 202.

well as retrieving the entry for the whole compound.[26] This "doubling up" by accessing multiple entries is perhaps surprisingly inefficient, minimizing neither mental effort in computation nor storage space, but it maximizes opportunity of access through redundancy, probably to allow the greatest processing speed possible.[27] As far as the data show, the brain follows both avenues, rather than choosing one over the other, and then employs the most-quickly-accessed information.[28] Thus, at some level, compounds are always processed as compounds, and that would have been the case for Anglo-Saxons as well, since the human brain has not fundamentally changed in the comparatively brief time since the early Middle Ages.

Many of the experiments leading to this "maximized opportunity" theory rely on literacy and the action of reading.[29] That restriction is of course not entirely problematic for Old English texts, especially the *Boethius* and Cynewulf's poems, which were certainly produced in a literate fashion to some degree and were likely consumed visually by at least portions of their audiences. The visual representation of Old English compounds in manuscripts in fact probably augmented the awareness of compounds qua compounds. Hyphenation or space between constituents of compound words in modern texts generally encourages morpheme- or constituent-based rather than whole-word processing, most likely because it overtly marks the division between the two constituents of a

26 Isel et al., "Prosody-Assisted Head-Driven Access"; Andrews, Miller, and Rayner, "Eye Movements and Morphological Segmentation of Compound Words"; Fiorentino and Poeppel, "Processing of Compounds Words"; Gagné and Spalding, "Constituent Integration During the Processing of Compound Words"; Häikiö, Bertram, and Hyönä, "The Development of Whole-Word Representations in Compound Word Processing"; Marelli and Luzzatti, "Frequency Effects in the Processing of Italian Nominal Compounds"; and Marelli et al., "Multiple-Lemma Representation," 860.

27 Libben, "Why Study Compound Processing?" 6–10. See also Jarema, "Compound Representation and Processing," and Fehringer, "The Lexical Representation of Compound Words in English."

28 See, for example, MacGregor and Shtyrov, "Multiple Routes for Compound Word Processing in the Brain."

29 A notable exception is MacGregor and Shtyrov, "Multiple Routes for Compound Word Processing in the Brain."

compound.[30] The irregularity of word divisions and the common division of Old English compounds in manuscripts probably produced the same result, since it too overtly demarcates the constituents of a compound. For example, "þeodcyninga" [nation-kings] in *Beowulf* line 2 appears in the manuscript as two separate words, "þeod cyninga."[31] Anglo-Saxon reading practices, moreover, differed greatly from modern practices, and readers probably did not skim, likely making such separation of constituents very effective in encouraging constituent-based processing.[32] Thus, visually encountering compound words when reading manuscripts would likely have emphasized the presence of, or at least the decompositional method of processing, compound words in Old English, again supporting a fundamental cognitive awareness of compounds as different from simplices.

Many Old English texts, however, were probably consumed aurally, either when read aloud or when performed, as with homilies. Much less research has addressed the auditory over the visual processing of compounds, but there is enough to make useful conclusions. For example, the symptoms of aphasia affect production of compounds both in speech and in writing, suggesting that the same process of lexical access underlies both.[33] In terms of speaking, aphasia inhibits the production of compounds in ways that support the theory that they are stored both as whole words and as separate constituents.[34] Compounds spoken by neurologically normal

30 Inhoff, Radach, and Heller, "Complex Compounds in German"; Juhasz, Inhoff, and Rayner, "The Role of Interword Spaces in the Processing of English Compound Words"; Pollatsek and Hyönä, "The Role of Semantic Transparency in the Processing of Finnish Compound Words"; Frisson, Niswander-Klement, and Pollatsek, "The Role of Semantic Transparency in the Processing of English Compound Words"; Häikiö et al., "The Development of Whole-Word Representations"; and Bertram and Hyönä, "The Role of Hyphens at the Constituent Boundary in Compound Word Identification."

31 London, British Library, Cotton Vitellius A. xv, folio 129r, line 2; textual quotations from Fulk, Bjork, and Niles, *Klaeber's Beowulf*. See also Fulk, Bjork, and Niles, *Klaeber's Beowulf*, xxxii.

32 See O'Brien O'Keeffe, *Visible Song*, especially 14–21.

33 Bi, Han, and Shu, "Compound Frequency Effect in Word Production." Aphasia is "the loss or impairment of language function caused by brain damage," according to Benson and Ardila, *Aphasia: A Clinical Perspective*, 3.

34 Eiesland and Lind, "Compound Nouns in Spoken Language Production," and Fehringer, "Lexical Representation."

people also support the "maximized opportunity" theory, since characteristics of the individual constituents in addition to those of the whole word work together to govern the assignation of stress (or prominence) in speech.[35] In terms of comprehension, listeners both break down compounds into constituents and employ whole-word access for processing, just as readers do in the studies discussed above. German listeners, for example, certainly employ decompositional processing – breaking a compound into its constituents – when the compound head is "transparent" as opposed to "opaque."[36] Other studies show that German listeners also decompose even opaque, supposedly lexicalized compounds in processing, for example assessing the gender of first (non-head) constituents, even though it does not affect the gender of the compound as a whole.[37] German listeners also begin assessing the semantic relationship of compounds before hearing the final (head) constituent, which requires accessing the lexical entries for the individual constituents on the fly.[38] Comparing German to Old English should be fairly uncontroversial, given that both are Germanic languages and since the findings correlate so well across languages.[39] Thus, as with the visual mode, oral production and aural processing of compounds involves a dual storage method, in that compounds are accessed both as whole words and also as individual constituents, the relationships between which are then interpreted and constructed.

35 For recent studies, see Plag, "The Variability of Compound Stress in English"; Plag, Kunter, and Lappe, "Testing Hypotheses about Compound Stress Assignment in English"; Plag, Kunter, Lappe, and Braun, "The Role of Semantics, Argument Structure, and Lexicalization"; Plag, "Compound Stress Assignment by Analogy"; Kunter, *Compound Stress in English*; Arndt-Lappe, "Towards an Exemplar-Based Model"; Bell and Plag, "Informativeness is a Determinant of Compound Stress in English."

36 Isel et al., "Prosody-Assisted Head-Driven Access."

37 Koester, Gunter, Wagner, and Friederici, "Morphosyntax, Prosody, and Linking Elements"; Koester, Gunter, and Wagner, "The Morphosyntactic Decomposition and Semantic Composition of German Compound Words"; and Holle, Gunter, and Koester, "The Time Course of Lexical Access in Morphologically Complex Words."

38 Koester, Holle, and Gunter, "Electrophysiological Evidence for Incremental Lexical-Semantic Integration."

39 Myers, "Processing Chinese Compounds," 194.

Given the fundamental cognitive patterns demonstrated by modern linguistics experiments and the awareness implied by Old English metrical restrictions, one can thus conclude with relative safety that Anglo-Saxons processed and recognized compounds as fundamentally distinct from simplices, allowing Anglo-Saxon authors and audiences – whether readers or listeners – unique lexical, grammatical, and stylistic options. With regard to the present discussion, just as sentence-length glosses gave glossators the opportunity for greater complexity and specificity than single-word glosses, so too did compounds for translators. Whether exploited or not, the variety of relationships between the two constituents of a compound at least allowed a complexity and semantic depth similar to sentences.

Turning to the specific texts at question in this chapter, one finds that the two versions of the *Boethius* seem to recognize this opportunity for complexity and depth, displaying notable consistency in the compounds used for construal. For example, the prose sections shared by the two versions of the *Boethius* frequently employ *anweald* [authority, power] to construe *potentia* [might, power] and *potestas* [ability, power].[40] In fact, no other compound construes *potentia* or *potestas* in the *Boethius*; there seems to have been a direct mapping of the two Latin words onto *anweald* in the translation process. *Anweald*, however, does occasionally construe other power words such as *valentia* [bodily strength, capacity] and *virtus* [strength, capacity] or other words relating to a ruler's position of power such as *honor* [honour, repute] and *dignitas* [authority, rank]. Thus, although there is still no one-to-one correspondence between *anweald* and a single Latin word, the vast majority of the uses of *anweald* for direct construal (40 of 48) consistently target *potentia* or *potestas*. Likewise, *woruld*–compounds frequently appear in the prose sections of the two versions construing *Fortuna* and her related benefits, such as *uoluptas* [pleasure], *delectatio* [delight], *ops* [power, wealth], and *divitiae* [riches].[41] In fact, the translator appears to have created a compound specifically for translating the word *fortuna*: *woruldsælða* [worldly fortune], which also occurs as *woruldgesælða*.[42] The same consistency, albeit on a smaller scale, also

40 See also Godden and Irvine, *The Old English Boethius*, 1:75.

41 See also Godden and Irvine, *Boethius*, 1:74–6.

42 See also Godden and Irvine, *Boethius*, 1:77, and below for further discussion of the *woruld*– compounds.

appears in the uses of *lichoma* [body] to construe *corpus* [body] and of *gesceadwis* [intelligent, wise] and its derivatives to construe *ratio* [reason, understanding] and its derivatives.[43] This consistency suggests an attempt to represent the original Latin with great fidelity through the careful use of specific compounds; the Old English *Boethius* does not match the rigidity of the Benedictine Reform "method," but that same sense of respect for the Latin original seems to be present.[44]

These consistent choices seem to demonstrate an awareness of the semantic and stylistic opportunities made available by compound structures. *Anweald* allows great specificity in the type of power at issue, activating more important associations than the simple, prefixed noun *geweald* [power]. The *Boethius* does, in fact, use *geweald* on its own and as a constituent in the compound *gewealdleðer* [rein, bridle], but rarely. Clearly the prefixed word, although available for valid use in the translation, was nonetheless not preferred. The major semantic difference between the two words, of course, arises due to the compound nature of *anweald* and the type of power specified by *an–*. While *geweald* expresses "power" simply, *anweald* provides the more complicated senses of "sole authority," "complete authority," or "a ruler's authority."[45] *An–* specifies the type of power under discussion in a way that the prefix *ge–* cannot. The emphasis on the solitary possession of power by God or of earthly rule by the king expressed through the constituent *an–*, therefore, must have made *anweald* preferable to *geweald*. Indeed, the *Boethius* is concerned not with the control that anyone can have – such as the control over a horse via a bridle – but rather with the unique power specifically of a king as the earthly extension of the heavenly King. Thus, in a few important instances,

43 *Lichoma* translates *corpus* twelve times out of its fifty-four occurrences in the all-prose version. This includes one instance in which *corpus* in the Latin refers to a generic, round object (*corporis rotunditatem* [Bieler, *Boethii Philosophiae Consolatio*, V.p.4, line 69]); the Old English translation of this part specifies the human body (Godden and Irvine, *Boethius*, 1:378, line 118). Apparently *corpus* necessarily implied the human body to the translator, at least in this instance. *Gesceadwis* and its derivatives translate *ratio* and its derivatives thirteen times out of sixty-three occurrences in the all-prose version of the *Boethius*.

44 On the patterns of vocabulary and translation choices in texts associated with Benedictine Reform, see, among others, Gneuss, "The Origin of Standard Old English"; Hofstetter, *Winchester und der spätaltenglische Sprachgebrauch*; and Gretsch, *The Intellectual Foundations of the English Benedictine Reform*.

45 BT, s.v. *anweald*; *DOE*, s.v. *ānweald*.

the translation subtly utilizes the complexity of compound structures to produce greater precision along with consistency.

Cynewulf's texts, on the other hand, do not employ compounds for construal as frequently as the *Boethius* translations, nor do they display the same level of consistency, but some small patterns arise from an inspection of the data. In at least a few instances, the poems seem to take advantage of compounds' capacity to compress long phrases into single words, as is the case with "burgsittendum" [city dwellers] which translates "qui in eadem erant ciuitate" [those who were in that same city].[46] Old English could express the concept of "one who dwells in a city" in a multi-word phrase, but that phrase perhaps would have been too long for a single Old English alliterative half-line.[47] One group of compounds covers terms that have technical senses, such as *praefectus* [overseer] and *tribunal* [place of judgment]. It is not clear whether Anglo-Saxons would have known the technical senses or cultural resonances of these words, but the translations clearly eliminate all but the essential meaning (just as my modern English glosses do).[48] For example, *praefectus*, often originally associated with the government of a territory in the Roman empire and generally tacitly assuming a higher authority as the source of the prefect's authority, is rendered as *folcagend* [people-ruler], stripping away the trappings of Roman cultural reference along with the implied higher authority.[49] Elsewhere in the Old English corpus, *folcagend* is applied to Beowulf and the phoenix; a *folcagend* was apparently the highest link in the chain of earthly authority.[50] Similarly, construing *tribunal* as *domsetl* [judgment-seat] eliminates the original cultural resonances, retaining only the essential meaning.[51] One could potentially infer from the *–setl* constituent a possible reference to the Roman magistrate's three-legged chair, which was

46 Gradon, *Elene*, line 276; Mombrizio, *Sanctuarium*, 1:376, lines 47–8.

47 A half-line to itself, "burgsittendum" is a type D verse, scanned / | / \ x (see Terasawa, *Old English Metre*, 40–1).

48 Sauer, "Language and Culture," especially 463–7, addresses this issue of Anglo-Saxons' lack of knowledge of the original cultural context. See also Abraham, "Cynewulf's *Juliana*: A Case at Law"; Law, *Grammar and Grammarians*, 208–10; and Ogura, "Camel or Elephant?"

49 *Oxford Latin Dictionary*, s.v. *praefectus*.

50 Although the phoenix accrues sacred signification, *folcagend* is applied to it in terms of its rule over a land which, although not earthly, is also not heavenly; the parallel seems to be an earthly ruler.

51 *Oxford Latin Dictionary*, s.v. *tribunal*.

placed upon the platform and which was literally denoted by *tribunal*, but this possibility seems unlikely. It is more probable that Cynewulf's translation choices follow what was likely Anglo-Saxon scholarly tradition, as *domsetl* appears as a gloss for *tribunal* in other contexts.[52] It also seems likely, however, that *Juliana* and *Elene* may have been intentionally eliminating information which has no bearing on the essential story and could only clutter the poetry and confuse the audience.[53] They remove the Roman-specific details, putting the emphasis more on the fundamental narratives than on their Latin cultural sources.

These examples illustrate a strategy which negotiates the translator's difficult task of retaining both adequacy and acceptability in the new text. By definition, no translation can recreate its source with perfect accuracy; some information – whether semantic, stylistic, or otherwise – inevitably disappears in the process of translation, thus decreasing the adequacy of the translation. Nonetheless, one task of a translator is to strive for some sort of adequacy. A competing claim on a translator's efforts, however, is the acceptability of the newly created text in the target language: the new text must fit the milieu of the target culture and not seem so foreign as to alienate any possible new audience. In the examples from Cynewulf's poems, the Old English compounds eliminate some original semantic details, thus decreasing the text's adequacy but also increasing its semantic acceptability in Anglo-Saxon culture. The construing compounds, lacking any of the Roman connotations, fit more easily into an Anglo-Saxon mental framework – if not one representing an actual reality of the time, then one representing the framework for understanding Christian narratives and vernacular poetry. For example, Anglo-Saxons did not consider Roman authorities to be divinely ordained, making *folcagend* the most appropriate construal of *praefectus*.

The need to augment semantic acceptability for the target culture must also fuel the use of compounds to construe of words that carry not Roman but biblical connotations in Cynewulf's poems. For example, the construal

52 For example, *domsetl* glosses *tribunal* in two different glosses on Hymn 75, verse 2; see Gneuss, *Hymnar und Hymnen*, 362, and Milfull, *The Hymns of the Anglo-Saxon Church*, 301.

53 See also Frederick, "Warring with Words."

of *propheta* [prophets] as *fyrnwita* [ancient sage] also "Anglicizes" the text. *Witega* is the common gloss for *propheta*, and it specifically implies a superhuman source of knowledge.[54] *Fyrnwita*, on the other hand, does not normally appear as a gloss for *propheta*, even though it is associated with prophecy once, when applied to King David.[55] Nonetheless, *Elene* employs *fyrnwita* over *witega*, reflecting the source with less than perfect adequacy, for *fyrnwitan* has connotations unrelated to the Latin original that influence the meaning of the Old English text; these unrelated connotations, however, must have created additional acceptability in the new text. The constituent *fyrn–* most commonly appears in texts with religious themes or assocations, usually as an element of *fyrndagas* [olden days]. *Fyrndagas* in those texts functions as a narrative signal that the temporal setting for the narrative is pre-Christian, most often Judaic pre-Christian, but occasionally pagan. In particular, *fyrn–* generally became associated with pre-Christian times, due to its frequent collocation with pre-Christian (pagan) Anglo-Saxons.[56] *Fyrn–* thus introduces a pre-Christian connotation in Cynewulf's texts, reinforcing the source's reference to the prophets with an Old English lexical item associated with the time period of the Old Testament, but also incorporating a non-Christian implication. That implication aligns *Elene* with other Old English poetry more than with its source, with acceptability in the form of semantic cultural resonance apparently influencing word choice over and against an interest in adequate fidelity to the source.

A similar linguistic-cultural resonance likely motivated the construal of *lignum* [tree] as *sigebeam* [victory-tree] in *Elene* line 420. In all likelihood, *beam* [tree] alone would have been a perfectly adequate construal in terms

54 BT, s.v. *witega*.

55 The other occurrences of *fyrnwita* are at *Andreas*, line 784; *Beowulf*, line 2123; and *Genesis A*, line 1154. Without a definite source text for *Andreas*, it is impossible to know *fyrnwita*'s role in the translation, although it is applied to Abraham. The occurrence in *Beowulf* clearly is not a translation, and, referring to *Æschere*, does not include the notion of prophecy. The occurrence in *Genesis A* is part of the translation of Genesis 5:9–14, which deals with Enos and does not contain the word *propheta*. Interestingly, all occurrences of *fyrnwita* except the one in *Elene*, line 1153, are part of the phrase "frod fyrnwita." This fact may suggest that the other occurrences are formulaic, as problematic as that claim is, and that the occurrence in *Elene* is a careful choice.

56 Robinson, "A Sub-Sense of Old English *fyrn*(–)."

of basic semantic denotation. The addition of *sige–*, however, provides several valuable features, such as the creation of alliteration with *secan* in the first half of the line. Moreover, the *sige–* constituent aligns the compound powerfully with stereotypical Old English poetic discourse, introducing to Christ's act of submission the idea of martial victory. As elsewhere in Old English literature, notably in *The Dream of the Rood*, Christ's surrender to a painful, humiliating death on the cross is transformed into a conqueror's victory. In *The Dream of Rood*, Christ takes on the role of military commander, actively mounting the cross, and his disciples become thegns; there is no reference to passivity or surrender on Christ's part.[57] This same adumbration of martial concepts presents itself concisely in *Elene* through the constituent *sige–*, which transforms the cross, originally a means of humiliation and torture, into the route to glorious conquest. Thus, construing *lignum* as *sigebeam* instead of simply *beam* taps into an existing mode of Anglo-Saxon thought, again tailoring Cynewulf's translation to its target culture.[58]

Similar effects occur in the *Boethius* with *woruld–* compounds, which bring to the fore the ultimately transitory nature of worldly wealth, worldly power, and the world itself that lies at the heart of Boethius's consolation. Often figured in the Latin source as the fickle *Fortuna*, or Lady Fortune, the apparent dominance of the earthly over the divine in human life plagues Boethius. The four instances in which *woruldsælða* construes *fortuna* all cluster in the translations of the first two proses of Book II, which introduce the image of the wheel of fortune.[59] These compounds bring the dichotomy of world and heaven into focus through specification. They make explicit the earthly, non-divine nature of *Fortuna*'s possessions: the point that *Philosophia* must prove to Boethius in the Latin becomes overtly expressed and assumed essentially a priori

57 See lines 39–42 in Krapp, *The Vercelli Book*, 62. For a discussion, see Duncan, "'Quid Hinieldus cum Christo?'" For a discussion of modifying content to fit cultural expectations, see Wilcox, "Vernacular Biblical Epics."

58 The concept of victory through the Crucifixion is, of course, present in all forms of Christianity, and the trope of the *miles Christi* [soldier of God] appears in many Christian works outside of Anglo-Saxon England, such as Prudentius's influential *Psychomachia*, in which the vices and virtues are allegorized in a massive battle over the human soul. However, Anglo-Saxons in particular seem to have embraced this version of Christianity vigorously.

59 *Woruldsælða* translates *fortuna* in the following places: Godden and Irvine, *Boethius*, 1:251, line 4; 1:252, line 25; and 1:253, lines 60 and 64.

in the Old English through these compounds. Indeed, there can be little argument about the worldly nature of riches when the very words expressing those riches contain the word *woruld* [world]. Thus, the Old English translation condenses the Latin source's line of reasoning into a single constituent, short cutting several steps of logical argumentation to highlight the contrast between heavenly and earthly goods. Riches and power were not completely to be shunned at all times, but poverty and humility were holy attributes and virtues for the translation's audience to a greater degree than for the original audience.[60] Although produced before the tenth-century Benedictine Reform, the *Boethius* assumes and taps into a Christian paradigm of eschewing worldly wealth that developed most fully after Boethius's original composition. Thus, the unargued assumption of a worldly nature for *Fortuna* again resonates with an Anglo-Saxon world view, supporting semantic-cultural acceptability over adequacy.

The pattern of using compounds for construal in these texts, then, is not one of creating translations of the greatest adequacy but one of eliminating the resonances of the source culture and introducing elements that resonate instead with the target culture of the Anglo-Saxons. Of course, the changes that these translations have effected on their sources have not gone unnoticed by scholars.[61] What the scholarship has not attended to is the fact that it is the complexity of compound structures that allows this subtle realignment of the texts. As with *anweald* and the *worold–* compounds in the *Boethius* translations, employing compounds for construal allows the translations to produce subtle effects that would be more difficult or even impossible to achieve with simplices. Without the opportunity for compounding, introducing the pre-Christian connotation of *fyrn–* and the martial connotation of *sige–*, for example, would likely have been more difficult or at least clunkier. Thus, both camps – represented by the *Boethius* on one hand and Cynewulf's poems on the other – recognized the utility of compound structures for construal and put them to work.

This pattern of compounds' utility in direct construal, however, is notably minor overall. While the *Boethius* displays at least a moderate

---

60 Boethius's Latin text famously makes no overt reference to Christianity.

61 See, for example, Bately, *Literary Prose*; Payne, *King Alfred and Boethius*; Cook, "Philosophy's Metamorphosis into Wisdom"; Discenza, "Power, Skill, and Virtue"; Szarmach, "The *Timaeus* in Old English"; and Discenza, *The King's English*.

level of consistency, there is no consistency regarding which compounds in Cynewulf's poems construe a Latin word from the source and which do not. For instance, *fyrngewrit* occurs four times in *Elene*, but only once does it construe a word in the source, *lex* [law].[62] Similarly, *heofoncyning* [heaven-king] appears once in *Juliana* construing *deus* [God],[63] but it appears two more times in *Elene*, without construing anything directly.[64] Moreover, *deus* is construed by various phrases and simplices other than *heofoncyning* at several points. God superficially disappears altogether from the construal of "hominem dei" [man of God] as "soðfæstum" [righteous, pious] in *Juliana*, although the implication is surely still there.[65] This variation, coupled with the fact that *heofoncyning* is a common appellation for God in Old English literature generally, reduces the significance of the fact that *heofoncyning* construes *deus* twice. Rather, those two instances come to appear accidental in context, as *heofoncyning* clearly did not target *deus* in Cynewulf's texts in the way that *anweald* did power words in the *Boethius*. This variation occurs with compounds throughout Cynewulf's two poems, suggesting a widespread inconsistency in translation choice. Clearly, no consistent method for treating appearances of *deus*, *lex*, or any other given word in the sources is at play in Cynewulf's translations.

What remains consistent about Cynewulf's translation method instead is that compounds rarely do the work of directly construing Latin words or phrases. Rather than rely on compounds for construal, *Juliana* and *Elene* overwhelmingly tend to use simplices to construe words and phrases from

62 Gradon, *Elene*, line 373; Mombrizio, *Sanctuarium*, 1:377, lines 13–14; the other three occurrences of *fyrngewrit* are in lines 155, 431, and 560.

63 Woolf, *Juliana*, line 360. The Latin source is edited in Lapidge, "*Passio*"; the *deum* in question appears on 160. For an earlier discussion of the differences between *Juliana* and a Latin version of the *passio*, see Garnett, "The Latin and the Anglo-Saxon *Juliana*."

64 Gradon, *Elene*, lines 367 and 747; Mombrizio, *Sanctuarium*, 1:377, lines 7–8 and 378, lines 22–3.

65 Lapidge, "*Passio*," 160; Woolf, *Juliana*, line 362. Further examples of construals of *deus* are "cyninga Cyning" (Woolf, *Juliana*, line 289; Lapidge, "*Passio*," 160), simply "God" (Woolf, *Juliana*, line 47; Lapidge, "*Passio*," 157), and "dryhten" (Gradon, *Elene*, line 292; Mombrizio, *Sanctuarium*, 1:376, line 51); "deus deus" becomes "dryhten hælend" (Mombrizio, *Sanctuarium*, 1:378, line 18; Gradon, *Elene*, line 725).

their Latin originals, leaving compounds to provide expansions on the source texts.[66] These expansions can be rather extensive, sometimes with multiple lines growing from a single word in the source. For example, when the Jews hand Judas over to Elene, the Old English goes into detail concerning the extent of their fear:

Ða wurdon hiȩ deaðes on wenan,
ades 7 endelifes 7 þær þa ænne betæhton
giddum gearusnottorne – þam wæs Iudas nama
cenned for cneomagum – þone hie þære cwene agefon,
sægdon hine sundorwisne, "He þe mæg soð gecyðan,
onwreon wyrda geryno swa ðu hine wordum frignest,
æriht from ord[e] oð ende forð;
he is for eorðan æðeles cynnes,
wordcræftes wis 7 witgan sunu."[67]

Then they expected death – the funeral pyre and the end of life – and then handed over the one who was extremely wise in the proverbs – he was named Judas among his kinsmen. They gave him to the queen and said that he was very wise. "He can reveal the truth to you, unveil the secrets of the events just as you ask him in words, the law from the beginning all the way to the end. He is of the region's noble lineage, knowledgeable in rhetoric and the son of a prophet."

The source reads:

At illi timentes tradiderunt Iudam dicentes: "Ecce uir iustus et prophetae filius qui legem optime nouit domina et quaecumque desyderat cor tuum ostendet tibi diligenter."[68]

But, fearful, they handed over Iudas, saying: "Here is a just man, the son of a prophet, who knows the law well, mistress, and will reveal to you carefully whatever your heart desires.

66 As noted above, only 12 per cent (31 of 254 occurrences) of the compounds in *Juliana* and 10 per cent (51 of 489) in *Elene* directly construe anything in the source.
67 Gradon, *Elene*, lines 584b–92.
68 Mombrizio, *Sanctuarium*, 1:377, lines 54–6.

From the single, general word *timentes* [fearful] in the source, the Old English grows to two half-lines (584b–585a) with distinct information about the Jews' thoughts. The Jews are specifically concerned about death and also the funeral pyre itself as a metonym for death. Interestingly, the translation does not describe the Jews as fearful but simply as in a state of expectation, albeit expectation of normally frightening things. These details complicate Elene's character, with the Jews' fears further bolstering her similarities to the pagan interrogators in *passiones*.[69] In a precursor to the reaction to Judas's treatment, the audience's sympathy begins to recede from Elene and move towards the Jews as their fears and confusion repeatedly surface, showing them to be less malevolent than simply ignorant, pointedly not casting them as clear-cut villains. In terms of translation details, the compounds mostly remain restricted to the expansions. Only *æriht* could possibly be taken to construe anything specific from the source (perhaps *legem*), but if so the translation is quite altered and reformulated compared to the original; most probable is that *wyrda geryno* translates *legem*. The other four compounds – *endelif*, *gearusnotor*, *cneomæg*, and *sundorwis* – are clearly new to the translation. As for *æriht*, although it certainly could translate *lex*, it is not straightforwardly presented as something Judas knows, as it is in the Latin; *æriht* as the object of knowledge is only implied in the Old English. Moreover, the clause in which *æriht* appears functions as an appositional variation on *soð* in line 588, not as an independent translation.

In another example of expansion, the demon at one point gives the following confession during his struggle with Juliana:

Oft ic syne ofteah,
ablende bealoþoncum beorna unrim
monna cynnes, misthelme forbrægd
þurh attres ord eagna leoman
sweartum scurum, 7 ic sumra fet
forbræc bealosearwum, sume in bryne sende,
in liges locan, þæt him lasta wearð
siþast gesyne;[70]

69 See Bjork, *Old English Verse Saints' Lives*, 62. On the other hand, Olsen, "Cynewulf's Autonomous Women," 225, claims that disapproval of Elene as torturer arises from a misunderstanding of heroic women in Germanic literature.

70 Woolf, *Juliana*, lines 468b–75a.

> Often, with evil intent, I deprived of sight and blinded countless warriors from the race of men; I snatched away the light of their eyes with a covering of mist, through a poisoned spear point, with dark clouds. Also, with evil deceit, I crushed the feet of some, sent some into the fire, into the flame's embrace, so that that was the last their tracks were seen.

The demon here provides quite a few details, greatly extending the length of his confession through appositional variation. In the Latin source, this passage in the demon's confession lacks comparable rhetorical decoration, tending instead towards plain, simple speech:

> Daemon respondit: "Ego multorum oculos extinxi, aliorum pedes confregi, aliorum pedes in ignem misi ..."[71]

> The demon responded: "I put out the eyes of many, crushed the feet of some, put the feet of others into the fire ..."

The Latin passage focuses on factual presentation without any characterizations of the demon's mental state nor with many details about the actions themselves, two things which the Old English translation takes care to provide. Very little of the Old English actually directly construes what appears in the Latin: the phrase "ic syne ofteah ... unrim" functions, as it were, as the skeleton onto which are added several appositional variations. The phrase renders the four words of the Latin, "Ego multorum oculos extinxi," as directly as the original. The sense of the words in Old English does not exactly reproduce the original, but they express the essential point as briefly as the Latin. The treatment of the rest of the Latin passage proceeds in the same way: "ic sumra fet forbræc" and "sume in bryne sende" are as terse and forthright as their Latin sources, and the rest of the Old English passage – most of it, in fact – does not correspond to anything in the source but instead expands upon the basic outline provided in the Latin.

Although they stand in the supposedly opposing camp, the *Boethius* translations also expand upon the source in similar manners. In fact, the *Boethius* amplifies its source even through the regular employment of *anweald*. Although the discussion above highlights the use of *anweald* to achieve translation adequacy, the word occurs another ninety-nine times

71 Lapidge, "*Passio*," 161.

in the shared prose sections in addition to the occurrences in which it construes a specific word or phrase from the Latin text. For example, in the translation of Boethius's II.p.6, a cluster of occurrences of *anweald* appears with no power words in the original Latin:

> Gif hit þonne æfre gewurð swa hit swiðe seldan gewyrð þæt se anweald and se weorðscipe becume to godum men and to wisum, hwæt bið þar þonne licwyrðes buton his god and his weorðscipe, þæs godan cyninges næs þæs anwealdes? Forþam þe se anweald næfre ne bið god buton se god sie þe hine hæbbe. Þe hit bið þæs monnes god nas þæs anwealdes gif se anweald god bið. Forþam hit bið þætte nan man for his rice ne cymð to cræftum and to medemnesse, ac for his cræftum and for his medumnesse he cymð to rice and anwealde. Þi ne bið nan mon for his anwealde na þe betere, ac for his cræftum he beoð god gif he god bið, and for his cræftum he bið anwealdes weorðe gif he his weorðe bið.[72]

> If it then ever happens – as it very rarely happens – that power and honour should fall to a good and wise man, what is praiseworthy in that [fact] other than his goodness and honour, that of the king and not of the power [itself]? Therefore, power is never good unless he who has it be good. Therefore, if the power is good, it is [because of] the goodness of the man and not of the power [itself]. Thus it is that no man comes to virtues and worthiness due to his authority, but due to his virtues and due to his worthiness he comes to authority and power. Thus no man is the better because of his power, but because of his virtues he is good if he is good, and because of his virtues he is worthy of power if he is worthy of it.

This passage expands on a comment on the source of honour and power in the Latin original:

> At si quando, quod perrarum est, probis deferantur, quid in eis aliud quam probitas utentium placet? Ita fit ut non uirtutibus ex dignitate sed ex uirtute dignitatibus honor accedat.[73]

---

72 Godden and Irvine, *Boethius*, 1:272, lines 23–33.

73 Bieler, *Boethii Philosophiae Consolatio*, II.p.6. For attribution of this Latin passage as the source of the Old English passage, see Godden and Irvine, *Boethius*, 2:309, note to 16.23–33, and source detail C.B.9.3.150.01, 2001, Fontes Anglo-Saxonici Project, *Fontes Anglo-Saxonici.*

> But if ever they [power and honour] are conferred upon estimable men, which is very rare, what is pleasing in those men other than the exercising of virtue? Thus it happens that honour proceeds not to virtue from rank but from virtue to rank.

While the basic thrusts of the original and the translation are effectively similar, the Old English significantly expands the moment in its explanation of the fairly terse logic of the Latin. The most obvious changes are the lengthy, additional rephrasing and the addition of the king, which betrays a fundamental concern of the Old English *Boethius* that is not present in the original. The occurrences of *anweald* in the passage are also technically additions, since no power words overtly appear in the specific source section of Latin. Power is clearly part of the overall discussion at this point in the Latin, but the Old English overtly names it in this passage in what seems to be an attempt at clarity. At most, one could take *dignitas* [rank] as the source for some of the ocurrences of *anweald*, since with rank would come power. The two occurrences of *dignitas*, however, cannot account for the proliferation of occurrences of *anweald*; at least some must be taken as expansions. The rest of this section of the *Boethius* expands even further, with no apparent basis in the Latin source, but with several more occurrences of *anweald*. This expansion is so extreme, that it leads Godden and Irvine to comment that "There is nothing in [the] DCP [*De consolatione Philosophiae*] or the glosses to match this remarkable passage about wisdom and power. Its claim that wisdom and virtue naturally bring power seems indeed very much at odds with the general argument of the DCP."[74] In the midst of using *anweald* fairly consistently to construe Latin words of power, the Old English translation also peppers it throughout a modification and significant expansion of the Latin source's content.

These additions in the *Boethius*, *Juliana*, and *Elene* thus expand upon the contents of their Latin originals but most importantly recalibrate the translations for their new audience. For example, power and the unsuitability of many who hold it are major issues in Boethius's original Latin, but power takes on a subtly new role in the Old English *Boethius*. Presented as the product of a ruler and not a captive, the translation develops a different conception of power, one in which earthly power has its uses and benefits. Addressing future wielders of power, the Old English *Boethius*

74 Godden and Irvine, *Boethius*, 2:309–10, note to 16.33–8.

therefore offers advice on the proper uses of power and does not completely decry it.[75] Importantly, in the expansion quoted above, the source of goodness is carefully explained in a manner and level of detail not found in the original Latin. This different conception is in many ways distilled in the additions of compound *anweald*, which expands the work done in construing power words such as *potestas* and *potentia* with *anweald*. The specific type of power at issue and its positive value becomes much more prominent through additional occurrences of *anweald* than would have been the case otherwise. The increased presence of *anweald* also connects the Old English *Boethius* with other texts associated with Alfred's translation initiative, specifically the Old English *Orosius* and *Bede*.[76] In these texts, the succession of *anweald* becomes the expression of providential history, a history which links Alfred to a long line of divinely chosen rulers.[77] The *Boethius* complements the historical translations of *Orosius* and *Bede* by addressing individual power within that line of providential succession, and its frequent use of *anweald* without a corresponding power word in the Latin reveals the importance of the theme to the translator, emphasizing it beyond its original place, and recalibrating the kind of power being discussed.

This realignment of Boethius's original text to fit an Anglo-Saxon cultural context becomes even more clear with the several *woruld*– compounds clustered in *Meter 7*. One of these, *woruldsælða*, is taken directly from the prose version of this metre, and one, *woruldgitsung* [covetousness], is an elaboration of *gitsung* [avarice] in the prose version.[78] The rest of the compounds, however, are original additions to *Meter 7*: *woruldearfoð* [earthly misery], occurring three times; *woruldmen* [earthly men], occurring once; and *woruldsælða* occurring once in addition to the instance that borrows from the prose.[79] This clustering of *woruld*– compounds in *Meter 7* can hardly be an accident, given that the *Meter* treats the metaphorical places

75 See Nelson, "Power and Authority at the Court of Alfred," 311–12; Discenza, "Symbolic Capital in the Translations of Alfred the Great," 453; and Discenza, "The Influence of Gregory the Great on the Alfredian Social Imaginary."

76 Bately, *Old English Orosius*, and Miller, *Bede's Ecclesiastical History*.

77 Kretzschmar, "Adaptation and *Anweald*," 142–3.

78 Godden and Irvine, *Boethius*, 1:406–7, lines 52 and 12, respectively, for *Meter 7*, and Godden and Irvine, *Boethius*, 1:264, line 7, for the prose.

79 Godden and Irvine, *Boethius*, 1:406–7, lines 26, 35, and 49 for *woruldearfoða*, line 41 for *woruldmen*, and line 54 for *woruldsælða*.

on which one should build the foundation of wisdom, a thematic extension of the dichotomy between earth and heaven. One should, advises the text, found one's wisdom and the *modes hus* [house of the mind] on eternal, divine elements, not on transitory worldly features.[80] The addition of *woruld–* compounds heightens the contrast at work in the Latin source, with the compounds reiterating the earthly, undesirable side of the equation. The repetition refuses to allow the concept of worldly destruction to recede from focus for long, overtly emphasizing the contrast between the earth and the proper foundation for wisdom, which is only suggested in the Latin original. As noted earlier, Anglo-Saxons were not expected to shun riches and power completely and at all times, but poverty and humility were positive pursuits for the overtly Christianized culture in Alfred's time. Heavenly pursuits purportedly surpassed worldly ones for Anglo-Saxons, and the *woruld–* compounds thus again realign the original argument, increasing the translation's cultural acceptability.

Similar to *Meter 7*, *Meter 20* adds new compounds to increase its acceptability. Specifically, several compounds denoting some type of water-body appear without directly construing any specific word from the Latin source, Boethius's best known poem, III.m.9, his distillation of Plato's *Timaeus*. Four of these compounds occur close together and contain the second constituent *–stream*: *lagustream* [water, sea, ocean], *merestream* [sea-water], and two occurrences of *egorstream* [sea, ocean].[81] Another water compound, *laguflod* [wave, stream, waters] occurs some fifty lines later.[82] These five compounds, coming in the midst of the long explanation of the nature of the four elements, insert extra water imagery into the versification that is not present in the original Latin or its prose translation. Interestingly, this explanatory passage contains no compounds at all in the forty lines preceding the water compounds, a rare occurrence in the *Meters*. The appearance of the water compounds, then, marks the reintroduction of compounds to the explanatory section, making their presence particularly noticeable in comparison with the preceding lines. Remarkably, none of the other three elements (fire, air, earth) merits compounds; while all four are expressed variously with simplices, only water is ever expressed with compounds.

80 Godden and Irvine, *Boethius*, 1:407, line 32.

81 Godden and Irvine, *Boethius*, 1:463–71, lines 111, 114, 118, 122, respectively.

82 Godden and Irvine, *Boethius*, 1:468, line 173.

The location of the fifth water compound, *laguflod*, reveals some of the effect of expressing only the element of water with compounds. *Laguflod* occurs as part of the description of the world as an immobile yolk within a moving egg:

> þæm anlicost þe on æge bið
> gioleca on middan, glideð hwæðre
> æg ymbutan. Swa stent eall weoruld
> stille on tille, streamas ymbutan,
> lagufloda gelac, lyfte and tungla,
> and sio scire scell scriðeð ymbutan
> dogora gehwilce, dyde lange swa.[83]

> It is most like what is inside an egg: a yolk in the middle, about which the egg yet glides. In this way the entire world stands immobile on its foundation; streams – the tumult of waters [and] of the sky and the stars – and the bright shell move all about [it] every day [and] have done so for a long time.

Lagufloda gelac in line 173 is an appositional variation of *streamas* in line 172, emphasizing the water, or perhaps a nonspecific fluid, surrounding the earth. This image of the world as an egg yolk likely makes reference to commentary on the *materia fluitans* [fluid matter] in line 5 of the original Latin metre.[84] Concerning this fluid matter, one version of the Remigian commentary tradition gives several possible explanations, including the following: "terra namque operta erat aqua licet tenui veluti nebula aeris" [alternatively, the earth had been covered by water, albeit a thin layer, just like a thin film of air].[85] It is possible that *Meter 20* conflates this conception of the earth with its egg description, imagining a round centre

83 Godden and Irvine, *Boethius*, 1:467–8, lines 169–75.

84 According to Griffiths, *Alfred's Metres of Boethius*, 36–7, the image of the world as an immobile yolk stems from a commentary tradition of the Anonymous St Gall type and extends ultimately to Empedocles, although the Old English Martyrology contains a similar image which may depend upon an Irish source, according to Cross, "*De Ordine Creaturarum Liber* in OE Prose." See also Dronke, *Fabula*, 79–99; Anlezark, "Three Notes on the Old English *Meters of Boethius*," 13–14; and Szarmach, "Boethius's Influence in Anglo-Saxon England," 234–5.

85 Silk, *Saeculi noni auctoris in Boetii Consolationem philosophiae commentarius*, 333.

surrounded by liquid. This liquid is simultaneously air, which is yet again similar to water – the *streamas* that are also the *lyft* and *tunglas* but still the *lagufloda gelac*. Such a conflation would explain the emphasis on water created by the insertion of *laguflod* and the other four water compounds. The significant role that fluid matter plays in the various conceptions of the universe, and also in the creation of the universe, makes water more than just one element out of four. It is connected in the commentary tradition to the underlying nature of reality in a much deeper way than the other three elements. The increased emphasis on fluid created through the insertion of the water compounds brings the verse translation further in line with the interpretation of Boethius's text that the intellectual elite in its Anglo-Saxon audience would have held, given the influence of the commentary tradition.

In addition to these cultural realignments, compounds also increase the formal acceptability in the *Meters*, *Juliana*, and *Elene*, often by creating the alliteration expected of Old English poetry. In many cases, the prose translation of one of Boethius's poems uses a simplex which then becomes the second constituent of a compound in the verse version. The first constituent of these compounds usually conforms to the alliterative needs of the line, suggesting that the compounding itself was undertaken, at least partially, to adhere to the rules of Old English verse.[86] For example, the prose version of II.m.5 employs *gitsere* [miser], which becomes *feohgitsere* [money-miser] in the verse, alliterating with *forma* earlier in the line.[87] The beginning of the sentence remains unchanged except for the addition of the *feoh*– constituent, suggesting that only the formal, alliterative element is at issue in the versification at this point. A similar alteration of *gitsere* also occurs in the beginning of the translations of III.m.3, becoming *woruldgitsere* [world-miser] in the metrical version, alliterating with *welegan* [wealthy].[88]

Beyond alliteration, Cynewulf's poems employ compounds to create other large-scale formal features, such as echoic patterns. An example of the latter can be seen in *Juliana* lines 468b–75a, the part of the demon's

86 For discussions of "poetic compounds" as motivated mainly or even solely by needs of alliteration, rhythm, and tradition, see Niles, "Compound Diction"; Russom, *Old English Meter and Linguistic Theory*, 92–7; Mazo, "Compound Diction"; and Russom, "Aesthetic Criteria in Old English Heroic Style," 71.

87 Godden and Irvine, *Boethius*, 1:271, line 21, and 1:414, line 55, respectively.

88 Godden and Irvine, *Boethius*, 1:296, line 78, and 1:444, line 1, respectively.

long confessional speeches quoted above. The two compounds *bealoþoncum* (line 469a) and *bealosearwum* (line 473a) create a parallelism absent in the source: both almost immediately follow terse translations and share a very similar verse structure.[89] In both instances, these verses are built around the constituent *bealo–* compounded with a second constituent generally denoting thought of some kind, both of which together follow a polysyllabic verb, modifying it adverbially. Both half-lines follow the reiteration of the personal pronoun *ic* in metrically similar b-verses.[90] Of course, none of these characteristics appears in the Latin original, which provides no adverbial modifiers.[91] The multi-point parallelism of these two passages is characteristic of the repetitive nature of echoic composition, a common device in Old English and early Germanic poetry.[92] Specifically, the *bealo–* compounds are literal echo-words, with each one containing

89 Although no other lines closely resemble these two, one might describe lines 469a and 473a as members of a "formulaic system," a term which denotes the fundamental pattern underlying a collection of related passages, often half-lines. The members of a system are related through the repetition of a single word or morpheme coupled with the limited variation of the rest of the text in question, normally requiring at least similar if not identical rhythms. Fry, "Old English Formulas and Systems," first proposed this concept for Old English poetry, and Niles subsequently refined it in "Formula and Formulaic System in *Beowulf*," which he later reworked as "Formula and Formulaic System" in his *"Beowulf": The Poem and Its Tradition*, 121–37. Riedinger, "The Old English Formula in Context," puts forward the concept of the "set," which is less restrictive than the concept of formulas but more restrictive than that of systems: a set entails members of a system limited to employing one fixed, stressed word and only one synonymously varied word. Foley, *Traditional Oral Epic*, 235, concludes that the formulaic system is too restrictive a concept to describe Old English traditional poetics accurately by itself, although it remains useful for certain purposes; see also Tyler, *Old English Poetics*, 101–23.

90 The half-lines containing *ic* are metrically similar although not perfectly identical; both are type B verses: line 468b, "oft ic syne ofteah," scanned x x / | x x /, and line 472b, "7 ic sumra fet," scanned x x / | x / (see Terasawa, *Old English Metre*, 38–9). This similarity may point to their membership in a formulaic system.

91 Lapidge, "*Passio*," 161.

92 For a detailed discussion of echoic repetition, see Battles, "The Art of the Scop," 168–208. For earlier important work on echoes, see Beaty, "The Echo-Word in *Beowulf*"; Rosier, "The Literal-Figurative Identity of *The Wanderer*"; Kintgen, "Echoic Repetition in Old English Poetry"; Rosier, "Generative Composition in *Beowulf*"; and Foley, *Traditional Oral Epic*, 340–4, in which echoic repetitions are discussed as "responsion."

the same morpheme and thus creating "proximate repetition."[93] Although similar devices are described in Latin rhetorical treatises, this phenomenon is also clearly a traditional, non-Latinate stylistic element.[94] Moreover, the addition of *misthelme* [covering of mist] in line 470 adds appositional, varied description of the blindings and provides the necessary alliteration with *monna*. The addition of these three compounds, then, creates formal stylistic features characteristic of Old English verse in general: alliteration, variation, and echoic parallelism. Not necessarily furthering any specific theme, these compounds instead imbue the translation with the characteristics of Old English poetic discourse; they infuse the text with the formal features expected by and appropriate for the literary culture of the target audience.

The *Boethius* translations similarly employ compounds to create echoic patterns, specifically in the metrical translations of Boethius's poetry.[95] In the case of the water compounds discussed above, the four that cluster close together are all formed on the second constituent *–stream* in the following passage:

Ne meahte on ðære eorðan awuht libban
ne wuhte þon ma wætres brucan,
on eardian ænige cræfte
for cele anum, gif þu, cyning engla,
wið fyre hwæthwugu foldan and *lagustream*
ne mengdest togædre, and gemetgodest

93 A literal echo, according to Battles, "The Art of the Scop," 176, involves the repetition of the same identical morpheme, as opposed to etymological echoes, in which the repeated morphemes are only etymologically related.

94 Battles, "The Art of the Scop," 174–5. For the knowledge of classical rhetoric in Anglo-Saxon England, see chapter one above. For classical rhetoric in Cynewulf's poems in particular, see Wine, "*Juliana* and the Figures of Rhetoric"; Wine, *Figurative Language in Cynewulf*; and Steen, *Verse and Virtuosity*, 110–38.

95 On poetic diction in the *Meters*, see Metcalf, "The Poetic Language of the Old English *Meters of Boethius*"; Metcalf, "On the Authorship and Originality of the *Meters of Boethius*"; Metcalf, *Poetic Diction in the Old English Meters of Boethius*; Monnin, "The Making of the Old English *Meters of Boethius*"; Monnin, "Poetic Improvements in the Old English *Meters of Boethius*"; Yoshino, "Poetic Syntax in the Old English *Meters of Boethius*"; Griffith, "The Composition of the Metres"; and Mize, *Traditional Subjectivities*, 163–71.

cele and hæto   cræfte þine,
þæt þæt fyr ne mæg   foldan and *merestream*
blate forbærnan,   þeah hit wið ba twa sie
fæste gefeged,   fæder ealdgeweorc.
Ne þincð me þæt wundur   wuhte þe læsse
þæt ðios eorðe mæg   and *egorstream*,
swa ceald gesceaft,   cræfta nane
ealles adwæscan   þæt þæt him oninnan sticað
fyres gefeged   mid frean cræfte.
Þæt is agen eard   *eagorstreames*,
wætres, on eorþan   and on wolcnum eac
and efne swa same   uppe ofer rodere.[96]

Nothing would be able to survive on the earth, nor could anything make any more use of water, nor live on [the earth] with any success because of the cold alone if you, king of angels, had not combined earth and ocean to some degree with fire and regulated cold and hot through your power such that fire can not lividly burn up earth and sea-water, even though it is firmly composed against them, the old creation of the father. It is no less amazing to me that this earth and sea, such cold creations, cannot through any means completely extinguish the power of fire that remains fixed within them, combined through the lord's power. That is a peculiar home of the sea, water on earth and also in the clouds, and even just the same up beyond the sky.

In addition to the repetition of *stream* in each compound, the last two echo *egor* as their first constituent. These echoes must be deliberate, since three of the four compounds do not appear in the prose original – they are additions to the poetic version. Both *egorstream* and *merestream* in the verse replace the simplex *wæter* in the prose, and the abandonment of *wæter* in the formation of the compound signals an interest in the creation of *–stream* echoes in its place.[97]

96 Godden and Irvine, *Boethius*, 1:466, lines 107–24, emphasis added.
97 Godden and Irvine, *Boethius*, 1:316, lines 189 and 190.

Meter 7 also employs echoic composition, repeating many different words and morphemes throughout, including the several *woruld–* compounds.[98] Along with the *woruld–* compounds, *ren* [rain], *sond* [sand], *grund* [ground], *geme* [care], *mod* [mind], *wind* [wind], *heall* [hall], *hus* [house], and *fæst* [firm] are each repeated multiple times throughout the poem. For instance, the image of sand swallowing rain recurs several times in the first half of the poem, reinforcing the uselessness of building on shifting ground. Also, the concept of a firm foundation, a *grundweall* in line 34, contrastingly echoes the *grundleas gitsung* [bottomless avarice] of line 15. This contrast intensifies the metaphorical bottomlessness of greed by focusing on *grund* as the foundation, albeit a metaphorical foundation, for the *modes hus* [house of the mind] in line 33. The *woruld–* compounds also display additional echoes in their second constituents: *woruldearfoð* occurs three times; *woruldsælða* occurs twice with *gesælða* occurring twice on its own as well; and *woruldgitsung* is echoed by *gitsung*.[99] This plethora of echoing suffuses *Meter 7*, setting it firmly within the traditional formal patterns of Old English poetry. It does not just carry the label of poetry, having been introduced as a "song," but it also fully performs the rhetorical and stylistic moves expected of Old English poetry.

This discussion of the differences between the prose and verse versions of Boethius's poetry assumes that the verse is dependent upon the prose. This assumption follows the standard view of the textual relationship, namely that the verse was derived from the prose, frequently borrowing the prose's word choice and word order but also frequently making changes to accommodate poetic needs.[100] An important point that remains unknown is the identity of the versifier, that is, whether the same person

98 These repetitions could be taken as instances of envelope patterning, in which words and/or ideas are repeated at the beginning and end of a verse paragraph. On envelope patterns in the *Meters*, see Stévanovitch, "Envelope Patterns in Translation." On envelope patterns in general, see Bartlett, *The Larger Rhetorical Patterns in Anglo-Saxon Poetry*, 9.

99 *Woruldearfoð* occurs in lines 26, 35, and 49. *Woruldsælða* occurs in lines 52 and 54, and *gesælða* in lines 30 and 48. *Woruldgitsung* occurs in line 12 with *gitsung* in 15.

100 Griffiths, "The Composition of the Metres," 80 and 134, expressing the current general concensus of this issue, espouses this view on the direction of dependency; see also Mize, *Traditional Subjectivities*, 156–8. Kiernan, "Alfred the Great's Burnt *Boethius*," 13, dissents, suggesting that the prose paraphrases the verse, and Szarmach, "*Meter 20*," 31–2, also questions the accepted view, taking the different functions of the two versions ("pedagogical" for Bodley 180 and "high art" for Cotton Otho A. vi) as possible evidence that the prosimetric version predated the all-prose.

translated the prose version and then versified portions, or one person produced the prose version and another produced the verse *Meters*.[101] Both of these questions, however, are essentially immaterial in examining the effects of the differences between the two versions. It is certainly possible that the characteristics assumed to have been added in a process of versification may instead have been removed in a process of "prosification." In either direction, the composition of each version depended upon a translator's conception of what style, vocabulary, and rhetorical effects were appropriate for that version, whether prose or verse. Similarly, positing one author or two, or even more, still leaves two versions of the translation, versions which present very different conceptions of the text. The direction of dependency and the identity of the reviser are not unimportant issues, but they do not change the understanding of what each version of the *Boethius* achieves, or tries to achieve, in terms of adhering to the discursive patterns of the target culture of the Anglo-Saxons. In short, regardless of who did what, the two versions of the *Boethius* use compounds to adhere to the formal expectations of Old English discourses, just as do Cynewulf's two translations.

These different effects produced by the subtle choices and deployment of compound words in *Juliana*, *Elene*, and the *Boethius* underscore the complexity behind the famous Alfredian dichotomy of "word for word" and "sense for sense."[102] *Anweald*, for example, both maintains accuracy and simultaneously creates greater acceptability. On one level, the consistent deployment of *anweald* in construing power words supports the translation's fidelity to its source as part of an attempt to maintain a one-to-one relationship between source and translation. At the same time, the specificity of the *an–* consituent and the additions of extra occurrences of *anweald* subtly mould the text to the expectations and world view of its Anglo-Saxon audiences. Importantly, the Old English *Boethius* is quite interested in advertising its status as a translation. Alfred's political

101 For reviews of the evidence and debate, see Bately, "The Alfredian Canon Revisited"; Godden, "The Player King"; Keynes, "The Power of the Written Word"; Smythe, "King Alfred's Translations"; Discenza, *The King's English*, 139–40n1; Godden, "Did King Alfred Write Anything?"; Pratt, "Problems of Authorship and Audience in the Writings of King Alfred the Great"; Bately, "Did King Alfred Actually Translate Anything?"; Godden and Irvine, *Boethius*, 1:140–51; Rowley, *The Old English Version of Bede's "Historia Ecclesiastica,"* 37–46; and Lockett, *Anglo-Saxon Psychologies*, 360–73.

102 Sweet, *Pastoral Care*, 1:7, lines 19–20.

position in the late 870s and early 880s, facing a significant Viking invasion and its aftermath, was precarious in many ways, and his translation program was one method to shore up his social authority.[103] In the proem, the Old English *Boethius* announces itself as a translation, thereby appropriating authority and cultural capital from Boethius's reputation and grafting it onto Alfred's. Nonetheless, the text needed to remain acceptable to its audience even in the midst of this appropriation, lest it alienate the audience and thus undermine the appropriation. Thus *anweald* flexibly performs several different functions, balancing accuracy and acceptability.

Cynewulf's poems, on the other hand, have no interest in any cultural capital that might come from the specific identity of their sources. The fact of being Christian seems to have been enough, and so they hide their nature as translations nearly completely. To be sure, the time periods and the genres of the narratives by themselves strongly suggest Latin sources, but the poems are presented in such a way that the audience could, theoretically, ignore those aspects. The poems seem to have greater interest in acculturating Christianity to Anglo-Saxon expectations, and in pursuit of that goal they provide Old English poetic style on every level – the line, the type-scene, the world view. Rather than the fairly simple, word-for-word and sense-for-sense conception of translation posited in the preface to the Old English *Regula pastoralis*, this situation more closely resembles the complexity described in the Alfredian preface to the Old English translation of Augustine's *Soliloquies*:

> Gaderode me þonne kigclas and stuþansceaftas, and lohsceaftas and hylfa to ælcum þara tola þe ic mid wircan cuðe, and bohtimbru and bolttimbru, and, to ælcum þara weorca þe ic wyrcan cuðe, þa wlitegostan treowo be þam dele ðe ic aberan meihte, ne com ic naþer mid anre byrðene ham þe me ne lyste ealne þane wude ham brengan, gif ic hyne ealne aberan meihte; on ælcum treowo ic geseah hwæthwugu þæs þe ic æt ham beþorfte.[104]

> Then I gathered for myself cudgels and props, and handles and helves for each of those tools with which I knew how to work, and arch-timber and building-timber and, for each of those products that I knew how to make, the most beautiful trees from the portion that I could carry. Nor did I come

103 See Nelson, "Power and Authority," and Discenza, "Symbolic Capital."

104 Carnicelli, *King Alfred's Version of St. Augustine's Soliloquies*, 47, lines 1–6.

> home with a load that did not make me want to bring home all the wood, if I could carry it all; in each tree I saw something that I needed at home.

In this image, the translator collects pieces from many different sources and actively combines them; the source text provides the raw material, with which the translator builds a product in another instance of the craftsmanship metaphor discussed in chapter 1 above.[105] This image more accurately characterizes the translation process in *Juliana* and *Elene* than does the more famous Alfredian formulation, with the Old English poems blending a centuries older version of Christianity with the newer target culture and traditional literary style. Of course, to succeed at acculturating that Christianity, Cynewulf's poems must eliminate so much foreign material and add so much new material that stylistic adequacy nearly disappears. This balance, however, underscores again the danger in "word for word" and "sense for sense": the basic elements of the plot remain largely in place in Cynewulf's poems. So, while much of the translation process is one of change for the sake of acceptability, a core or backbone of adequate fidelity remains. Indeed, the *vita* of a saint allows only so much deviation before the identity of the saint becomes questionable. There are certain elements or events that Cynewulf's texts must hit in order to succeed as a life of Juliana or an account of Elene's search for the true cross.

Thus, the translation strategies of these Old English texts are rather complicated and distinctive, yet surprisingly similar on one level. Each translation blends acceptability and accuracy, with the differences between the two supposedly opposed camps coming in which elements need to be retained to remain accurate and which aspects of the target language and culture were considered necessary for acceptability. Indeed, each translation must blend "word for word" and "sense for sense" to create the right mixture of acceptablity and accuracy in ways unique to each text. Within this balancing of adequacy and acceptability, the opportunities for semantic precision provided by compound structures were evidently not a primary attraction. All-in-all, compounds play an important role in Old English translations of Latin sources, but not a role in directly construing specific words and phrases in a source. Rather, in each text, compounds create patterns and emphases that generate or highlight aspects deemed

---

105 See also the discussion in Zacher, *Preaching the Converted*, 106–7, which further cites the use of this passage in Scragg, "Source Study," 39–58.

most important for making the text more acceptable to the audience. That acceptability looks different for each because of the different cultural contexts and goals of the texts, but the fundamental application of compounds remain the same. Compounds clearly perform important discursive work in these texts, but their utility in the translation process grows out of other, apparently more fundamental uses for compounds in Old English literature, not their semantic complexity. The next chapter turns to that fundamental use and explores the rhetorical impact of compound words in various types of texts from various periods.

3 Compound Interest

While participating in important ways in translating from Latin to Old English, compounds, as the previous chapter demonstrates, were not most useful for directly construing specific words and phrases from a source. Rather, compounds acted most commonly to realign the translations by introducing formal and semantic elements appropriate for an Anglo-Saxon cultural context. This work that compounds do in Cynewulf's translations and the Old English *Boethius* texts clearly depends less on the flexibility of the semantic complexity offered by compound structures than on the rhetorical impact of those structures. In fact, the most important and fundamental feature of compound words in Old English literature generally is the rhetorical emphasis that they provide. This use of compounds appears almost ubiquitously in the Old English corpus, as this chapter shows with examples from different types of texts and a range of time periods: *Beowulf*, *The Wanderer* and *The Seafarer*, and homilies by Wulfstan. In these texts, one finds compounds emphasizing different themes important to each individual text, but in each case the emphasis is created in the same manner: the exploitation of the rhetorical impact inherent in the structural complexity of compound words coupled with, almost secondarily, their semantic content. *Beowulf*, in addition to the uses discussed in chapter 6 below, uses compounds to foreground war-gear and violence, especially at politically sensitive moments when they could produce egregious havoc. In shorter texts, the divergent interests of *The Wanderer* and *The Seafarer*, so alike in many ways, become powerfully clear through an examination of their compounds, with the mind as an enclosure fascinating one and the sea as an open metaphor the other. Compounds in Wulfstan's Old English homilies emphasize dangers to socio-political cohesion in the midst of the eleventh-century Danish attacks. In each case, while rhetorical emphasis can of course be achieved in other ways, compounds form a primary and fundamental source of emphasis for these texts.

The discussion of recent linguistic experiments in chapter 2 above adduces the evidence, direct and indirect, that Anglo-Saxons were aware of compound words as distinct from other types of words. The features that distinguish compounds from simplices have effects well beyond that simple classificatory awareness, specifically producing much greater expressive force for compounds than for simplices. This expressive force depends to a large degree on the unique structure of compounds and on the ways in which the brain processes that kind of structure. The demands that compounds impose on mental processing subtly shift the balance of influence slightly from content towards form. Through this shift, they participate more deeply in Roman Jakobson's poetic function, becoming more rhetorically weighty than other kinds of words. Importantly, these claims depend not solely on theories about the structure of compound words or on theories of rhetoric but also on data from empirical linguistic experiments. Compounds are simply, demonstrably, fundamentally unique and expressive.

The assumption of a "deep structure" hidden beneath the surface form of compound words has long informed scholarship on compounds, beginning with the original classification of Sanskrit compound types,[1] and recent scholarship supports the development of at least certain types of compounds from phrasal structures.[2] Such classification systems rely upon the different relationships assumed to be present in the paraphrase of a compound, such as interpretting *watchmaker* as signifying "one who makes watches." Studies that specifically treat Old and Middle English compounds from a structural standpoint continue that practice: Theodor Storch and Charles Carr retain the Sanskrit system mainly intact,[3] dissertations from the 1960s and 1970s apply it in studying style or supplement it with reference to

1 The basic Sanskrit system divides compounds into five groups based on the relationship between the constituents and between the compound and its referent; the groups are named in Sanskrit: *Dvandva*, *Tatpuruša*, *Karmadhâraya*, *Dvigu*, and *Bahuvrihi*. See Whitney, *Sanskrit Grammar*, 480–515.

2 Kiparsky, "Dvandvas, Blocking, and the Associative."

3 Storch, *Angelsächsische Nominalcomposita*, and Carr, *Nominal Compounds*.

attested Old English sentences or Case Grammar,[4] Hans Sauer extends the system to early Middle English,[5] and Dieter Kastovsky and Roger Lass mostly silently retain the Sanskrit system and meld it with more contemporary linguistic issues.[6] More recent theoretical approaches to compounds suggest semantic in addition to syntactic "deep structure," but they still retain the assumption of a structural complexity beyond what simple (monomorphemic) words can produce.[7] Only in the past decade or two have empirical experiments on the processing and mental representations of compounds reached a critical mass and begun to bear out these assumptions.[8]

One of the earliest findings of those recent experimental studies, however, goes against the fairly common assumption that compounds should take longer to process mentally than monomorphemic words because of their complex structures.[9] At the very least, runs this argument, if

4 Koban, "Substantive Compounds in *Beowulf*"; Reibel, "A Grammatical Index to the Compound Nouns of Old English Verse"; Gardner, "Semantic Patterns in Old English Substantival Compounds"; Overholser, "A Comparative Study of the Compound Use of *Andreas* and *Beowulf*." The first expression of Case Grammar is Fillmore, "The Case for Case." Case Grammar essentially posits that all languages share a universal set of syntactic relationships that lie behind the surface representations of sentences. The verb is taken as the sentence's conceptual centre, which selects many of the sentence's characteristics, and the theory would thus assume an underlying structure dependent on a verb to organize the relationship between the constituents of a compound. See also the discussion of compounds in Robinson, *Appositive Style*, 14–19, which relies on the concept of a deep structure lying behind the surface realization.

5 Sauer, *Nominalkomposita im Frühmittelenglischen.*

6 Kastovsky, "Semantics and Vocabulary," 362–77, and Lass, *Old English*, 194–8.

7 See, for example, Fabb, "Compounding." The most prominent approaches to categorizing compounds in modern linguistic work are Lees, *The Grammar of English Nominalizations*; Downing, "On the Creation and Use of English Compound Nouns"; Levi, *The Syntax and Semantics of Complex Nominals*; and Warren, *Semantic Patterns of Noun-Noun Compounds*. For overviews of these approaches, see Benczes, *Creative Compounding in English*, 15–39, and Spencer, "What's in a Compound?"

8 According to Gagné, "Psycholinguistic Perspectives," 255, the amount of psycholinguistics research on compounds nearly doubled from 1986 to 2006. A good, recent example of theory based on empirical data is Spalding et al., "Relation-Based Interpretation of Noun-Noun Phrases."

9 Taft and Forster, "Lexical Storage and Retrieval of Prefixed Words," and Taft, "Interactive-Activation as a Framework for Understanding Morphological Processing."

many compounds have probably lexicalized (i.e., become represented as a single word mentally stored in one lexical entry), they should take as long to be processed as any other word.[10] If, on the other hand, continues this argument, compounds are not simply lexicalized but in fact are taken as the combination of two or more monomorphemic words, the brain should need to access multiple entries in the mental lexicon and construct a meaning from there, which takes time.[11] As discussed in chapter 2, experiments show that compounds in fact never fully lexicalize, with the brain instead employing two routes of processing: one that activates the whole-word entry for the compound and one that activates the individual entries for the compound's constituents. Although all this evidence about compound storage seems indirectly to support the initial assumption suggesting that the processing of compounds should be comparatively slow, other evidence directly shows that the brain can actually process compounds more quickly than it does monomorphemic words.[12] First, the brain understands transparent compounds like *blueberry*, the meaning of which can be derived from the constituents alone, more quickly than opaque compounds like *strawberry*, whose meaning is partially independent of its constituents.[13] Second and perhaps most surprisingly, transparent compounds are processed more quickly even than simple, monomorphemic words. At least for high-frequency (i.e., commonly occurring) compounds or compounds with high-frequency first constituents, activation of the entries for each constituent at the lexical level must bolster the activation of the whole-word entry for the compounds through "facilitative links."[14] Those links speed along the processing, leading the brain to the meaning of the compounded forms very quickly and making it paradoxically faster than the processing of simple words. Any difference in expressive force between simplices and

---

10 Butterworth, "Lexical Representations."

11 Lehtonen et al., "Recognition of Morphologically Complex Words in Finnish."

12 Juhasz, "Effects of Word Length and Sentence Context on Compound Word Recognition"; Fiorentino and Poeppel, "Compound Words and Structure in the Lexicon"; Drieghe et al., "Parafoveal Processing during Reading Is Reduced across a Morphological Boundary"; and Ji, Gagné, and Spalding, "Benefits and Costs."

13 On *blueberry* versus *strawberry*, see Libben, "Why Study Compound Processing?" 10–16.

14 Ji, Gagné, and Spalding, "Benefits and Costs," 415. See also Schreuder and Baayen, "Modeling Morphological Processing," and Libben, "Semantic Transparency in the Processing of Compounds."

compounds, then, must not come from a (non-existent) delay in processing compounds, since in fact they are the first kind of word understood by the brain as a person reads or listens.

The differences in processing transparent compounds and opaque compounds points to the real source of that expressive force: complex structures and the mental effort of processing the semantic relationships created by those structures. Opaque compounds, such as *strawberry*, benefit from the same facilitative links on the lexical level that transparent compounds enjoy, but not to the same degree, because the meanings of their individual constituents are not fully (or sometimes not at all) employed in the whole-word meaning. In base-line experiments, opaque compounds were processed faster than monomorphemic words, but not as fast as transparent compounds.[15] However, in experiments that encouraged the processing of compounds via decomposition into individual constituents (by, for example, distinguishing constituents with a medial space or with different textual colour), opaque compounds lost their advantage over monomorphemic words.[16] Opaque compounds and monomorphemic words in these experiments were processed at relatively the same speed. The only explanation for opaque compounds only sometimes being processed faster than monomorphemic words is that the brain is taking two steps to understand compounds: first, lexical activation, and second, semantic composition. The facilitative links on the lexical level support the processing of opaque compounds when the brain pursues whole-word processing more actively than the decomposition route. On the other hand, when the presentation of a compound pushes the brain to decompose it into contituents and then recompose them on the semantic level, the task of resolving the difference between the meaning of a whole compound and those of its consituents extends the processing time. Transparent compounds suffer no such delay, since the meanings of their constituents are fully involved in the meaning of the whole compound. These differences in the processing times for transparent compounds, opaque compounds, and monomorphemic words demonstrates that while lexical retrieval is involved with all three, semantic processing plays a special role in the treatment only of compounds and not of other words.

It is important to note that the brain assesses semantic relations for all types of compounds, both opaque and transparent, and this treatment of

15 Ji, Gagné, and Spalding, "Benefits and Costs."
16 See experiments 4–6 in Ji, Gagné, and Spalding, "Benefits and Costs," 413–17.

transparent compounds is of particular interest for studies of Old English compounds, since effectively all of the compounds in such studies are transparent. Although opaque compounds see the greatest delays in processing due to the need for semantic resolution, transparent compounds go through similar semantic evaluation, simply without the conflict between the meaning of the whole-word entry and the meaning constructed by the brain from the constituents. Indeed, the delay caused by resolving the conflict between the whole-word meaning of opaque compounds and the meanings of their constituents is only one piece of evidence of the semantic aspect of processing compounds. Other experiments show that the interpretation of transparent compounds occurs more quickly when the brain is "primed" by compounds with a similar semantic relation connecting their constituents than by compounds with a different relation.[17] In these experiments, subjects briefly see a stimulus word – known as the "prime" – before seeing the target word being tested; the priming word can be shown long enough to be consciously recognized (unmasked priming) or hidden in such a way that it does not register consciously (masked priming).[18] For example, subjects in one set of experiments would see one of three different words (*snowfort*, *snowshovel*, or *gearshift*) before being shown the target, *snowball*, and being asked to indicate whether it had a "sensible interpretation."[19] Subjects assessed the target words more quickly when primed by compounds that employed the same underlying semantic relationship. For example, *copper horse*

17 Gagné, "Relation and Lexical Priming"; Gagné, "Lexical and Relational Influences"; Gagné and Shoben, "Priming Relations in Ambiguous Noun-Noun Combinations"; Estes, "Attributive and Relational Processes"; Gagné and Spalding, "Effect of Relation Availability"; Estes and Jones, "Priming via Relational Similarity"; Raffray, Pickering, and Branigan, "Priming the Interpretation"; Gagné and Spalding, "Constituent Integration"; Spalding and Gagné, "Relation Priming"; and El-Bialy, Gagné, and Spalding, "Processing of English Compounds."

18 On masked priming, see originally Forster and Davis, "Repetition Priming and Frequency Attentuation in Lexical Access."

19 Gagné and Spalding, "Constituent Integration," 24, 25, and 33. Other priming experiments require different tasks: for example, the experiments recounted in Raffray, Pickering, and Branigan, "Priming the Interpretation," called for subjects to select one of two pictures that best matched the meaning of an ambiguous prime. Nonetheless, all priming experiments use the same fundamental method, regardless of the task required. For an analysis of the efficacy of the priming methodology, see Hutchison, "Is Semantic Priming Due to Association Strength or Feature Overlap?"

primes *glass eye* since both evidently employ the MADE OF relation, and so *glass eye* is processed more quickly when the subject sees *copper horse* beforehand than after seeing no prime at all or a prime involving a different semantic relationship.[20] These results demonstrate that the brain is better prepared for understanding a target compound when that compound's semantic structure is already actively in mind because of prior exposure to a related priming compound.[21] The changes of response times in these experiments shows that the brain semantically assesses all types of compounds, whether transparent or opaque. Facilitation at the purely lexical level certainly occurs, but again semantic composition plays a large role in processing compound words in a way that is absent for other types of words.

Processing compounds on a semantic level does not simply extend or shorten the processing time for certain compounds; rather, it places a greater load on the brain, whether that load is relatively short- or long-lived. Experiments measuring response times or tracking eye movement in reading effectively measure the presence of semantic processing through the back door, as it were, analysing behavioural responses that generally occur after the fact. These types of experiments, however, cannot directly measure the load imposed on the brain by semantic processes. The best tool currently available for assessing that load is the electroencephalographic (EEG) measurement of the electrical activity of the brain in response to specific stimuli. By averaging and comparing the levels of this activity over time, one can isolate reactions to individual stimuli, known as event-related potentials (ERPs).[22] These measurements are highly temporally sensitive, with different response types characterized by their time of occurrence in milliseconds. One such response relates directly to the semantic processing of language and is known as the N400, a negative relative peak of electrical activity reaching its

20 Estes and Jones, "Priming via Relational Similarity," 90. The various systems classifying the relationships between constituents are theoretical and some may not accurately reflect mental structures as well as others; see Estes and Jones, "Priming via Relational Similarity," 100, for a discussion of how the different systems can affect experimental outcomes.

21 Priming experiments have been very popular in the past decade, but other types of experiments can produce similar results, such as in Marelli and Luzzatti, "Frequency Effects."

22 Kutas and Federmeier, "Thirty Years and Counting," 622.

maximum around 400 milliseconds after a stimulus.[23] The amplitude, or size, of the N400 peak roughly tracks the ease of processing the stimulus eliciting the N400 effect, with an "easier-to-understand" stimulus producing smaller peaks than a stimulus that is more difficult to parse.[24] The N400 offers especially useful evidence for the current discussion, since it provides more targeted information than response times in that it indexes specifically the process of semantic judgment, whereas response times vary based on several additional factors.[25] Moreover, N400 effects appear in response to both visual and auditory stimulus,[26] meaning that these results are not specific only to reading but also address listening. This cross-modality is highly useful for studying Old English compounds, which, as discussed in chapter 2 above, may have been encountered in oral performance or reading.

The main measurable feature for the N400 effect is its amplitude, that is, the size of the deflection of electrical potential from the baseline level. Analyses of the differences in N400 amplitudes in response to various stimuli lead to two main conclusions: first, the N400 reacts differently to compounds and non-compounds, and, second, it reacts specifically to the semantic relation between compound constituents. Compound words elicit larger negativities than non-compound words; that is, the brain's electrical potential drops lower when processing a compound than when processing a monomorphemic word.[27] This comparison suggests that the brain must simply work harder to understand compound words than simple words. Similarly, transparent compounds produce a larger negativity than opaque compounds, in this case reflecting the greater semantic demands of constructing meaning from the constituents rather than simply preferring the whole-word meaning.[28] The degree of the N400 dip can also be controlled by priming a particular semantic relationship, in the manner discussed above. Specifically, the target compound elicits smaller N400 dips if its constituents are linked by the same semantic relation as in

23 The N400 effect is particularly sensitive to semantics in language processing, but meaningful non-linguistic stimuli also produce it. Kutas and Federmeier, "Thirty Years and Counting," 622–3 and 625; see also Kutas and Federmeier, "Electrophysiology."

24 Kutas and Federmeier, "N400."

25 Kutas and Federmeier, "Thirty Years and Counting," 628, and Holcomb, "Semantic Priming."

26 Kutas and Federmeier, "Thirty Years and Counting," 627.

27 Chiarelli et al., "Electrophysiological Correlates."

28 Koester, Gunter, and Wagner, "Morphosyntactic Decomposition."

the priming compound, again suggesting that the prime makes the target easier to process.[29] Ultimately, these studies show that compounds induce greater processing costs at the semantic level than non-compounds and that these costs are a result of having to construct a meaning by placing the constituents of compounds within some semantic relationship.[30]

These processing costs associated with semantic integration of the constituents are not the only additional costs induced by compound words. Another electroencephalographic measurement known as the left-anterior negativity (LAN) demonstrates a syntactic element to the processing of compounds. The LAN specifically responds to morphosyntactic violations, which the brain must resolve, thus linking it to syntactic processing generally.[31] Similar to the N400 in that both are negative dips in the brain's electrical potential, the LAN appears earlier than the N400 and in a different area of the scalp. Just as with the N400, compounds elicit larger negative LAN dips than do non-compounds.[32] This larger dip again demonstrates that the brain works harder to process compounds than non-compounds, but this time on a syntactic level. At the very least, the brain assesses gender on the syntactic level, since gender incongruity between constituents in German compounds elicits greater negative LAN dips than congruity.[33] This deflection in response to gender incongruity implies that the brain processes each constituent of a compound in a syntactic relation to the other constituent(s) in addition to the semantic relations discussed above. While the fulness of various syntactic relations suggested by Case Grammar are probably not at play, there is some level of syntactic information involved. Gender incongruity or other syntactic relationships within a word are impossible for non-compounds, and the fact that the brain reacts to compounds in this way shows that the processing of compounds involves multiple tasks that are simply not necessary for non-compounds.

These experimental observations apply to any compound word, but they are particularly germane for low-frequency (i.e., rarely occurring)

---

29 Jia et al., "Electrophysiological Evidence."

30 Bai et al., "Semantic Composition."

31 For a review of the connection between LAN and syntax, see Hoen and Dominey, "ERP Analysis of Cognitive Sequencing."

32 El Yagoubi et al., "Neural Correlates."

33 Koester, Gunter, Wagner, and Friederici, "Morphosyntax, Prosody, and Linking Elements," and Koester, Gunter, and Wagner, "Morphosyntactic Decomposition."

compounds. Specifically, several experiments demonstrate that frequency significantly affects processing time and demands. Changing the frequency of a compound – or one of its constituents – facilitates or impedes compound processing; specifically, high-frequency constituents lead to faster response times in lexical decision tasks and shorter fixation times in eye-tracking experiments than do low-frequency constituents.[34] The frequency of a compound's second constituent also affects EEG measurements like the N400, with low-frequency second constituents producing a more significant negative dip than common ones.[35] These differences illustrate the additional cost of processing a rare compound or a rare constituent and constructing the whole-word meaning, presumably as a result of the fact that the whole-word meaning of the rare word or constituent is relatively difficult to activate and use because it is not reinforced through regular use. In applying these experimental conclusions to Old English studies in particular, it may seem perilous to argue from a frequency standpoint with a corpus that may have suffered remarkable decimation over the centuries. After all, dozens of other, say, vernacular epics could have existed alongside *Beowulf*, the state of whose manuscript prominently reminds us of the precarious circumstances through which so many manuscripts travelled to reach the current day. Nonetheless, it is very unlikely that many other poems like *Beowulf* ever existed, considering the nature of the other surviving manuscripts, with homilies, histories, and even glossaries vastly outnumbering the poetic works.[36] The degree of overlap between *Beowulf* and other poems such as *Andreas*[37] are enough to suggest that the vast majority, if not all, of words that are unique in the corpus as we currently know it were unique always. Moreover, while individual words currently thought to be unique might be proved common if many more manuscripts had survived, clusters of unique or rare compounds, as discussed below, would likely remain significant. The probability of, say, all five rare compounds

34 Andrews, "Morphological Influences"; Hyönä and Pollatsek, "Reading Finnish Compound Words"; Pollatsek, Hyönä, and Bertram, "The Role of Morphological Constituents"; Juhasz et al., "Effects of Morphology"; Duñabeitia, Perea, and Carreiras, "Role of Frequency"; and Marelli and Luzzatti, "Frequency Effects."

35 Vergara-Martínez et al., "ERP Correlates." See also MacGregor and Shtyrov, "Multiple Routes."

36 Such a calculation becomes more complicated if one accepts Ælfric's homilies as poetry, as argues Bredehoft, *Early English Metre*. The significant difference in content and style between Ælfric's works and *Beowulf* supports my claim nonetheless.

37 See, for example, Peters, "*Andreas* and *Beowulf*."

in a given cluster of rare words having been, in fact, common is so low that it seems quite safe to base arguments on the currently available evidence. Thus, the experimental research on the effects of compound frequency should apply to Old English and the corpus as we have it.

This mass of experimental data coalesces around the conclusion that compounds are indeed fundamentally different from simple, monomorphemic words in several, demonstrable ways, most importantly in the complexity of their structures and in the cognitive demands of processing them. The experiments elucidating the semantic processing of compounds show that the brain expends a great deal of effort in understanding their meanings, but that work is a reaction to the structural complexity of those meanings, not their content. Certainly, complex meanings are not unique to compound words, as many morphologically simple words signify very complex concepts. Accessing the complex meanings of such words, however, does not take the same effort as (re)constructing the meaning through syntactic and semantic composition. Processing any word involves activating its lexical entry, effectively remembering the word's meaning, but compounds add the two layers of assessing additional syntactic information and composing a new meaning from the semantics of the constituents. The N400 and LAN effects demonstrate the additional mental effort needed to process these two layers, extra effort that is caused specifically by compound structures. Consequently, although meaning is not absent, compound structure has a significant presence and influence on a subconscious level.

This recognition of structure as a dominant factor for compounds leads into Roman Jakobson's concept of the poetic function of language. In Jakobson's schema, each verbal expression, which he conceptualizes as a message connecting an addresser to an addressee, involves several functions, such as emotive, referential, and poetic.[38] It is effectively impossible to find a message performing only one function, but one function or another will tend to dominate in any given message.[39] The poetic function

38 In total, Jakobson delineates six functions: emotive, referential, poetic, phatic, metalingual, and conative. Jakobson, *Language in Literature*, 66–71. For an in-depth and helpful discussion of Jakobson's schema specifically in relation to Old English literature, see Beechy, *Poetics of Old English*, 6–12.

39 Jakobson, *Language in Literature*, 66. However, he suggests that infants first acquire solely the phatic function, which consists of "messages primarily serving to establish, prolong, or discontinue communication," without the ability to communicate information through the other functions (*Language in Literature*, 68–9).

constitutes a "focus on the message for its own sake," and its dominance characterizes verbal art.[40] This focus on the message takes precendence when "the word is felt as a word and not a mere representation of the object being named."[41] In other words, a message with a dominant poetic function attends primarily to the rhythm of its words, the likeness of their sounds, the similarity of sound to reality, or other elements not directly related to the meaning it denotes – in short, the shape and feel, as it were, of the message. Importantly, the poetic function need not be dominant to be present, as any expression – not just "poetry" – can secondarily attend to its shape and feel while focusing primarily on its content.[42] That secondary attention to a message's form "reinforces its impressiveness and efficacy";[43] in other words, the expressive force of a message increases through attention to its form. This reinforcement is exactly how compounds fit into a great deal of Old English literature: the demands of their complex structures subtly (subconsciously) require greater attention to their formal (syntactic and semantic) structures and augment expressive force beyond their content.

This focus on form and structure connects interestingly with so-called "poetic compounds," the form of most of which, insofar as they fulfil the needs of metre and alliteration, seems to be their only important feature.[44] These "pleonastic" compounds are generally restricted to poetry, and their first constituents seemingly contribute nothing of semantic significance.[45] As discussed briefly in chapter 1 above, compounds are key to several of the most important aspects of traditional Old English poetry: metre,

40 Jakobson, *Language in Literature*, 69.

41 Jakobson, *Language in Literature*, 378.

42 Jakobson, *Language in Literature*, 70; see also Beechy's discussion of this point in *Poetics of Old English*, 10–11.

43 Jakobson, *Language in Literature*, 70.

44 Brodeur, *The Art of "Beowulf,"* 14–17; Russom, *Old English Meter*, 92–7; and Russom, "Aesthetic Criteria," 71. The approach taken to determining "poetic" in these studies is markedly different from that in Chapman and Christensen, "Noun-Adjective Compounds."

45 See for example Russom, *Old English Meter*, 94: "When these appear with words referring to military equipment, as often happens, they create a striking effect of redundancy. The base *bill* 'sword,' for example, appears in *guð-bill* 'war-sword' ([*Beowulf*] 803a, 2584b); *hilde-bill* 'battle-sword' ([*Beowulf*] 557a, 1520a, 1666b, 2679a); and *wig-bill* 'combat-sword' ([*Beowulf*] 1607a)." On "pleonastic compounds," see also Lass, *Old English*, 197–8.

alliteration, repetition, variation, and the linkage to the cultural context of the tradition. Pleonastic compounds sometimes seem most important as an element of metrical theory, but an analysis within a Jakobsonian framework informed by the experimental data outlined above expands their significance. While their pleonastic nature may not allow much complexity in their final meaning, these compounds still must be (and must have been) processed as compounds, that is, with the brain assessing syntactic and semantic relationships between the two constituents. Indeed, these pleonastic compounds still "count as two words," that is, they retain the stress pattern and linguistic structure of completely unlexicalized compounded words, regardless of their "deviant semantics."[46] These poetic compounds call attention to their structures, and thus, in Jakobson's words, they reinforce the "impressiveness and efficacy" of the passages in which they appear, augmenting the expressive force of those passages. From this point of view, they are not simply present to make alliteration and metre function correctly, although those aspects must certainly have been part of their appeal. Rather, that utility with regard to alliteration and metre is only one product of their compound structures, with the creation of additional expressive impact being another evidently more significant aspect.

The semantics of compounds, even seemingly pleonastic compounds, nonetheless remains significant. The facts that compound structure requires more (subconscious) mental effort in processing and that the structure itself therefore becomes prominent does not vitiate the actual meaning produced by the processing. Rather, that meaning becomes all the more prominent within the immediate context of the passage in which it appears because of the cognitive demands of producing it. While the meaning of *guðbill* [battle-blade], for example, is ultimately straightforward and perhaps little different from that of the simplex *bill*, it is nonetheless cognitively different. It requires more of the brain in terms of the amount of effort and the areas employed than *bill*.[47] Moreover, an assessment of seemingly synonymous compounds within context yields the convincing conclusion that each individual word produces different connotations, even

46 Russom, *Old English Meter*, 95.

47 Syntactic and semantic composition occur in different parts of the brain than simple lexical activation of a monomorphemic word.

though modern translations tend to obscure that fact.[48] Compounding thus emphasizes structure due to its processing demands, and that emphasis in turn highlights the meaning of the particular compound in a way that monomorphemic words cannot achieve.

Good examples of this interaction and creation of emphasis occur in several passages describing war-gear and violence in *Beowulf*. Weapons and armour of course seem nearly ubiquitous in the poem, but their presence becomes especially important in a few passages in particular. The potentially politically dangerous role of war-gear first surfaces in the Geats' landing on the shores of Denmark. The coastguard challenges the Geats, noting that their weapons and armour have aroused his suspicions; the guard's duty, after all, is to watch for hostile raiding parties armed just as are Beowulf and his men. The war-gear, however, takes a back seat, as it were, to Beowulf's stature during this encounter, with the guard remarking that Beowulf would stand out without any weapons.[49] In a sense, the weapons are less important because the coastguard catches the Geats before they can move inland. A few lines later, however, he shows them the way directly to Heorot, and they carry their weapons with them:

Stræt wæs stanfah, stig wisode
gumum ætgædere. Guðbyrne scan
heard hondlocen; hringiren scir
song in searwum. Þa hie to sele furðum
in hyra gryregeatwum gangan cwomon,
setton sæmeþe side scyldas,

48 See the discussions and citations in Brady, "'Weapons,'" 81; Brady, "'Warriors,'" 200; and Harbus, *Life of the Mind*, 50–5.

49 The impact of the guard's comments and the exact meaning depend to a degree on the punctuation of lines 249b–50a: "nis þæt seldguma / wæpnum geweorðad." Mitchell and Robinson, *Beowulf*, put no comma at the end of line 249, although one does appear in that spot in Fulk, Bjork, and Niles, *Klaeber's Beowulf*. Fulk, Bjork, and Niles, *Klaeber's Beowulf*, thus depends on *seldguma* [retainer] implying a rank not befitting someone of Beowulf's stature (see 133, note to line 249b), leading to a translation along the lines of "that is no [mere] retainer, exalted by weaponry." Removing the comma, however, allows the negation to migrate, producing a meaning more like "that retainer is exalted not by his weaponry," suggesting that the honour comes from something other than the weapons. While the weapons are dismissed as less important in both readings, the comma-less punctuation makes the redundancy of the weapons most clear.

rondas regnhearde wið þæs recedes weal;
bugon þa to bence. Byrnan hringdon,
guðsearo gumena; garas stodon,
sæmanna searo samod ætgædere,
æscholt ufan græg; wæs se irenþreat
wæpnum gewurþad.[50]

The street was stone-paved; the path guided the warriors together. The hard, hand-linked battle-byrnie shone, the bright iron-ring of the armour resounded, when they set out first for the hall in their awe-inspiring armour. The sea-weary men set down their wide shields, those exceptionally hard rounds, against the wall of the building; they bent down onto the bench – the byrnies, the warriors' war-gear, rang; the spears stood, the gear of the sea-men gathered together, an ash-grove topped with gray; the armed troop was honoured by the weapons.

This passage contains a cluster of eleven compounds, eight of which denote or describe war-gear in some way, and the fact that so many compounds appear so closely together becomes significant in comparison to the average rate of occurrence of compounds in *Beowulf*.[51] Not only do the compounds create cognitive demands individually here, but the cluster also amplifies the effect, reproducing the processing demand over and over. Thus, the piling up of emphasis specifically draws attention to the presence of the war-gear in the passage in a unique manner.

From one perspective, this concatenation of emphasis highlights the high rank of the warriors.[52] Although Beowulf himself, according to the coast-guard a few lines before this passage, needed no gear to demonstrate his stature, his Geatish companions in this passage are "wæpnum gewurþad" [honoured by the weapons], the quality of which weapons demonstrates that they are not rabble. From a different, stylistic perspective, however,

50 Fulk, Bjork, and Niles, *Klaeber's Beowulf*, lines 320–31a.

51 Specifically, I calculate that on average a compound appears approximately every 2.17 lines in *Beowulf*. See chapter 6 below for a full discussion of the statistical significance of clusters of compounds in *Beowulf*. In short, these lines contain more than two standard deviations worth of compounds beyond the average, which makes them statistically significant.

52 See, for example, Fulk, Bjork, and Niles, *Klaeber's Beowulf*, 137–8, note to lines 321b–3a.

the subtle details of the descriptions also participate in the formulaic language of oral-traditional composition. In particular, the noise and shining of the armour invoke the approach-to-battle type-scene, thus making the Geats' approach problematic and possibly threatening. While the details may seem minor in this passage, audiences would have caught even small allusions to traditional diction.[53] The metonymic nature of oral-traditional composition would then lead them to extrapolate from small details to the larger context of the entire canon, producing in this instance connotations not just of social status but also of militaristic aggression.[54] The flashing light is evidently most characteristic of the "hero-on-the-beach" theme, but that moment on the beach is often followed by the beasts of battle, which are frequently tied to approach-to-battle scenes.[55] The flashing light alone, then, would have primed the original audience for the progression from the beach, through a journey, and finally to the noise of the beasts of battle.[56] The noises of the armour further correlate to the noises of battle and partially fulfil the expectations for elements of a battle scene following the shining light reflecting off the armour.[57] These details thus produce connotative meaning in the passage, linking it to battle and violence, even though the overt content remains pacific. Beowulf may espouse friendship, but the stylistic details of the passage retain the violent implications that lead the Danes to follow protocol carefully before allowing him into Hrothgar's presence. Those stylistic details are produced mainly through the cluster of compounds, demonstrating the rhetorical power produced by the linguistic characteristics and cognitive demands of compound structures.

War-gear again leaps to the fore a few lines later in Wulfgar's announcement to Beowulf and his companions that Hrothgar will see them:

"Eow het secgan   sigedrihten min,
aldor East-Dena,   þæt he eower æþelu can,

53 Fry, "Themes and Type-Scenes," 41.

54 Foley, *Immanent Art*, 7.

55 On the "hero-on-the-beach" preceding the beasts of battle, see Crowne, "Hero on the Beach," 372, and Fry, "Themes and Type-Scenes," 42–3. On the beasts of battle as an important aspect of the approach to battle, see Ramsey, "The Theme of Battle," 71 (cited by Fry, "Themes and Type-Scenes," 36), and Jorgensen, "The Trumpet and the Wolf," 322.

56 Fry, "Themes and Type-Scenes," 44.

57 See Jorgensen, "The Trumpet and the Wolf."

ond ge him syndon ofer sæwylmas
heardhicgende hider wilcuman.
Nu ge moton gangan in eowrum guðgetawum,
under heregriman Hroðgar geseon;
lætað hildebord her onbidan,
wudu wælsceaftas worda geþinges."[58]

"My victory-lord, the chief of the East-Danes, has commanded that you be told that he knows your noble lineage and that you hard-thinking men from over the sea-rolls are welcome to him. Now you may go in your war-gear, under war-masks, to see Hrothgar; let the battle-shields, the wooden slaughter-spears, await the result of the discussion here."

Several compounds again cluster in this passage, with four of them appearing in quick succession in the quotation's final four lines expressing arms and armour in different ways, again becoming significant in comparison to the rate of occurrence in the rest of the poem. That this particular and significant cluster of compounds should appear at this point in the narrative makes excellent sense in relation to the poem's depiction of the safety measures and obstacles faced by Beowulf and his men as they approach Heorot. Their encounter with the coastguard upon first landing in Denmark makes it perfectly clear that the Danes remained vigilant against heavily armed war bands: the arms and armour in particular attract the coastguard's interest, and he initially challenges them largely because of their war-load. While they are allowed to retain their armour and helmets in their audience with Hrothgar, the poem emphasizes that the weapons are still not welcome. Even though Hrothgar knows their *æþelu* [noble lineage], precautions against violence must still be taken. Indeed, several vignettes and allusions in the poem depict violence erupting in the hall even in the face of agreements or familial ties.[59] In such a delicate situation as this passage depicts, then, the poem makes clear that the Danes preclude the opportunity for violence

58 Fulk, Bjork, and Niles, *Klaeber's Beowulf*, lines 391–8.

59 For example, see the prolepsis of the enmity between son-in-law and father-in-law (*aþumsweoras*) in lines 83–5 and the Finnsburg episode, in which truce is overwhelmed by vengeance in lines 1060–1159a. On the connection between violence, war-gear, and royal succession in particular, see Biggs, "*Beowulf* and Some Fictions," and Biggs, "The Politics of Succession."

and implies the alternative by foregrounding the Geat's war-gear with compounds.

The clusters of compounds in these passages are naturally not the only uses of compounds to denote weapons and amour in the poem. Indeed, such compounds appear frequently throughout the entire poem, in line with the traditional interest in war-gear as treasure.[60] Specifically, there are ninety-four occurrences of compounds expressing weapons and/or armour in *Beowulf*.[61] There are, of course, many more occurrences of simple words denoting weapons and armour, such as *sweord* [sword], *seax* [short sword], *bill* [blade], etc. Unsurprisingly, *Beowulf* has a marked interest in the trappings of war. That interest, however, is not entirely consistent: the first five hundred lines of the poem contain twenty compounds for war-gear, but the next five hundred only seven. The contents of those portions make some sense of that divergence, with the journey of armed men in a foreign land in the first section and the battle in which Beowulf and Grendel both eschew weapons and armour in the second. Significantly, those seven compounds in the second section come at points at which the presence or concept of weaponry is particularly important: the swimming match with Breca, Beowulf's divesting himself of weapons and armour before his combat with Grendel, and the Geats' failed attempts to harm Grendel with weapons.[62] Presumably, it should be impressive for Beowulf to have entered the swimming match wearing armour and toting a weapon; certainly, Beowulf's choice to face Grendel unarmed is meant to be impressive and appropriate; and the Geats' failed attacks lend evidence to Beowulf's insight and Grendel's otherworldly protection. The pattern in the second five hundred lines, then, complements my argument concerning the scenes in which Beowulf and his men approach Heorot and then are called in to see Hrothgar: compounds (as opposed to simplices) for weapons and armour appear when those items play a particularly significant role in the narrative. The large number of simplices for war-gear demonstrate the poem's general interest in the topic, but the compounds come out when it needs to take centre stage.

60 See Tyler, *Old English Poetics*, 26.

61 On compounds for weapons in *Beowulf*, see Brady, "'Weapons,'" and Orchard, *A Critical Companion*, 69–72.

62 Fulk, Bjork, and Niles, *Klaeber's Beowulf*, lines 550, 552, 557, 671, 674, 803, and 804, respectively.

For example, war-gear again receives the emphasis of compound structures as Beowulf prepares to face Grendel's mother. In this case, the violent applications of weapons and armour come to the fore in addition to their role as precious heirlooms:

Gyrede hine Beowulf
eorlgewædum, nalles for ealdre mearn;
scolde herebyrne hondum gebroden,
sid ond searofah, sund cunnian,
seo ðe bancofan beorgan cuþe,
þæt him hildegrap hreþre ne mihte,
eorres inwitfeng, aldre gesceþðan;
ac se hwita helm hafelan werede,
se þe meregrundas mengan scolde,
secan sundgebland since geweorðad,
befongen freawrasnum, swa hine fyrndagum
worhte wæpna smið, wundrum teode,
besette swinlicum, þæt hine syðþan no
brond ne beadomecas bitan ne meahton.
Næs þæt þonne mætost mægenfultuma
þæt him on ðearfe lah ðyle Hroðgares;
wæs þæm hæftmece Hrunting nama;
þæt wæs an foran ealdgestreona;
ecg wæs iren, atertanum fah,
ahyrded heaþoswate;[63]

Beowulf geared himself with warrior's armour, mourned by no means for his life; the war-byrnie, woven by hand, large and cunningly decorated, was to test the water, [because] it knew how to protect the bone-coffer so that the battle-clutch, the malicious grasp of the angry [enemy], could not harm his heart, his life; moreover the shining helmet protected his head – it was to stir up the mere-bottom, seek the water-commotion adorned with treasure, encircled by lordly bands, as the smith of weapons had worked it in ancient days, formed it wondrously, set it with boar-images so that afterwards no brand nor battle-blade could bite him [it?]. What Hrothgar's deputy lent him in his hour of need was not the meanest of mighty supports; the name for that

63 Fulk, Bjork, and Niles, *Klaeber's Beowulf*, lines 1441b–60a.

> hilted-sword was Hrunting; it was peerless among ancient treasure; the edge was iron, adorned with poison-stripes, hardened by battle-blood.

Contrasting greatly with Beowulf's preparations for facing Grendel, this passage details the armour and weapon with which he gears himself against Grendel's mother. As with the other passages focusing on war-gear discussed above, these lines emphasize the preparations with a significant cluster of compounds. This cluster, however, mixes compounds not related directly to equipment with those that denote or describe war-gear: at most ten out of the seventeen compounds apply to the armour or Hrunting, and only if one includes in that count almost tangential features (such as the *freawrasene* [lordly bands], *swinlic* [boar-images], and *atertanas* [poison-stripes]). The other seven compounds lend their weight to, for example, the act of attacking itself (*hildegrap* [battle-clutch] and *inwitfeng* [malicious grasp]) or aspects of the mere (*meregrundas* [mere-bottom] and *sundgebland* [water-commotion]). The focus of this arming scene expands, as it were, beyond the arming itself to the mere with its ominous implications and the bodily danger Beowulf will soon face. The violence, left implied in the previous passages, becomes more overtly palpable through the compounds *bancofa* [bone-coffer] and *heaþoswat* [battle-blood].

The violent uses of war-gear – as opposed to its role as treasure within a gift economy – are more prominent in this arming scene than in the scenes discussed above because Beowulf faces a more difficult battle than before with a foe that proves to be more dangerous than Grendel. The decision to forego armour and weapons in battling Grendel emphasizes Beowulf's physical might and sets up the comparison between those two opponents. War-gear is not involved with that form of violence; instead, it often primarily takes on the role of treasure in that section, for example in the form of the sword that Hrothgar bestows on Beowulf in return for killing Grendel. Grendel's mother, however, uses weapons and proves to be so dangerous that Beowulf only survives because his armour protects him. Moreover, he can only overcome his second foe with the help of weaponry, specifically the "sigeeadig bil, / ealdsweord eotenisc" [victory-blessed blade, a giant, ancient sword] too big to be hefted by anyone other than Beowulf.[64] This arming scene thus highlights the violent applications of weaponry in preparation for the actual clash, pushing the imminence of that violence closer to the forefront again.

---

64 Fulk, Bjork, and Niles, *Klaeber's Beowulf*, lines 1557–8 and 1560.

The arming passage nonetheless also mixes the violent applications of war-gear with their wider social context, particularly through Hrunting. Unferth's gift had been a reliable weapon, but it is also a valuable heirloom, a piece of treasure beyond its pragmatic applications in battle. The reminder that it was "ahyrded heaþoswate" [hardened by battle-blood] ensures that Hrunting never loses its violent connotations, but the sword nevertheless becomes symbolic of the ties of loyalty that are so important within the heroic world depicted in *Beowulf*.[65] The act of gifting treasure creates a relationship between the two men outside of battle, the kind of relationship that binds together that heroic world.[66] Moreover, with the loan, Unferth demonstrates his repentence over his initial challenge to Beowulf – or his judgment of Beowulf as worthy of recognition as a great warrior, depending on one's interpretation of Unferth.[67] Whatever one thinks of Unferth, his act of gifting Hrunting to Beowulf goes well beyond the battle with Grendel's mother and places the weapon and its capacity for violence within a complex cultural matrix that the poem both celebrates but also subtly questions.[68] The compounds in this arming passage, then, weave together those aspects, emphasizing both the violent and the social applications of war-gear. The cluster of compounds applies the emphatic rhetorical force of compound structures to both sides of that coin, implying that violence generally – and especially the violence about to ensue – inextricably produces ramifications throughout the culture. As with the possibility of the destabilizing consequences of the violence threatened by the war-gear in the Geats' approach to and arrival at Heorot,

---

65 For example, later in *Beowulf*, Wiglaf focuses on the waste of Beowulf's giving treasure to the craven warriors, using that treasure as a metonym representing the relationship between lord and retainer (Fulk, Bjork, and Niles, *Klaeber's Beowulf*, lines 2864–72). See O'Brien O'Keeffe, "Values and Ethics in Heroic Literature."

66 On the relationship between gift giving and violence, see Baker, *Honour, Exchange, and Violence*. On gift giving from an anthropological point of view, see Mauss, *The Gift*. On gift giving in *Beowulf*, see Donahue, "Potlatch and Charity"; Hill, "Beowulf and the Danish Succession"; Enright, "Lady with a Mead-Cup"; Bjork, "Speech as Gift"; Hill, *The Cultural World in "Beowulf,"* chapter 4 (85–107) and its notes (180–9); and Thieme, "The Gift in *Beowulf*."

67 On the challenging character of Unferth, see, among many others, Hollowell, "Unferð the *þyle*"; Clover, "The Germanic Context"; Enright, "The Warband Context"; Donovan, "*Þyle* as Fool"; and Baker, *Honour, Exchange, and Violence*, 77–102. For an account of earlier interpretations of Unferth, see Bjork, "Digressions and Episodes," 205–8.

68 The poem's conflicted depiction of violence is explored further in chapter 6 below.

here violence can produce ripple effects throughout society through the relationships that it establishes. For Unferth, Beowulf's hypothetical success with Hrunting in battle would have improved the *þyle*'s social standing, thus producing non-material profit from the violence.

While this arming scene introduces the possible positive aspects of violence, such as the building of relationships and accrual of honour, the negative cultural consequences of violence return to the fore in the final third of *Beowulf*.[69] The frequent digressions recounting the long-standing feud between the Geats and the Swedes lays the foundation for this persistent and dangerous aspect of violence. Recurring clashes threaten to destabilize the Geats' kingdom, with, for example, Hygelac's son Heardred being killed in a clash after providing help for Ohtere's sons Eadgils and Eanmund.[70] His death in a feud-driven battle followed, of course, Hygelac's own feud-driven death that threatened Geatish stability to such an extent that Hygd initially preferred Beowulf as his successor over her own son.[71] Without the exceptional and intimidating Beowulf finally bringing stability, the Geats would have been unlikely to see peace. Fear of that feud's return suffuses the final third of the poem, and Beowulf's fight with the dragon frequently foreshadows his death in parallel with references to events in that feud with the Swedes, implying the dire consequences through narrative apposition.[72] As a result of these juxtapositions, two particular moments accrue special significance narratively and, moreover, contain significant clusters of compounds. In each, war-gear and violence, whether actual or implied, interact with wider implications for the Geats.

First, the moment of Nægling's failure:

Þa wæs beorges weard
æfter heaðuswenge on hreoum mode,
wearp wælfyre; wide sprungon
hildeleoman. Hreðsigora ne gealp
goldwine Geata; guðbill geswac

69 Baker, *Honour, Violence, and Exchange*, takes a more positive position on the end of the poem than I; see the full discussion in chapter 6 below.

70 Fulk, Bjork, and Niles, *Klaeber's Beowulf*, lines 2379b–90.

71 Fulk, Bjork, and Niles, *Klaeber's Beowulf*, lines 2354b–79a.

72 See Robinson, *Appositive Style*, for a discussion of the processes and possibilities of apposition.

nacod æt niðe, swa hyt no sceolde,
iren ærgod.[73]

Then after the battle-stroke, the guardian of the mound was in a savage state, [it] slung out slaughter-fire; battle-flames burst forth widely. The gold-friend of the Geats did not boast of glory-victories; the battle-blade failed, naked in need, as it should not, [since it was] a proven iron.

Here, Beowulf's long-proven sword, Nægling, proves instead to be useless in its final battle. The blade's name, however, is not revealed for another hundred lines; that name is not important at this point. More telling than that omission, however, is the epithet used for Beowulf, "goldwine Geata" [the gold-friend of the Geats]. Of the many available epithets, such as "sunu Ecgðeowes" [son of Ecgtheow] or even "mæg Higelaces" [Hygelac's kinsman], in this passage Beowulf's position as leader of the Geats receives emphasis, although in the very next line he returns to being "maga Ecgðeowes" [son of Ecgtheow].[74] To be sure, epithets in oral-tradition style invoke a character's entire career, activating all the various incarnations and understandings of a character simultaneously.[75] Nonetheless, the overtly named aspect must remain dominant over the others, which here foregrounds Beowulf's stewardship of the Geats. That specification in turn activates an awareness of the consequences that would attend to the king's death. Beowulf does not die at this very point, but this passage marks the first fulfilment of the preceding comments foreshadowing his death. The sword's failure in this moment of violence, then, has much greater consequences within the poem than this single moment.

The poem matches the far-reaching narrative significance of this moment in its style, packing seven compounds into its twelve half-lines. Only a few of the compounds relate to war-gear, but *hildeleoma*, here meaning "battle-flames," provides an important connection, since in its other occurrence in *Beowulf* (line 1143) it is a kenning for a sword.[76] *Hildeleoma* here denotes the dragon's flames in a literal sense but recalls that earlier use as

73 Fulk, Bjork, and Niles, *Klaeber's Beowulf*, lines 2580–6a.

74 Fulk, Bjork, and Niles, *Klaeber's Beowulf*, line 2587; for the former epithets see, for example, lines 1550 and 737, respectively.

75 Foley, *Immanent Art*, 197.

76 See Brady, "'Weapons,'" 99–101.

a kenning and perhaps also the term *beaduleoma*, used previously to refer to Hrunting in line 1523.[77] The shift from kenning to literality erases the idea of "sword" from the term's semantics, which subsequently highlights the actual presence and then failure of Beowulf's sword in the next few lines. The use of *nacod* [naked] may also interact with this subtle wordplay: it overtly describes the sword but may subtextually also apply to Beowulf himself by recalling his preference to fight unarmed, as he did against Grendel and Dæghrefn.[78] The loss of his sword at least leaves him metaphorically naked for a moment in the face of the dragon's flames, against which he needs even more protection than he did against Grendel's mother. The high number of compounds but low proportion of compounds for war-gear thus fit the content of this passage quite well, since they lend additional rhetorical force to the important moment of failure and, through absence, highlight that failure.

The poem's final significant cluster of compounds appears when Wiglaf sends a messenger to the retainers who await news of the fight's outcome:

> Heht ða þæt heaðoweorc   to hagan biodan
> up ofer ecgclif,   þær þæt eorlweorod
> morgenlongne dæg   modgiomor sæt,
> bordhæbbende,   bega on wenum,
> endedogores   ond eftcymes
> leofes monnes.[79]

> Then he commanded that the battle-work be announced on the entrenchment up above the cliff-edge, where that sad-minded warrior-band sat, [although they were] shield-bearers, through the morning-long day in expectation of two [outcomes]: the end-day [or] the return of the dear man.

War-gear seems not to play a major role in this passage, with only *bordhæbbende* [shield-bearers] denoting it directly. Other compounds, such as

77 Talentino, "Fitting *Guðgewæde*," demonstrates that multiple occurrences of a given compound in *Beowulf* tend to share thematic emphases, such as *guðgewæde* occuring in passages concerned with "the essential bond between a lord and his followers" (594).

78 For Beowulf's claim of killing Dæghrefn bare-handed, see Fulk, Bjork, and Niles, *Klaeber's Beowulf*, lines 2501–10.

79 Fulk, Bjork, and Niles, *Klaeber's Beowulf*, lines 2892–7a.

heaðoweorc [battle-work] and *eorlweorod* [warrior-band], strongly imply violence, but they do not overtly reference weapons or armour. *Bordhæbbende*, however, produces a strongly ironic condemnation of the retainers through its apposition: they sat sad and idle awaiting the outcome of the fight, even though they had their shields. Their inactivity and failure to earn the gift of those shields becomes a major factor in the passage and in the poem. In the lines immediately preceding this passage, Wiglaf excoriates the hand-picked troop that had accompanied Beowulf on the journey to the dragon's barrow only to stand back while Wiglaf alone finally came to his king's aid. That context highlights this ironic implication for *bordhæbbende*, for Wiglaf predicts that "Nu sceal sincþego ond swyrdgifu … alicgean" [Now the gifts of treasure and swords must cease].[80] Their failure to use the gifts of weapons and armour must now lead to the loss of those gifts, and the description of the other retainers awaiting news also as *bordhæbbende* plays into this same reversal. Thus the absence of compounds for war-gear again highlights its failure.

The moment described in this passage may initially seem less important than the surrounding events, since it narrates not the tragic outcome of the fight itself but only Wiglaf's order to spread the word of that outcome, but the dire consequences of Beowulf's death depend on the dissemination of that news. Just as Beowulf's long-foreshadowed failure finally begins in earnest with Nægling's failure, the messenger's announcement will make Beowulf's death a public reality and set in motion attacks by the Swedes and other groups kept in check only by Beowulf's presence. Wiglaf recognizes this fact, noting that the punishments for the cowardly retainers will occur only "syððan æðelingas / feorran gefricgean fleam eowerne" [after noblemen from afar learn of your flight].[81] The messenger also makes clear that he expects *orleghwile* [time of war] only "syððan underne / Froncum ond Frysum fyll cyninges / wide weorðeð" [after the fall of the king becomes widely known among the Franks and Frisians].[82] This point in the poem, then, marks the first step in renewing the prosecution of old feuds against the Geats ultimately because of their failure to act correctly with their gifted war-gear. The clustering of compounds therefore again aligns in this passage with moments in which war-gear and

80 Fulk, Bjork, and Niles, *Klaeber's Beowulf*, lines 2884–6a.
81 Fulk, Bjork, and Niles, *Klaeber's Beowulf*, lines 2888b–9.
82 Fulk, Bjork, and Niles, *Klaeber's Beowulf*, lines 2911–13a.

violence – specifically knowledge of the violence and the failure to use war-gear correctly in this case – produce or threaten significant and often political consequences.

This use of compounds in *Beowulf* accords with the implications of the experimental linguistic evidence above: compounds produce greater emphasis than simplices. Simplices denoting war-gear could have proved equally serviceable in grammatical and metrical senses at the points at which war-gear is particularly significant in *Beowulf*, but they would not have produced the same rhetorical foregrounding that the compounds do. For example, if the compounds in Wulfgar's invitation to go in to Hrothgar, quoted above, were replaced with simplices, the final four lines might have little more interest than "check your umbrellas at the door." Significantly, almost all of the compounds denoting war-gear in that passage – and in fact in all of the passages discussed here – are unique to *Beowulf*, with almost all the non-unique compounds being rare.[83] This point too accords with the implications of the experimental evidence, in that low-frequency compounds, especially unique creations, cannot have lexicalized to any significant degree and thus require the most mental effort in processing. Indeed, as discussed above, low-frequency compounds take longer to process than high-frequency compounds, in addition to the basic mental effort. Many of these compounds qualify as so-called "pleonastic" or "poetic" compounds that seem to gain no benefit from their compound structures.[84] These examples from *Beowulf* demonstrate that, while little semantic complexity is created through the compounding, the syntactic and cognitive complexity nonetheless interacts with the rest of the surrounding passage to create stylistic emphasis. On the level of individual words, the compound structures of these words do very little; on the levels of sentences and larger discourse units, on the other hand, the compound structures do important stylistic work unattainable by simplices. *Beowulf* thus employs unique or rare compounds in ways that emphasize weaponry and armour exactly when they emerge from the poem's heroic "background," as it were, and play a prominent role in the narrative, thereby illustrating the most basic and useful application of compounds in Old English literature.

83 Of the forty-nine compounds in these passages, thirty-seven (75.5 per cent) are unique to *Beowulf*, and seven (14.3 per cent) are rare in the corpus.

84 On such compounds, again see Brodeur, *The Art of Beowulf*, 14–17; Russom, *Old English Meter*, 92–7; and Russom, "Aesthetic Criteria," 71.

Another good example of compounds creating emphasis appears early in *The Wanderer*, with a cluster of several compounds expressing some aspect of the mind:

> Nis nu cwicra nan
> þe ic him modsefan minne durre
> sweotule asecgan. Ic to soþe wat
> þat biþ in eorle indryhten þeaw,
> þæt he his ferðlocan fæste binde,
> healde his hordcofan, hycge swa he wille.
> Ne mæg werig mod wyrde wiðstondan,
> ne se hreo hyge helpe gefremman.
> Forðon domgeorne dreorigne oft
> in hyra breostcofan bindað fæste;
> swa ic modsefan minne sceolde,
> oft earmcearig, eðle bidæled,
> freomægum feor feterum sælan.[85]

> There is no longer anyone alive to whom I would dare openly speak my mind. I know as truth that it is an honourable habit for a noble man to bind fast his mind, hold shut his treasure chest, think as he wants. The weary mind cannot withstand fate, nor can the tempestuous thought give help. The ambitious [virtuous?] therefore often bind the dreary fast in their minds; in this same way, I – often miserable, deprived of my homeland, far from my kinsmen – have had to confine my mind with fetters.

In these twelve-and-a-half lines appear five compounds relating to the mind: *ferðloca*, *hordcofa*, *breostcofa*, and *modsefa* twice. In particular, this cluster of compounds depends on a conception of the mind itself *as* an enclosure, not simply *in* an enclosure.[86] In other words, the mind is not simply enclosed within a particular part of the physical body; the mind

85 Krapp and Dobbie, *The Exeter Book*, 134, lines 9b–21.

86 Mize, "Representation of the Mind," especially 62–4. See also Low, "The Anglo-Saxon Mind"; Harbus, *Life of the Mind*, 50–5; Matto, "A War of Containment"; and Lockett, *Anglo-Saxon Psychologies*. *Hordcofa* by itself simply means "treasure coffer" and only through the extension activated by its parallelism with the other words for mind does it come to express an aspect of the mind; see BT, s.v. *hordcófa* and the discussion of *hord* in Mize, "Representation of the Mind," 68.

is itself an enclosure containing thoughts, emotions, etc. Understandings of the mind and interior mentality, though perhaps stereotypically unrecognized by some scholars of other periods, are fundamental to much of Anglo-Saxon literature. *The Wanderer*, often paired with *The Seafarer*, is one principal instance of the exploration of the issue of the life of the interior – the self – and how one should relate to the exterior world; indeed, the issue has occupied scholars for decades.[87]

Feeding into this theme of interiority, the collocation of these four compounds (in five occurrences) in such close proximity further underscores the importance of this concept of mind-as-enclosure at the opening of the poem.[88] In fact, the concept of mind-as-enclosure becomes fully expressed in this passage only through the compound structures of the words.[89] The words *loca* and *cofa* express the container aspect without denoting the mind, and the first constituent *ferhð* denotes the mind without a necessarily overt sense of containment.[90] Of these constituents, only *breost* can by itself imply containment and interiority in addition to connecting to the mind, although it can often mean simply the front of the chest without implying containment.[91] Its frequent association with the mind and mental activity is not always direct, usually requiring additional apparatus such as prepositions or, as in this passage, compounding with another word overtly denoting the mind.[92] Thus, the amalgamated concept of the mind as a container in and of itself only overtly arises in this passage through the combination of the various pieces in these compounds. The mind/container amalgam could theoretically be expressed

87 In addition to the works cited in the previous note, see Clemoes, "*Mens absentia cogitans*"; Godden, "Anglo-Saxons on the Mind"; Jager, "The Word in the 'Breost'"; Lucas, "The Language of the Loner"; Low, "Exile"; Harbus, "The Medieval Concept of the Self"; and Matto, "True Confessions."

88 Few other compounds denoting the mind occur in *The Wanderer*: *ferðloca* and *modsefa* each occur once more outside of this cluster in lines 33 and 59, respectively, but no other compounds for mind appear.

89 *Modsefa* does not imply any sense of enclosure; it is only through its parallelism with the other compounds that it participates in that theme; see Mize, "Representation of the Mind," 63–4.

90 BT, s.v. *loca*; *DOE*, s.v. *cofa* and *ferhð*. See also Lockett, *Anglo-Saxon Psychologies*, 33–5 and 52–3.

91 *DOE*, s.v. *brēost*; Jager, "The Word in the 'Breost'"; and Lockett, *Anglo-Saxon Psychologies*, especially 54–109.

92 See the discussion of *breostsefa* in Lockett, *Anglo-Saxon Psychologies*, 54–7.

through phrases, but that method would lack the structural, subconscious unification achieved through compounding. The fact that *ferðloca*, *hordcofa*, and *breostcofa* are relatively low-frequency in the corpus suggests that they would necessarily have been processed through the decomposition/recomposition route, which emphasizes their compound structures.[93] That emphasis builds their impact, consequently giving much more expressive force to the concept of mind-as-enclosure than would have been possible without the compounds.

The concept of enclosure of course constructs the dichotomy of interior and exterior, with the implications that some elements can be locked within and that others can be excluded.[94] The narrator of *The Wanderer* keeps the contents of his mind locked in and any companions or interlocutors out. This interest in both protecting and excluding aligns with the emphasis on the mind as an enclosure and must motivate the employment of the compounds discussed above. This concern for exclusion runs through the entire text, with the compounds laying the groundwork for it at the beginning; in a sense, they prime the concept that then underlies the rest of the poem. The interest in isolation and mental seclusion, ironically, becomes obvious in *The Wanderer* through various direct, gnomic statements, but the sense of the mind as an enclosure is introduced and concretely laid out largely through these compounds.

The voice of *The Seafarer*, in contrast, openly desires to reveal his thoughts:

Mæg ic be me sylfum   soðgied wrecan,
siþas secgan,   hu ic geswincdagum
earfoðhwile   oft þrowade,
bitre breostceare   gebiden hæbbe,
gecunnad in ceole   cearselda fela,
atol yþa gewealc,   þær mec oft bigeat
nearo nihtwaco   æt nacan stefnan,
þonne he be clifum cnossað.[95]

93 *Fer(h)ðloca* occurs in four texts total, *hordcofa* in five, and *breostcofa* in six. See the *DOEC*.

94 Mize, "Representation of the Mind," 72.

95 Krapp and Dobbie, *The Exeter Book*, 143, lines 1–8a. See also the discussion in Matto, "True Confessions," 161–2.

> I can relate a true tale of myself, tell of my travels, how I often suffered wretched times in toilsome days, how I have endured severe sorrow, have experienced at the keel many places of sorrow, the terrible churning of waves, where the anxious night-watch often seized me at the ship's prow, when it strikes near the cliffs.

These opening lines achieve the exact opposite of what the voice of *The Wanderer* seeks, actively opening up the enclosure of the mind. For all their other similarities, the two poems are in this way diametrically opposed, and it is thus unsurprising that they also diverge in their uses of compound words. Although *The Seafarer* contains *breostcearu* [breast-sorrow], which highlights the enclosing breast, and two other compounds relating to the mind as an enclosure (*breosthord* [breast-hord] in line 55 and *hreþerloca* [breast-locker] in line 58), these compounds do not create the same emphasis on containment as do those in *The Wanderer*. True, all three of these mind-as-enclosure compounds are rare in the corpus, as were those in *The Wanderer*, but there are fewer of them, and they do not cluster together in the same fashion. Attention seems to turn to the mind in lines 50 through 64, but that moment comes late in *The Seafarer*, compared to the fairly immediate concern for the mind as an enclosure in *The Wanderer*. Moreover, the senses of containment and exclusion are not supported in this passage, with the mind instead leaving the body to revisit what it misses. The only exclusion here comes from external loss, not from intentionally shutting others out. *The Seafarer* instead emphasizes the sea as its central image through seven compounds relating to water in some way, several of which are unique to the poem.[96] This fact is relatively unsurprising, considering the importance of the sea and sea journeys in Anglo-Saxon culture,[97] but the interest is particularly pronounced in *The Seafarer*.[98] The different emphases of the two poems thus manifest powerfully in their compounds, and the individuality of the two poems, so similar in other ways, becomes markedly clear.

---

96 The unique compounds relating directly to water are *merewerges* (line 12), *brimlade* (30), *sæfore* (42), and *anfloga* (62); two more are rare in the corpus: *sealtyþa* (35), and *flodwegas* (52); and one is uncommon: *mereflode* (59). There are also two compounds relating to ice: *isceald* (14 and 19, rare in the corpus) and *hrimgicel* (17, unique to *The Seafarer*). See the *DOEC*.

97 See Howe, *Migration and Mythmaking*; Sobecki, *The Sea*; and Rudolf, "The Spiritual Islescape."

98 See, for example, Holton, "Old English Sea Imagery."

It is unfortunately nearly impossible to place *The Wanderer* and *The Seafarer* in a specific cultural context.[99] Both appear in The Exeter Book, which was likely produced in the second half of the tenth century and included in Leofric's donations to Exeter.[100] The manuscript's history before the donation remains speculative, and the linguistic features of its contents offer little specific help. This situation is of course standard for Old English poetry, which cultivates a timeless, almost ahistorical character as part of its aesthetic.[101] Discussions and interpretations of much of Old English poetry must therefore rely on the features of its general poetic culture and comparison between different members of the corpus, as with the above comparision of *The Wanderer* and *The Seafarer*.[102]

It is much easier to place compound words within a cultural context in Old English prose texts, which do not cultivate the same timeless aesthetic. Moreover, as noted above, the expressive force of compound words depends on their structure and its cognitive effects, which occur whether a compound appears in poetry or prose. The Old English homilies of Archbishop Wulfstan provide a particularly striking prose example of the creation of rhetorical emphasis through the strategic deployment of compound words with an eye to specific cultural contexts.[103] Although not as prolific an author as his contemporary Ælfric, Wulfstan produced a large corpus of Old English and Latin homilies and other prose works during the late tenth century and early eleventh century. During that period, he was also closely involved in many of the major political changes that the Anglo-Saxons witnessed, serving as advisor to several kings in succession. The influence of Wulfstan's political activities on his writing is most readily apparent in his treatise on the organization of society, his laws, and some of his most clearly political homilies, but the political and social motivations of his style extend throughout the rest of the homilies

99 See chapter 6 below for a discussion of putting *Beowulf* in a cultural context.

100 Exeter, Exeter Cathedral Library MS 3501. See Ker, *Catalogue*, no. 116; Muir, *Exeter Anthology*, 1:1–3; Gneuss, *Handlist*, no. 257; and Gneuss and Lapidge, *Anglo-Saxon Manuscripts*, no. 257.

101 Tyler, *Old English Poetics*, 2.

102 The discussion in the next chapter of *Juliana* within the cultural context of the Exeter Book's copying would be difficult to apply to *The Wanderer* and *The Seafarer*, since I am unaware of any features of the two elegies that resonate with the Benedictine Reform.

103 A version of the portions of this chapter discussing Wulfstan's homilies previously appeared in Davis-Secord, "Rhetoric and Politics."

as well.[104] Indeed, the patterns of compound occurrence in Wulfstan's Old English homilies highlight the archbishop's concern with the social and political problems facing the Anglo-Saxons during his archepiscopacy.[105] The great instability in England in his time, according to Wulfstan, required special addressing by the church, and, in response to this perceived need, he crafted his rhetoric – especially the employment of rare or unique compounds – around the cause to engage his audience and advance his social vision.

The utility of these compounds for Wulfstan and his sensitivity to the rarity of compounds become particularly clear in *De septiformi spiritu* (Bethurum IX), a reworking of an Ælfrician text. Through line 106 of the homily, Wulfstan reworks Ælfric's explanatory text relatively faithfully in terms of the content, but, after that point, he departs from the source onto his own line of thought, contemplating the advent of the Antichrist. Most insidiously, the Antichrist has allies among the people spreading his message, which constitutes for Wulfstan the worst threat posed by the Antichrist. This final section of the homily, lines 107–51, employs several compounds that are unique to Wulfstan's writings. Of these, three are in fact *hapax legomena*, each appearing only this one time in the entire corpus of Old English.[106] Some common compounds do occur in this section, but always in the context of a rhetorical structure such as parallelism or

104 I accept the list of legitimate Old English homilies by Wulfstan in Wilcox, "Dissemination of Wulfstan's Homilies," 200, with the additions and subtractions suggested in Lionarons, *Homiletic Writings*, 23–42. According to Wilcox, Wulfstan's vernacular homiletic corpus consists of the material in Bethurum, *Homilies*; homilies I, XXIII, XXIV, XXV, XXVII, XXXV, XXXVI, XXXVIII, L, LI, LII, LIII, LIX, LX, LXI in Napier, *Wulfstan*; the Copenhagen fragment, printed in Ker, "The Handwriting of Archbishop Wulfstan"; the traces in London, BL Add. 38651, folios 57–8; and the works printed in appendices A, B, C, E, and K in Jost, *"Institutes of Polity."* Lionarons suggests the removal of Napier XXXVI from Wulfstan's corpus and the addition to it of Napier XLVII and Jost's appendices F, G, L, and I.

105 On Wulfstan's social concerns, see Wormald, "Archbishop Wulfstan," and Wormald, *Making of English Law*, 457. Chapman's work also addresses Wulfstan's use of compounds, but he generally does not explore the non-stylistic motivations for their presence in the homilies: "Stylistic Use"; "Pragmatics"; "Motivations"; "Poetic Compounding"; and "Germanic Tradition."

106 The three *hapax legomena* are *gearawitolnys* [sagacity], *rihtlicetere* [complete liar], and *þeodlicetere* [deceiver of the people]. See the *DOEC*.

punning, as is the case in the rest of the homily.[107] On the other hand, almost none of the *hapax legomena* or the other unique compounds participate in any overt rhetorical devices.[108] It is striking that in this final section Wulfstan's style changes in terms only of compound usage. It is not the case that only once free of the confines of his source does he feel free in his form of expression, for Wulfstan actively rewrites Ælfric's style throughout the entire homily.[109] He alters sentences to reflect his own sense of rhythm, grammatical parallelism, and style of vocabulary. It is only the frequent use of rare and unique compounds which is restricted to the final section. The increased occurrence of this type of compound evidently reflects the shift in focus to a topic which clearly exercises the archbishop elsewhere in similarly exhortatory homilies.

This stylistic change takes advantage of the impact of low-frequency compounds. Especially without any other such compounds occurring earlier in the homily, the rare and unique compounds in the final section stand out prominently, thereby emphasizing their semantic content through their formal features and cognitive demands. Of particular interest are the three compounds *þeodlicetere*, *þeodfeond*, and *þeodloga*, which are all unique to Wulfstan's writing (*þeodlicetere* is a *hapax legomenon*).[110] Bethurum claims that the *þeod–* constituent of these compounds serves only to add intensifying force to the condemnation of the Antichrist, thus translating these three compounds as "arch-hypocrite," "arch-fiend," and "arch-liar," respectively.[111] She gives no explanation, however, for the collocation of these three compounds in the final section of this homily. Placing the three compounds in their context reveals a strong concern for the Anglo-Saxon

107 For example, in "ne eac mæðe ne geseo on his underþeoddum ne on his efengelican" (lines 97–8), *underþeod* and *efengelic* form grammatical parallelism as objects of the two occurrences of *on*. In the first section of the homily compounds are either glosses of Latin terms or members of simple, short rhetorical structures such as this.

108 Only *manswican* (line 126) creates paranomasia with *swiciað* later in that line. This sound play, however, is not of the same degree as the echoing parallelism noted by Chapman, "Stylistic Use." The fact that *unsoðfæstnyss* (line 131) is rare can be disregarded as an accident of Wulfstan's clear affinity for the prefix *un–* since *soðfæstnyss* is common throughout the Old English corpus.

109 Orchard, "Crying Wolf," 244.

110 Bethurum, *Homilies*, 189–90, lines 16, 17, and 33 respectively.

111 Bethurum, *Homilies*, 90.

community, that is, for the *þeod* as translated literally: people, tribe, nation, state. Wulfstan makes it clear in this section of Bethurum IX that the greatest threat from the Antichrist is his treacherous deception which infects more and more people as they themselves become treacherous deceivers, spreading the Antichrist's lies far and wide. Society, the *þeod* itself, begins to break down. Given this clear resonance between the theme underlying Wulfstan's expansion of Ælfric's text and the specific language employed therein, translating *þeod* literally in the three compounds is more appropriate than Bethurum's suggestion. Understanding the Antichrist as the deceiver or the enemy of the people (*þeodlicetere* or *þeodfeond*) and his victims also as deceivers of the people (*þeodlogan*) links very well with Wulfstan's overall interest in the topic. The archbishop was concerned not just for his flock's spiritual lives but for their lives *in middangeard* and in the *þeod* as well, thus supporting the literal interpretation of these three compounds.

This single example of reevaluating the *þeod*– compounds in light of Wulfstan's political and social thought acts as a microcosm for understanding his use of compounds in general, which all cluster around Wulfstan's social concerns: stability of, purity of, and respect for the church as the support of society as a whole. The following quotation sums up much of Wulfstan's point of view on this topic:

> Leofan menn, lagjað gode woroldlagan and lecgað þærtoeacan, þæt ure cristendom fæste stande, and þæt ures hlafordes kinedom up arise, and þæt ealles folces frið wyrðe betere, þonne hit git sig.[112]

> Dear people, ordain the worldly laws for God and moreover arrange them so that our Christendom shall stand fast and so that our lord's kingdom will spread and so that the refuge of all people will become better than it yet is.

The laws of the world are put in place for God and for the benefit of Christendom in the human world. Worldly law and sacred power are intertwined.[113] This quotation also contains a perfect instance of ambiguity in the word *hlaford*, for it could refer to the Lord God or to the worldly lord, the king. To be sure, as a churchman, the archbishop sought

112 Napier, *Wulfstan*, homily LI, 274, lines 7–10.
113 See also Treharne, *Living Through Conquest*, 61–8.

to extend the kingdom of God on earth, but, as a political figure, he also showed great concern for the welfare of the king. If not for a specific king, Wulfstan's involvement with royal legal issues show that he cared at least for the role and position of the king as a source of social order. While this concern could have been motivated by the political opportunism of a shrewd, politically minded ecclesiast, the actions themselves cannot be construed as completely negative, and the emphasis on social well-being suggests unselfish motivations.

The *Sermo Lupi* in particular reveals this concern for kingship, with its railing against traitors to the king (*hlafordswican*).[114] Wulfstan condemns specific acts of treachery against kings: the murder of Edward the Martyr and the exile of Æthelred.[115] These deceitful and traitorous acts, according to Wulfstan, aroused God's anger and invited his punishment in the form of the Viking attacks. The specific kings, however, are not as important as the royal throne itself. Indeed, Wulfstan originally supported Æthelred's exile only one year before delivering his condemnation of it.[116] Apparently a canny political player, Wulfstan carefully negotiated the ebbs and swells of Æthelred's popularity. The archbishop also skilfully avoided losing his position after Æthelred's death and the subsequent changes of kingship, and in fact just the opposite occurred, as Wulfstan became one of Cnut's trusted advisors and legislators. Although Wulfstan may have been an anti-royalist from one point of view,[117] his actions supporting and working for several different kings show that, while perhaps not loyal to an individual, he was always loyal to the throne. This loyalty may have been opportunistic, but the fact remains that Wulfstan lent his support to each successive monarch and worked to maintain social stability on the island during the transitions.

Whether Wulfstan agreed with individual kings or even with the system of royalty is in a way irrelevant to the fact that he saw the throne as a powerful force for social stability. His support for the throne stemmed from his interest in the well-being of Anglo-Saxon society in general, an interest overt in his work on the structure of society, the *Institutes of Polity*, but also permeating the rest of his writings. This concern underlies the addition to Bethurum IX: it is the Antichrist's threat to society that worries Wulfstan.

---

114 Bethurum, *Homilies*, 270, line 72.

115 Wilcox, "Political Performance," 383.

116 Wilcox, "Political Performance," 387.

117 Bethurum Loomis, "*Regnum* and *sacerdotium*."

The specific sins are of course censured, but a real danger lies in the social instability they engender.[118] In normal times, the institution of the monarchy ensured stability for the Anglo-Saxons, fulfilling a valuable role in Wulfstan's vision of society. As the monarchy's ability to guarantee stability waned in the early years of the eleventh century, so did Wulfstan's estimation of it. A revision of the *Institutes of Polity* removes the references to royal divinity, reflecting this changing perception of the monarchy's power.[119]

But the monarchy was never the sole source of social stability for Wulfstan: he subscribed early on to the threefold ordering of society into warriors, churchmen, and workers,[120] as can be seen in following passage:

> Ælc riht cynestol stent on þrym stapelum, þe fullice ariht stent: an is *oratores*, and oðer is *laboratores*, and þrydde is *bellatores. oratores* syndon gebedmen, þe gode sceolon þeowjan dæges and nihtes for þæne cyngc and for ealne þeodscipe þingjan georne. *laboratores* syndon weorcmen, þe tiljan sceolan þæs, þe eall þeodscipe big sceal lybban. *bellatores* syndon wigmen, þe eard sculon werjan wiglice mid wæpnon. on þysum þrym stapelum sceal ælc cynestol standan mid rihte ...[121]

> Each upright royal throne which stands truly upright stands on three pillars: one is the *oratores* [those who pray], and the second is the *laboratores* [those who work], and the third is the *bellatores* [those who fight]. The *oratores* are the priests who must eagerly intercede with God day and night on behalf of the king and on behalf of the entire people. The *laboratores* are the workmen who must work because all the people must live by [them]. The *bellatores* are the war-men who must defend the country with their weapons. On these three pillars must each royal throne properly stand ...

This passage comes not from Wulfstan's social tracts but from a homily, edited in Napier's collection. Again, the concern for social order surfaces throughout Wulfstan's entire corpus. The king and his authority must be backed by a correctly structured society, which, moreover, must be based on the word of God to be truly successful.[122]

118 Wormald, *Legal Culture*, 245.
119 Bethurum Loomis, "*Regnum* and *sacerdotium*," 137.
120 Wormald, "Archbishop Wulfstan," 19.
121 Napier, *Wulfstan*, homily L, 267, lines 9–17.
122 Wormald, "Archbishop Wulfstan," 21.

According to Wulfstan, as the priests and monks go, so go the people, and during his lifetime this point was of particular significance. The social situation in England was in upheaval following the sudden death of Edgar in 975 and then the murder of his son and successor Edward in 978.[123] The rule of Æthelred, Edgar's second son and Edward's successor, offered little stability, seeing internal political manipulation, the resurgence of external invasions, and natural disaster.[124] Æthelred's power eroded, and in the course of only three years beginning in 1013 the monarchy suffered still more disorder as the kingship passed from Æthelred to Swein, back to Æthelred, briefly to Edmund, to both Edmund and Cnut, and finally to Cnut *in toto* near the end of 1016.[125] Wulfstan was intimately involved with at least some of these transitions, possibly influencing the judgments of the English council and probably ever attempting to maintain social stability.[126] In those days of unrest, the church must have seemed to be the sole alternative to the monarchy as a source of stability. Without a strong monarchy to hold the fracturing country together, the only other "nation-wide" entity in existence needed to step in: the church, one of the three pillars of society, had to fill the breach being created in the military and political tug of war. Wulfstan, as the influential second highest-, and for a time the highest-, ranking church official on the island during this period of supreme disorder,[127] was clearly well suited to push the church in this direction. Many of his homilies to general audiences, presumably containing lay people, urge repentance and social reform, and some of his homilies to limited religious audiences call for pure living and adherence to the rules. The two emphases intertwined: purifying the church and increasing its regulation of society would in turn facilitate his other push to reform lay society. Wulfstan was, in a sense, working from two different angles to achieve one goal: to maintain Anglo-Saxon society, both the people and the church needed to work together.

Wulfstan worked to achieve his goals of social maintenance and reform through his rhetoric. The unique compounds found at the end of Bethurum

123 Stenton, *Anglo-Saxon England*, 372.

124 Keynes, *Diplomas*, 186 and 215.

125 Stenton, *Anglo-Saxon England*, 384–93; and Keynes, *Diplomas*, 226–7. For a useful summary, see also Keynes, "Appendix: Rulers of the English," 515.

126 Wilcox, "Political Performance," 387.

127 Wilcox, "Political Performance," 380–1. Ælfheah, Archbishop of Canterbury, was martyred on 19 April 1012, and his successor, Lyfing, was not elevated to the position until 1013.

IX bring to the forefront the threats to social stability which the Antichrist poses. Interestingly, Wulfstan's other homilies on the Antichrist do not show these same uses of compounds to heighten the rhetorical style. This absence is perhaps because these non-compounded homilies were written early in Wulfstan's career, before he became archbishop of York.[128] The homilies using heightened rhetoric to push the issue of social order came later, after Wulfstan had assumed the larger responsibilities of an archbishop and the invasions progressed. The political problems of the day presumably also became of greater concern to Wulfstan as the years passed. In a sense, then, this concern for social order is a chronological development, but not one simply tied to Wulfstan's age. The historical events, the dangers posed to the emerging English state, his new position as leader of the English church, all these things clearly influenced Wulfstan's thoughts, concerns, and writings, making themselves felt in the archbishop's use of compounds as rhetorical markers in a way that could not be achieved with simplices.

The diverse examples in this chapter – from the epic (or at least long-form) *Beowulf*, the elegies (or at least short-form) *The Wanderer* and *The Seafarer*, and Wulfstan's Old English homilies – demonstrate that the utility of compound words spans generic and even supposedly temporal divides. In each type of text, compounds, often low-frequency or entirely unique, highlight important themes or features. In *Beowulf*, compounds provide additional emphasis on important moments, especially highlighting weapons and armour when they play important roles poetically or politically. For *The Wanderer*, compounds emphasizing the structure of the mind as an enclosure open the poem, laying a groundwork for the concerns discussed throughout the rest of its lines. *The Seafarer* eschews the reticence of *The Wanderer* and concentrates instead on the sea and water imagery in the *soðgied* that it shares. Wulfstan's exhortatory homilies draw upon rare or entirely new compounds to call attention to the concerns regarding the social influence of the Antichrist. In all of these examples, compound structures serve different final goals, but each text is drawing from the same well. The cognitive demands of compounds and the mental costs of processing them, as opposed to simplices, create fundamentally greater expressive force on a structural level than a simple word can have. That structure can then become the vehicle for any expression, making compound words unique and powerful features of Old English language and style.

128 Wormald, "Archbishop Wulfstan," 26.

4 Compound Discourses in the Old English *Boethius* and *Juliana*

In the opening scenes of Cynewulf's poem celebrating her martyrdom, Juliana spurns Heliseus's advances and refuses to tolerate a *mægræden* [relationship] with him.[1] *Mægræden*, which construes *coniugium* from the source, is an uncommon word, but more importantly it is a word normally found in prose, not poetry; in fact, *Juliana* is the only poetic occurrence for *mægræden*.[2] Indeed, although her speeches incorporate some poetic vocabulary, she employs a disproportionate amount of common, prose words – particularly prose compounds – when compared to the rest of the poem. Rather than producing a heroic proclamation of faith, Juliana presents one that is prosaic not in a pejorative sense but in a generic sense. The prosimetric Old English *Boethius*, mixing prose and poetry, displays a similar interest in the generic affiliation of its compounds, severely restricting poetic compounds to its verse portions and prose compounds to its prose. These patterns depend on the rhetorical and cognitive emphasis created by compounds, discussed in chapter 3 above, and use that emphasis to invoke particular Old English discourses. The restriction of certain compounds to poetry has not gone without prior notice,[3] but the patterns

1 Woolf, *Juliana*, line 109. Cynewulf's version of Juliana's refusal actually softens the demands made in the source; see Olsen, "Autonomous Women," 228.

2 The word's other appearances come in a homily for the third Sunday in Lent, the Old English *Orosius*, the Old English translation of Gregory's *Dialogues*, and two glosses to the prose version of Aldhelm's *De virginitate*. Both glosses construe the phrase *propinquae necessitudinis* [close relative]. See the *DOEC*.

3 See among others Godden, "Literary Language"; Chapman and Christensen, "Noun-Adjective Compounds"; and Scragg, "The Nature of Old English Verse."

of deployment in *Juliana* and the *Boethius* powerfully demonstrate Old English discursive distinctions and the capacity for compounds to signal them strongly. Through careful use of the strong generic resonances made possible by compound structures, these texts create hybrid discourses that mix multiple registers or discourses in order to present stylistic illustrations of important themes in each work.

Hybridity of discourse, of course, features prominently in Mikhail Bakhtin's analysis of the novel, which he considers to be best characterized as mixing different registers and discourses. Bakhtin bases his formal, literary analysis on a paradigm that approaches language as a collection of "utterances" within specific contexts.[4] This theory of the utterance has been particularly influential in the development of stylistics,[5] and it resonates with this study in particular because of its emphasis on the social nature of language. The essential point in Bakhtin's philosophy of language is that the strongly bipolar situation suggested by Saussure's *langue* and *parole* is misleading.[6] Any instance of speech or writing – Bakhtin's "utterance" – is the result neither simply of the arbitrary choices of the speaking or writing individual nor of the imposed, normative "rules" of "unitary language."[7] For Bakhtin, an utterance is not an "either-or" proposition but the product of a give-and-take between the individual's choices and large language patterns. Utterances are thus "dialogic," balancing and incorporating the conflicting interests of both of the poles posited by Saussurian linguistics.[8] For Bakhtin, the dialogic nature of language transcends binarism and involves instead a "diversity of speech types," which he calls "heteroglossia," a web of multiple languages interacting.[9]

4 Bakhtin, "Discourse in the Novel," 269–72.

5 See Crowley, "Bakhtin and the History of the Language," 69.

6 For Saussure's "dualistic" theory of language, see de Saussure, *Writings in General Linguistics*, especially "Part I: On the Dual Essence of Language." On the relationship between Bakhtin's theories and Saussure's, see Holquist, *Dialogism*, 44–7 and 59–63.

7 Bakhtin, "Discourse in the Novel," 272.

8 Gordon, "*Langue* and *Parole*," defends Saussure's two poles, showing that *langue* and *parole* are in fact "complementary" and that Saussure conceived of them as "interactive" and not totally disengaged from one another. Bakhtin, "Discourse in the Novel," 269–70, nonetheless sees such an apparently dualistic conception as insufficient to account for the subtleties of language.

9 Bakhtin, "Discourse in the Novel," 263.

An integral part of this heteroglossia is the existence of a myriad of "speech genres" created through the interactive, social use of language, genres which define the patterns of speech and writing at all levels of discourse.[10] The concept of speech genres is similar to but distinct from – and more rigorously defined than – the stereotypical concept of genre, which encompasses such types as epic, romance, history, lyric, etc.[11] Rather than that classic concept of genre, Bakhtin's speech genres more closely align with the concepts of the branch of modern linguistics known as pragmatics, which recognizes the strong influences of various contexts on language and meaning.[12] Bakhtin's speech genres are thus essential in making linguistic communication possible:

> Speech genres organize our speech in almost the same way as grammatical (syntactical) forms do. We learn to cast our speech in generic forms and, when hearing others' speech, we guess its genre from the very first words; we predict a certain length (that is, the approximate length of the speech whole) and a certain compositional structure; we foresee the end; that is, from the very beginning we have a sense of the speech whole, which is only later differentiated during the speech process. If speech genres did not exist and we had not mastered them, if we had to originate them during the speech process and construct each utterance at will for the first time, speech communication would be almost impossible.[13]

Speech genres provide not only the internal, linguistic patterns of sentences but also the patterns of the discursive levels above the sentence, for example, the length and type of paragraphs. Speech genres, then, in a sense populate the conceptual space between Saussure's two linguistic poles of *parole* and *langue*: a genre is neither determined by an individual nor produced

10 Bakhtin, "Speech Genres," 60 and 78. The theory of speech genres was apparently the product not of Bakhtin alone but of Bakhtin and his associates V.N. Vološinov and P.N. Medvedev, all three of whom together are generally referred to as the "Bakhtin Circle." For a recent engagement with this issue, see Bronckart and Bota, *Bakhtine démasqué*, and its review by Zbinden.

11 For seminal discussions of this type of genre, see Derrida, "The Laws of Genre," and Cohen, "History and Genre."

12 Pragmatics, however, focuses mainly on meaning in spoken interactions, whereas Bakhtin's theories also encompass literary texts. See Birner, *Introduction to Pragmatics*, 1–35.

13 Bakhtin, "Speech Genres," 78–9.

by a "unitary" language system like, for example, grammar or phonology. Instead, genres provide the "typical forms of construction" deemed socially appropriate for an expression, forms that a speaker/writer may employ even without any overt recognition of their existence.[14] Importantly, this theory of genres stems from and necessitates a social view of language: no utterance is an isolated phenomenon; all utterances exist in relation to other utterances. An utterance is thus ontologically social: it is a concrete realization of language produced by an individual speaker or writer, "a *real unit of speech communication*."[15] The accumulation of similar utterances actually produced by a group of individuals – and nothing else – constructs a genre.

In producing an utterance, therefore, a speaker/writer necessarily builds upon previous utterances. No piece of speech or writing is ever truly originary, that is, completely without precedent or knowledge of previous speech or writing. Preceding utterances, moreover, do not simply provide the new utterance with linguistic and thematic patterns but enter into a dialogic relationship with it. The new utterance reacts to previous utterances, perhaps reinterpreting them, disagreeing with or reaffirming them, or simply referencing them; every utterance, according to Bakhtin, is "a link in a very complexly organized chain of other utterances."[16] These generic links of utterances affect not just the large patterns of an utterance but also the choices of individual words:

> When we select words in the process of constructing an utterance, we by no means always take them from the system of language in their neutral, *dictionary* form. We usually take them from *other utterances*, and mainly from utterances that are kindred to ours in genre, that is, in theme, composition, or style. Consequently, we choose words according to their generic specifications. A speech genre is not a form of language, but a typical form of utterance; as such the genre also includes a certain typical kind of expression that inheres in it. In the genre the word acquires a particular typical expression … This typical (generic) expression can be regarded as the word's "stylistic aura," but this aura belongs not to the word of language as such but to that genre in which the given word usually functions. It is an echo of the generic whole that resounds in the word.[17]

14 Bakhtin, "Speech Genres," 78.
15 Bakhtin, "Speech Genres," 67, original emphasis.
16 Bakhtin, "Speech Genres," 69.
17 Bakhtin, "Speech Genres," 87–8, original emphases.

In forming an utterance, the speaker/writer follows a genre's example both for the formation of discursive patterns, such as paragraph length or argument structure, and also for the vocabulary associated with the genre. Every word has its fundamental definition – its "dictionary form" – and also its associative characteristics accrued through its use in specific generic conditions. The types of text – that is, their content, style, and affiliations – in which a word appears become adumbrations to its "dictionary" definition, creating the word's "stylistic aura." Thus, every word becomes dialogically connected with a particular style or form of speech and carries those associations in every occurrence. By examining a text's dialogic connections, one can determine its "particular *definite* position in a sphere of communication."[18] That is, in the conceptual space of speech communication, each text fills a position defined by its dialogic relations – its affirmation, refutation, supplementation, modification, etc. – to other texts.

A corollary of this social view of language is that, to comprehend an utterance, one must understand both the fundamental grammatical "rules" of a language as well as the context of that individual utterance. Utterances not only respond to other utterances in their linguistic context but also to their "extraverbal context," factors and situations that inform language but are not overtly expressed linguistically.[19] The following, short example illustrates this point: "Two people are sitting in a room. They are both silent. Then one of them says, 'Well!' The other does not respond."[20] The meaning of this "conversation" only becomes clear with the explanation that the two people looked out the window together and saw it begin to snow even though it was May. Given the full extraverbal context, the utterance of "Well!" clearly becomes a (disappointed and frustrated) response to the May snowstorm. It is important to note that the utterance is not simply a reflection of the situation but an active response that dialogically becomes part of the situation: "utterances actively continue and develop a situation, adumbrate a plan for future action, and organize that action."[21] The extraverbal situation becomes an implicit element of the utterance, which in turn participates in the extraverbal situation. Moreover, the utterance

18 Bakhtin, "Speech Genres," 91, original emphasis.
19 Vološinov, "Discourse in Life," 99.
20 Vološinov, "Discourse in Life," 99; the explanation of this illustration continues on from page 99 onto 100.
21 Vološinov, "Discourse in Life," 100.

depends on the commonly shared understanding of the extraverbal situation; without a common point of reference, the exclamation of "Well!" would be meaningless. Utterances, then, are social in that they participate in their extraverbal context and depend on the common reference-point of those participating in the situation. The meaning of an utterance therefore can never be fully divorced from its context.

At this point, another brief, self-contained example of the application of these ideas would perhaps be helpful. In his piece "Pierre Menard, Author of the *Quixote*," Jorge Luis Borges presents a reflection on a fictional author who strove to rewrite word-for-word Miguel de Cervantes' *Don Quixote* in the twentieth century.[22] Borges's narrator makes very clear that this rewriting was no modernized version of the original nor a mere copying:

> Those who have insinuated that Menard devoted his life to writing a contemporary *Quixote* besmirch his illustrious memory. Pierre Menard did not want to compose *another* Quixote, which surely is easy enough – he wanted to compose *the* Quixote. Nor, surely, need one be obliged to note that his goal was never a mechanical transcription of the original; he had no intention of *copying* it. His admirable ambition was to produce a number of pages which coincided – word for word and line for line – with those of Miguel de Cervantes.[23]

Menard's fictional text is verbally identical to Cervantes' original, a phenomenon achieved through multiple revisions until the words become Menard's own as well as, almost accidentally, those of Cervantes. Thus, the originally seventeenth-century text becomes a product of the twentieth century. This conceit of placing the text in a new historical context completely alters the effects of the linguistic and stylistic patterns in *Don Quixote*, even though the words themselves remain superficially unchanged. The language constituting the contemporary vernacular in the seventeenth-century text becomes a nostalgic exercise in archaism in the twentieth-century text.[24] In Bakhtinian terms, Cervantes' text is in dialogue with other seventeenth-century and earlier texts and contexts,

22 Borges, "Pierre Menard."

23 Borges, "Pierre Menard," 91, original emphases.

24 As Borges's narrator notes, "The archaic style of Menard – who is, in addition, not a native speaker of the language in which he writes – is somewhat affected. Not so the style of his precursor, who employs the Spanish of his time with complete naturalness" ("Pierre Menard," 94).

while Menard's is in dialogue with those same texts and contexts but also Cervantes' original as well as those from the intervening three hundred years. Menard's text responds to texts that themselves responded to Cervantes' original, and it therefore constitutes a completely different utterance than the original. Thus, the twentieth-century text has completely new meanings, challenging its contemporary modes of thought and expression where the seventeenth-century text tacitly employs the contemporary modes of its time.[25] The alterations of generic relations and extraverbal context for *Don Quixote* begets a complete alteration of the text's identity, but without changing a word. The new text, although verbally identical to the original, becomes an entirely different utterance.

Oral Theory relies on a similar concept of external referentiality in that, at a basic level, as discussed in chapter 1 above, an oral work produces meaning primarily by referencing the context of its tradition: individual traditional elements of the work resonate with and metonymically invoke the entirety of the tradition.[26] That large tradition also subdivides further into registers, which are "major speech styles associated with recurrent types of situations" and "shared by many speakers and hearers."[27] Vocabulary, turns of phrase, levels of formality, assumptions of audience knowledge – many different elements combine in defining an individual register.[28] Each of those elements then links to the entirety of that register, and meaning becomes adumbrative instead of simply denotative:

> Because registers are more highly coded than everyday language, because their "words" resonate with traditional implications beyond the scope of multipurpose street language, they convey enormously more than grammars and dictionaries (based as they are on the everyday language) can record. For this reason – because they offer ready access to meaning that otherwise lies out of reach – registers can and do persist beyond live performance and into texts. Registers don't just get the composition job done; they connect oral poems to their oral traditions.[29]

25 Borges, "Pierre Menard," 94–5.

26 Foley, *Immanent Art*, 7. See also Foley, *Singer of Tales*, 1–59, and Tyler, *Old English Poetics*, 1–7.

27 Respectively, Hymes, "Ways of Speaking," 440, and Foley, *How to Read an Oral Poem*, 115.

28 Foley, *How to Read an Oral Poem*, 114–15.

29 Foley, *How to Read an Oral Poem*, 116.

Dictionaries again receive the short end of the stick, as it were, because registers involve much more than the base meaning of a word, implying also cultural assumptions, systems of knowledge, and stylistic expectations. Because registers are a product specifically of a speech community, a text's assumed audience would be aware of those implications. A non-poetic text is unlikely to employ poetic diction, since that diction would invoke much more than the individual words' meanings: it would also produce in the audience expections of content, style, modes of creating meaning, etc.

Michael Drout provides a modernized, perhaps scientific approach analagous and complementary to Bakhtinian speech genres and the registers of Oral Theory. He emphasizes the interactions between culture, tradition, cognitive patterns, and composition in the creation and definition of genres.[30] Applying paradigms of evolutionary biology, Drout explores "feature interlink" to understand those interactions as genre-defining connections.[31] Of prime importance for the present discussion is the significant role of vocabulary in identifying genres, authorship, and influence, a method of study termed "lexomics."[32] This approach assesses lexical patterns to determine similarities between texts, which can support claims of shared authorship or generic resemblance in cases of significant similarity. In test cases, Drout finds that lexical patterns align with conclusions reached from other bases of evidence, such as the differences between *Genesis A* and *Genesis B*, *Guthlac A* and *Guthlac B*, and the three *Christ* poems.[33] That alignment is an important aspect of "feature interlink": Drout argues not for the superiority of lexomics in these identifications but for its interface with evidence of metrical, thematic, semantic, or historical natures.[34] In this way, Drout's paradigm matches the emphasis on the social aspects of language in Bakhtin and Oral Theory: genre is a product of several individual patterns – lexical, cultural, etc. – that all work together. The patterns of words within larger cultural contexts define genres and help us understand how literature worked at any particular historical moment.[35]

---

30 Drout, *Tradition and Influence*.

31 Drout, *Tradition and Influence*, 5–6 and 105–10.

32 On lexomics of Old English literature, see Drout et al., "Lexomics," and Drout et al., "Of Dendrogrammatology."

33 Drout et al., "Of Dendrogrammatology," 315–23.

34 Drout, *Tradition and Influence*, 5.

35 Drout, *Tradition and Influence*, 5: "Similarly [to genes], the smallest part of a memeplex, the portion that cannot be further subdivided, even if it could be identified, is not interesting or significant outside of a larger context."

The speech genres of heteroglossia, registers, and lexomics therefore provide a framework for analysing the blending of linguistic and stylistic features from multiple traditions in *Juliana* and the Old English *Boethius*. Applying the framework of heteroglossia to Old English literature, however, requires the identification of different genres, which, as discussed above in chapter 1, remains problematic given the ambiguity of Anglo-Saxon words for genre and the fact that we have little access to unrecorded genres of quotidian interaction. The dichotomy of prose and poetry seems to comprise the most basic generic divide in the corpus, but even that distinction, again as discussed in chapter 1, is difficult to assess. Since the present discussion examines patterns of vocabulary, it seems best to rely not mainly on lexical patterns but rather on a metrical distinction between prose and poetry, lest the reasoning become circular.[36] Such a reliance, moreover, aligns with Anglo-Saxon distinctions between prose and poetry, which note metre as a fundamental dividing line between the two.[37] A reliance on metre as a distinguishing feature of "poetry" allows the identification of individual compounds as "poetic" without implying any value judgments regarding style or content, hopefully thus making the characterizations more rigorous and less subjective.

The three pieces of my framework make no mention of compounds in the discussions of speech genres, but the neurolinguistic details of compounds discussed above in chapter 3 make them excellent markers of discursive difference. The brain stores information about every word in its mental lexicon, which allows for the construction of Bakhtin's "stylistic auras," Oral Theory's registers, and Drout's interlinkages between the lexical and stylistic levels. The facilitative links connecting the mental representations of compound words and their constituents along with their processing demands make them neurolinguistically "heavy," as it were, with this information. In one sense, there are simply more opportunities for compounds to accrue generic associations, given the multiple lexical entries and links involved. In another sense, the additional processing required by compounds forces the brain to attend more to compounds than simplices, which, almost accidentally, makes compounds the most noticed type of word in any text. The generic identity

36 The kind of circular argument that I hope to avoid could take the form of claiming that, say, *hronrad* [whale-road, sea] is poetic because it appears in a text that employs poetic compounds such as, say, *hronrad*.

37 See chapter 1 above for Anglo-Saxon definitions of poetry relying on metre.

of a text should therefore most easily be associated with compounds, because they stand out the most, and they thus constitute one of the most important elements in identifying and analysing speech genres. In the supposedly basic distinction between poetry and prose, determining what constitutes a poetic compound seems clearer for Latin texts than Old English,[38] although certain types of Old English compounds appear primarily in metrical texts.[39] Isolating what features of those compounds make them "poetic" may be impossible, but such knowledge is not strictly necessary for this discussion with its reliance on metre as the distinguishing factor. In this paradigm, it is clear that neologisms – newly invented words, especially compounds – feature prominently in the discursive patterns of Old English metrical texts (poetry).[40] Non-metrical (prose) texts, in contrast, tend to contain a high share of common compounds not found in metrical texts.[41] On an individual basis, each compound has a type of text – metrical or non-metrical – with which it becomes primarily associated. Assessments of those associations for a text's compounds and the proportion of rare and common compounds in that text can provide evidence of the presence of various discourses blended into a single text.

38 Lapidge, "Old English Poetic Compounds." Lapidge's argument, however, is problematic in that it relies on overly restrictive filters on the data that ultimately distort the results unhelpfully. Mize, *Traditional Subjectivities*, 61n52, points out the incompatibility of Old English compounds with Lapidge's focus on tetrasyllabic Latin compounds and of Old English metrical lines with Lapidge's emphasis on Latin hexametrical lines.

39 Chapman and Christensen, "Noun-Adjective Compounds." Chapman and Christensen's argument, however, is problematic in that it relies on conflating "stylistic effect" with "poetry" (451). Beechy, *Poetics of Old English*, makes it clear that non-metrical texts certainly also pursue "stylistic effects," but ones different from those of metrical texts.

40 See, among others, Foley, *Traditional Oral Epic*, 201–39; Godden, "Literary Language"; Scragg, "The Nature of Old English Verse"; and Mize, *Traditional Subjectivities*, 61.

41 To be sure, not all prose compounds are common, and not all poetic compounds are neologisms or even rare. I arbitrarily denote a compound as rare if it occurs in five or fewer texts, uncommon if in six to ten texts, and common if in more than ten texts. I find no way to distinguish precisely between common and rare without either subjective metrics or arbitrary metrics. This system, while arbitrary, at least gives numerical rigour and meaning to the otherwise subjective categories "common" and "rare," with the category of "uncommon," frankly, being employed mainly to provide greater division between the two ends of the spectrum.

This pragmatic approach sheds interesting light on the differences between the two versions of the Old English *Boethius*, which provide an excellent case study of Anglo-Saxon understandings of differences between the prose and verse speech genres and the effect of mixing those genres. The *Boethius* is particularly fruitful in this regard because of the differences between its two versions and also because the two versions were produced with some relationship to the Alfredian translation program. The Alfredian program is largely responsible for developing Old English prose as a literary medium, which acts as an example of Drout's "adaptive radiation" phenomenon.[42] Adaptive radiations feature "a single species rapidly splitting into numerous lineages to fill all the available niches in the ecology," with greater differentiation developing between those lineages as they specialize.[43] Alfredian prose displays the beginnings of such specialization, and the *Boethius* in particular explores the differences between metrical and non-metrical literary composition. Several poetic features created in the *Boethius* by compounds have been discussed in chapter 2 above, but the concern here becomes the impact of the mixing of metrical and non-metrical portions in the prosimetric version and the ways in which the two versions demonstrate an awareness of speech genres in their Anglo-Saxon reception.

The creation of a prosimetric version from the base materials of the all-prose version implies an interest in realigning the discursive identity of the translation through changing its generic affiliations. The running prose aligns most obviously with prose discourse generally, while the alternation between metrical and non-metrical sections produces an entirely different generic alignment. The pertinent issue then becomes how the two different conceptions of the *Boethius* compare with Old English discursive norms, which we can understand as Bakhtinian speech genres. The texts of the Alfredian translation initiative were distributed to a privileged few, probably to various bishops and quite possibly to thegns and earldormen.[44] The preface to the Old English translation of the *Regula pastoralis* claims that the translation program was aimed at the children of free men, that is, the future nobility of the kingdom that Alfred was trying to create. These

42 Drout, *Tradition and Influence*, 146–7.

43 Drout, *Tradition and Influence*, 147.

44 See Keynes, "The Power of the Written Word." Keynes lists the bishops to whom we know copies of the Old English *Regula Pastoralis* were sent (193), and copies of the *Boethius* may have received similar treatment.

men would not have been educated, at least not in late-antique works like that of Boethius, although they would probably have been in contact with educated religious men whose opinion of the translations might have been influential.[45] One can assume, therefore, that the original audience of the Old English *Boethius* was not familiar with much of the content of the Latin original nor with its language and style. The audience for the translations would then have encountered the text with little or no preparation for its style and contents and therefore been forced to rely on knowledge of Old English speech genres to understand the texts.

Given the natures of the two versions, the difference in their impacts on the audience primarily stems from the divergent structures of the two versions: prose and prosimetric. The prosimetric version is obviously structurally closer to the Latin original than the prose in that it renders Latin metrical text as Old English metrical text.[46] Although, as discussed in chapter 2 above, the *Meters* employ distinctive features of poetic diction, the full extent of the differences between the verse and the prose versions of the *metra* have nonetheless come into question at a few points. For example, the Old English prose version of IV.m.7, along with the other prose translations of the *metra*, seems to display an "elevated" style appropriate for Old English verse, employing alliteration, two-stress phrases, and repetition similar to the echoic style discussed above in chapter 2.[47] These characteristics constitute signals that the prose version attempts to distinguish linguistically between the representations of Boethius's poetry and those of his prose, and the prose version thus represents the poetic nature of the Latin metres with Old English poetic diction, but without metre.[48] If such distinctions are indeed present, then the differences between the two Old English versions of the *Boethius* might be far less significant: a Latin metre's non-metrical translation employing poetic devices could be quite similar to a completely poetic (i.e., metrical) version. The degree of difference between prose and verse versions is further complicated by the "prosaic" vocabulary of the *Meters*, which "freely admit prose words," not just in the portions directly borrowed from the prose version but also in the additions to the prose.[49] Thus, just as the Old English prose versions

45 See Discenza, *King's English*, 14.
46 See Szarmach, "*Meter 20*," 31.
47 Irvine, "Authorship."
48 Irvine, "Authorship."
49 Stanley, "Prosaic Vocabulary," 387 and 390.

of the Latin *metra* employ poetic stylistic devices, the metrical versions employ prose vocabulary, resulting in an ill-defined distinction between the genres of the two renderings. In other words, the prose version seems much like poetry,[50] and the metrical version seems much like prose.[51]

Literate Anglo-Saxons approached written texts with great sensitivity to their discursive characteristics, at least as regards Old English poetry.[52] The comparative dearth of pointing and the orthographic irregularity in the manuscripts of Old English poetry required Anglo-Saxon readers to read such texts more actively and employ more contextual information than a modern reader with modern editions of the same texts. Anglo-Saxon readers required prior knowledge of the "rules" and traditions of Old English poetry, a specific speech genre, to compensate for the lack of visual cues provided by the manuscripts. As a result of this approach to consuming texts, an Anglo-Saxon audience should presumably have been sensitive enough to the poetic characteristics of the *Boethius* to recognize the supposedly poetic character of the prose translations of Boethius's poetry. An Anglo-Saxon reader would have been trained to note the style and structure of poetry such that he or she should have been able to recognize easily the same devices in an otherwise prose text. Essentially, the stylistic clues should have been enough to signal the presence of "poetry" or "prose." In an Anglo-Saxon audience's perception of the two *Boethius* versions, then, it seems that the distinctions between them would have been far less significant than the difference our modern editions present through different lineations and page presentations. In Drout's paradigm, this situation would be characteristic of a period early in a "radiation," during which time genres are only just beginning to diverge.[53] The two species – in this case prose and verse – still share many features and have very few distinctive differences. Metre seems to be the one solid constant here, with any lexical divergence separating poetic diction from prose not fully in place.

50 This is the argument of Irvine, "Authorship."

51 This is the argument of Stanley, "Prosaic Vocabulary."

52 As noted in O'Brien O'Keeffe, *Visible Song*, 21: "at whatever level one wishes to examine reading activity for Old English verse, the written text is relatively rich in orthographic surprise. The implication of this statement is that a reader of Old English necessarily brought a great deal of predictive knowledge to the text to be read, precisely because the manuscripts were low both in orthographic redundancy and in graphic cues. This knowledge came from a deep understanding of the conventions of Old English verse, marked as it is by formula, generic composition and repetition ..."

53 Drout, *Tradition and Influence*, 147.

The similarities studied so far thus suggest that, beyond the issue of metre, poetry and prose were barely distinctive in Alfred's time.

The patterns of compound usage, however, do not support such a strong conclusion. The prose translations of Boethius's poetry may employ aspects of Old English poetic diction in some ways, but they avoid compounds normally found in metrical texts. The prose *metra* certainly use compounds, but their usage pattern differs very little from that of the shared prose sections. On the other hand, although they contain a good number of prose compounds, the *Meters* contain a significantly greater proportion of poetic compounds than the all-prose version. Specifically, the metrical portions of the *Boethius* translations contain drastically more poetic compounds than the corresponding prose sections.[54]

Consequently, the prose *metra* align best – in terms of speech genres – with the rest of the prose translation, with all the prose sections employing nearly the same proportion of non-poetic compounds. On the other hand, the *Meters* invoke an overtly poetic discourse through the employment of such a comparatively high proportion of poetic compounds. Again, according to Bakhtin,

> Each words tastes of the context and contexts in which it has lived its socially charged life; all words and forms are populated by intentions. Contextual overtones (generic, tendentious, individualistic) are inevitable in the word.[55]

Every word, according to Bakhtin, brings with it its contextual relationships and its customary discourse. The poetic compounds of the *Meters*, in a Bakhtinian view, connect the translation generically with other Old English poetry.

Finding direct evidence of the efficacy of compounds in invoking various discourses and thereby signalling the presence of those discourses in the *Boethius* is difficult, and we must rely on the indirect evidence provided by the manuscript layouts of the two versions.[56] Those layouts provide insight into how each version must have been understood at least

54 36.17 per cent of the compounds (136 of 376) in the *Meters* are "poetic," compared to 2.83 per cent (6 of 212) in the prose *metra*.

55 Bakhtin, "Disourse in the Novel," 293.

56 Portions of this analysis of the *Boethius* manuscripts also appear in Davis-Secord, "Scribal Interpretations."

by the scribes that copied them, and perhaps by the original versifier as well. In particular, the page layouts of the two main *Boethius* manuscripts accord with the patterns of compounds described above and reinscribe the distinction between the all-prose and prosimetric structures of the two versions.[57] Oxford, Bodleian Library, Bodley 180, containing the all-prose version, separates its text into chapters, which often obscure the Latin source's five-book structure and alternation between prose and verse. London, British Library, Cotton Otho A. vi contains the prosimetric version, marking transitions between prose and verse with blank lines and enlarged initial capitals (or at least space for them), and lacks a chapter system. Moreover, in the prose version, three prose *metra* – I.m.6, II.m.2, and IV.m.7 – have no introductory statement marking them as prose translations of *metra*,[58] nor does the manuscript layout in Bodley 180 identify them with capitals or any other significant marking. Even with the presence of poetic diction (other than compounds associated with poetry) in the all-prose version, the Bodley scribe or his exemplar failed to identify those sections as "poetic." The versifier, presumably working from a manuscript with a layout similar or identical to that of Bodley 180, seems to have similarly failed, since those prose *metra* were left unchanged in the creation of the prosimetric version. The failure to identify and versify the three prose *metra* demonstrates that no feature of diction other than poetic compounds sufficiently signalled poetry to the versifier or the scribe of Bodley 180. Concomitantly, the layout in Cotton Otho A. vi demonstrates a recognition of the presence of two different discourses, with the incorporation of poetic compounds being the major distinguishing feature in addition to actual metre.

It is unlikely that the creation of the prosimetric version of the *Boethius* was motivated purely by literary aspirations of producing a more faithful translation of the Latin original. While the structure of the prosimetric version better reproduces Boethius's original structure, much more could have been altered to attain the goal of greater accuracy. Although, as discussed in chapter 2 above, translations must balance accuracy with acceptability, the changes made in creating the prosimetric version clearly target the issue of speech genres specifically and pay little to no attention to other features

57 For full descriptions of the manuscripts, see Ker, *Catalogue*, §167 and §305; and Godden and Irvine, *Boethius*, 1:14–16 and 23. See also Bately, "Book Divisions," 157.

58 Irvine, "Authorship."

that would increase accuracy without compromising acceptability. The modification of the speech genre of the *metra*, however, affects not just the text's accuracy but also its acceptability. The signposting statements that indicate the transitions between *prosa* and *metrum* routinely apply the term *gydd* to the *metra*, and it seems that such a use may have proved dissonant.[59] At its core *gydd* means "'poetic utterance,' ranging from 'proverb' to 'heroic lay,'" with some specialized meanings, and its use in the *Boethius* to construe Latin *cantus* supports the meaning of "sung poetry" specifically in that text.[60] That characterization may simply have been ill fitting for the prose *metra*, even given their various non-compound poetic features. Pairing *gydd* with language that, rhetorically patterned as it is, lacked metre and poetic compounds seems to have been something to be emended. The prosimetric version matches the intended use of *gydd* as a term for poetry in the *Boethius* with actual poetry by introducing two features that seem to have best defined the genre. By employing the generically appropriate language and form in this way, the prosimetric version must have become more acceptable to its Anglo-Saxon audience while simultaneously better reproducing the structure of the Latin original. This two-in-one change must have added to Alfred's legacy, regardless of the degree of his involvement, since the translation would still have been associated with his program, even if the versifier were not. It would therefore have presented Alfred as even more knowledgeable of late-antique intellectual culture and better skilled in his contemporary Anglo-Saxon literary culture as well.

The emphasis on the structure as found in the original Latin source would have built up the translation's cultural value. The *Boethius*'s faithfulness to its source in a way legitimates Alfred's entire translation project, marking the translations as authoritative.[61] The closer to the original structure, the more legitimate the translation would have appeared. Faithful rendering of the late-antique original would have inspired confidence in the few

59 The term "signposting" comes from Bately, "Book Divisions." An example of such a statement is "Þa se Wisdom þa ðis spel asæd hæfde, þa ongan he eft singan and ðus cwæð" [When Wisdom had finished this statement, then he began to sing again and said the following] (Godden and Irvine, *Boethius*, 1:293, lines 1–2).

60 Reichl, "Old English *giedd*," 358. See also *DOE*, s.v. *gydd*, for which "poem, song" is the first definition; Parker, "*Gyd*, *Leoð*, and *Sang*"; and Sheppard, "A Word to the Wise," 130–4.

61 Discenza, *King's English*, 13–14.

readers educated enough to recognize that faithfulness, and the authority of those readers would have influenced other, less well educated readers.[62] Indeed, the audience would have expected to discover foreign styles in the *Boethius*.[63] The unfamiliar aspects of the text would then have verified the text's foreign nature for an Anglo-Saxon audience, and that foreign nature was at least one part of what made the text so culturally valuable. The prosimetric structure, emphasized by the addition of metre and poetic compounds and subsequently recognized and presented as such in the Cotton manuscript, would have been one of those unfamiliar aspects. The basic concept of combining verse and prose was not completely unknown to any Anglo-Saxons literate in Latin, given, for example, their attraction to Latin *opera geminata* – that is, twinned works.[64] An *opus geminatum*, however, combines two complementary but distinct versions of a work, one in prose and one in verse, and it does not entail repeated alternation between the two forms. The alternation between prose and verse in a single, unified text is rare in Old English, leaving its use in the *Boethius* remarkable.[65]

62 Discenza, *King's English*, 14.

63 Discenza, *King's English*, 14, notes concerning uneducated readers, "Seeing unfamiliar textual elements handled consistently over a long text, however, they could conclude that Alfred followed the source text's ideas and usages."

64 See Godman, "Anglo-Latin *Opus Geminatum*"; Wieland, "*Geminus Stilus*"; Friesen, "*Opus Geminatum.*" Mize, *Traditional Subjectivities*, 161–3, suggests that the two version of the Old English *Boethius* are themselves the two halves of an *opus geminatum*, although they depart from the standard relationship of one half being entirely in prose and the other half entirely in verse.

65 The *Solomon and Saturn* texts provide the closest parallel in terms of prosimetric structure, suggesting that the structure was not completely unknown to Anglo-Saxons, but certainly rare. Poetic sections are interspersed among prose sections in the Vercelli Book (Vercelli, Biblioteca Capitolare, CXVII) and the *Anglo-Saxon Chronicle*, but the natures of those two works are very different from the *Boethius*. The Vercelli Book is not a unified, sustained work but a series of separate works in a compilation; the alternation of prose and verse then is not a text-internal phenomenon as it is with the *Boethius*. The poems of the *Anglo-Saxon Chronicle* also do not create the same sense of systematic internal alternation, even though one could take the *Chronicle* as a single, sustained work. The *Chronicle* does present a somewhat unified account of the royal line of the Cerdicings with some narrative vignettes spanning several year entries, but it has a very different character than the *Boethius*. The *Boethius* is presented as a long, sustained conversation, while the individual *Chronicle* entries are essentially self-contained and discrete. Thus, a sustained, coherent alternating, text-internal prosimetric structure in Old English appears only in *Solomon and Saturn* and the *Boethius*.

The creation of the prosimetric version of the *Boethius*, then, increased the text's cultural value as an ancient, foreign source and further bolstered the image of Alfred and his translation program.

The prosimetric structure thus produces far-reaching effects that depend on the invocation of various speech genres through the employment of compounds associated with them. The layouts of the two manuscripts react to the speech genres cultivated and invoked by the two versions, which in turn depend heavily on the types of compounds used. The layouts illustrate the scribal reactions to different genres and exemplify what was probably the reaction of the larger audience of the *Boethius*. From this evidence and chain of reasoning, then, we can conclude that compound words indeed strongly signal generic affiliations in the Bakhtinian sense. The prosimetric *Boethius*, linguistically and literarily similar to the entirely prose version in so many ways, highlights the importance and influence of compounds in that signalling. The poetic compounds constitute, perhaps second only to metre, a significant and influential feature marking the presence of poetry. Without attempting to define what makes a compound poetic or not, we can also conclude that individual compounds' patterns of occurrence illustrate the effects of generic associations beyond a dictionary definition. Some compounds traditionally belong to poetry, and the insertion of those compounds can thus alter the generic identity of a text. Attending to patterns of occurrence and the distribution of compounds of different types, one can discover the *Boethius*'s likely social impact and the importance of employing different types of compounds in different situations.

Applying this approach to *Juliana*, one finds a recurring prose discourse signalled by the significant presence of common and prose compounds in the poem. As translations, both *Juliana* and *Elene* combine remnants of the Latin, hagiographical discourse of their sources with the traditional diction of Old English "heroic" poetry. To be sure, not all of the compounds in the two poems, or any Old English poem for that matter, are found solely or even mostly in poetic works; many, in fact, occur commonly throughout the corpus. In *Juliana* alone, however, common and prose compounds gather in specific places in ways that invoke the discourses of Old English religious prose, adding to the hybridity of the poem's discourse. These common, prose compounds specifically cluster in Juliana's dialogue, deviating from the otherwise almost rigidly regular distribution of compounds in the two poems.[66] Thus, the poem mixes two different speech genres and thereby creates a hybrid of discourses. This admixture of a distinct speech genre in Juliana's dialogue differentiates Juliana from her adversaries, stylistically and discursively enacting a theme central to the poem. The manipulation of rhetorical devices and syntactic structures achieves a similar effect of differentiation, through which the saintly characters in *Juliana* and *Elene* display their spiritual superiority through their linguistic control.[67] This "iconographic style" of dialogue presents an image of static immutability of language meant to parallel the saints' immutability of soul just as does the visual iconographic style.[68] From one point of view, the deviation under discussion here plays a role in the creation of this linguistic immutability in that the fewer unusual lexical items in a saint's speech, the more universal that speech should appear. Unique or rare compounds presumably could individualize a saint in a manner contrary to the creation of an iconographic style. Thus, a larger proportion of common, prose compounds in her dialogue maintains Juliana's universality.

From a different point of view, however, Juliana's speech pattern serves to separate her from the rest of the poem in a very different manner, not creating a new, immutable discourse but instead inserting into the poem another, pre-existing discourse, a prose discourse.[69] In addition

66 According to the pattern of compound distribution in the rest of the poem, the lines of Juliana's dialogue should contain just under 18 per cent of the common compounds in the poem, but they in fact contain just over 29 per cent of the common compounds. While some inexactitude is to be expected from a work of linguistic art, this deviation exceeds expectation by more than two standard deviations, a common threshold for attaining statistical significance; no other character's dialogue has a similar deviation. Importantly, the probability that the deviations in Juliana's usage rates are random is rather low. Specifically, her results have a p-value of 0.025 (2.5 per cent likely to be random), while the demon's have a p-value of 0.471 (47.1 per cent likely to be random) and the narrator's a p-value of 0.566 (56.6 per cent likely to be random). A typical p-value threshold below which results are generally accepted as not random is .05 (5 per cent), below which Juliana's results easily fall.

67 Bjork, *Saints' Lives*. See also Erussard, "Language, Power, and Holiness."

68 Bjork, *Saints' Lives*, 26–7.

69 On such hybridity, see also Irvine, *Textual Culture*, 422–3; Lionarons, "Cultural Syncretism"; Harbus, "Articulate Contact"; and Godlove, "Apostolic Discourse."

to the deviation in the occurence of her common compounds, Juliana's vocabulary departs from the traditional, "poetic" language employed throughout the rest of the poem and resembles Old English religious prose.[70] To be sure, a larger than expected proportion of common compounds does not automatically signal prose diction since not all common words are automatically prose words, although most do tend to be. For example, *werþeod* [army] appears in fifteen poems and one gloss, making it, by my system, a common compound but certainly not a "prose" compound.[71] The patterns of occurrence alone suffice at this point to show that, for whatever reasons, *werþeod* is poetic but *middangeard* [earth], which appears in all types of texts, is not. In order to avoid any mistakes, I apply a strict and hopefully objective criterion: the large majority of a word's occurrences must come in either metrical or non-metrical texts to qualify as a poetic compound or a prose compound, respectively. Patterns of occurrence, of course, are not perfect indications of a word's generic characteristics, but they do reveal the types of discourse in which the word was apparently deemed appropriate. By examining the occurrences, general trends of usage become apparent which usefully inform our understanding of a word's poetic or prose resonances – that is, the speech genres to which the word links. Some words, however, have mixed patterns of occurrence, appearing in both metrical and non-metrical texts; for example, simple words such as many verbs, prepositions, demonstratives, simple nouns, etc., display no particular affinity to one group of texts over the other. In addition to vocabulary marked specifically as literary and poetic, poetry necessarily employs these shared words, but they do not become "poetic" in terms of their discursive resonances.[72]

By this standard, I have found that of the forty-five occurrences of compounds in Juliana's dialogue, twenty-one are non-poetic words, roughly

70 To a lesser extent, a similar phenomenon occurs in *Elene*, when Judas employs language reminiscent of sacramental formulas; see Johnson, "Hagiographical Demon."

71 See the *DOEC*.

72 See Hanson and Kiparsky, "Nature of Verse," and Beechy, *Poetics of Old English*, 12. Hanson and Kiparsky posit that Old English literary discourse (as opposed to quotidian language) was marked but that poetry was the unmarked form of that marked discourse and prose the marked.

47 per cent. This proportion is again far more than the share of non-poetic compounds appearing in, for example, the demon's dialogue, which by a liberal count is roughly 19 per cent. In Juliana's dialogue there are several compounds which do appear in many poems, but they also appear an extremely large number of times in an extremely large number of prose texts. *Middangeard*, for example, appears in more than forty poems by my count but in far more prose texts.[73] The large quantity of prose texts in which *middangeard* occurs, however, clearly discredits any attempt to label it as poetic and pushes the word into prose territory. Compounds in Juliana's dialogue with a pattern of occurrence similar to that of *middangeard* include *ælmihtig* [almighty], *mancynn* [humanity], *mægenþrymm* [mighty host], and *mundbora* [protector], among others. The former two of these four compounds are easily recognizable as common to prose discourse: *ælmihtig* occurs in more than thirty poems but many more times in many more prose texts, and *mancynn* in more than twenty poems and similarly many more prose texts.[74] The latter two compounds occur in fewer poems than the former and a large amount of prose texts. In each case, as with *middangeard*, the predominance of prose occurrences shows that these words are not marked as appropriate only for poetry. Of the greatest interest for identifying speech genres are the prose compounds for which *Juliana* is the sole poetic text in which they occur. For example, as noted at the beginning of this chapter, *mægræden* [relationship] occurs in very few texts other than *Juliana*, all of them non-metrical. In another example, *yfeldæd* [evil deed, sin] occurs in a large number of texts, all of which are also non-metrical other than *Juliana*, mainly homilies and glosses. The only appearance of *mægræden* in *Juliana* is in Juliana's dialogue, as is one of the two appearances of *yfeldæd* in the poem. Strikingly, in the immediate context of these occurrences, Juliana's speech draws upon prose vocabulary and language most appropriate to prose, religious discourses in other ways in addition to these compounds. The compounds are thus accompanied by other elements of prose discourse that support their generic resonances, connecting the passages to the larger discursive contexts of Old English literature and different speech genres than the rest of the poem.

73 See the *DOEC*.
74 See the *DOEC*.

Specifically, the dialogue containing *mægræden* closely resembles homiletic language, urging more eager (*geornor*) worship of God and employing prayerful language in the description of God:

> "Næfre ic þæs þeodnes þafian wille
> mægrædenne, nemne he mægna God
> geornor bigonge þonne he gen dyde,
> lufige mid lacum þone þe leoht gescop,
> heofon 7 eorðan 7 holma bigong,
> eodera ymbhwyrft. Ne mæg he elles mec
> bringan to bolde. He þa brydlufan
> sceal to oþerre æhtgestealdum
> idese secan; nafað he ænige her."[75]

> "I will never tolerate a relationship with this noble unless he more eagerly worships the God of hosts than he yet has, until he loves with sacrifices the one who created the light, heaven and earth, and the expanse of the oceans, the regions of the skies. He cannot bring me to his house any way else. He will have to seek conjugal love with possessions from another woman; he will not have any here."

This short speech sounds much like a preacher calling for increased dedication combined with prayer.[76] Although the concept of describing God as the creator of everything is not rare, the phrasing here is somewhat idiosyncratic. The phrase "heofon 7 eorðan" would constitute a standard binomial expressing all of creation by itself, but the presence of the third term ("holma bigong") and possibly a fourth, probably appositive, term ("eodora ymbhwyrft") is less common.[77] Perhaps the passage most closely resembling this one comes in *Meter 11* from the Old English *Boethius*: "He hafað þe bridle butu befangen / heofon and eorðan and eall holma begong" [He has grasped with the bridle both heaven and earth and the entire region of the seas].[78] The *Boethius* passage shares with *Juliana* the

---

75 Woolf, *Juliana*, 108–16.

76 For example, "Uton us nu ealle þe geornor warnian" [Let us now all the more zealously be on guard], from Vercelli Homily 20, line 22 in Scragg, *Vercelli Homilies*.

77 For a detailed account of binomials, see chapter 5 below.

78 Godden and Irvine, *Boethius*, 1:430, lines 29–30.

first three elements of the list, but it replaces *Juliana*'s sense of creation (*gescop*) with a sense of control (*bridle ... befangen*).

The focus on creation also connects the *Juliana* passage with prose texts more than poetic texts. For example, a very similar specification of God's creations appears in Wulfstan's translation of the creed (Bethurum VII): "gescop heofonas 7 eorðan 7 ealle gesceafta" [he created the heavens and earth and all of creation].[79] Although later than the composition of Cynewulf's poems, this occurrence shows that the phrase fit well into homiletic and prayerful language. This Wulfstanian parallel retains the creation – specifically *gescop* – and the order of the three main elements but replaces the reference to water with a reference to all of creation, thus still creating the sense of triadic fulfilment, albeit somewhat differently.[80] Other homiletic versions of this phrase that emphasize creation over control vary in the details, some retaining the reference to water but expanding beyond the triadic structure, as *Juliana* possibly does with "eodera ymbhwyrft." For example, Vercelli Homily 19 reads as follows:

> Ærest on frymþe he geworhte heofonas 7 eorðan 7 sæ 7 ealle þa þinc þe on him syndon.[81]
>
> In the beginning he first created the heavens and earth and the sea and all the things that are in them.

This passage also includes the creation terminology, using *geworhte* instead of *gescop*, but the sense of all-encompassing fulfilment is delayed until the fourth member of this list instead of the third. A version of the phrase earlier in the same homily retains the triadic structure but not the reference to water, presenting a nearly exact precursor to Wulfstan's version.[82] Vercelli Homily 19 is again likely later in date than the composition of Cynewulf's poems, but the compiler reworked older material and certainly employed commonplaces of the homiletic tradition which predated his own text.[83]

79 Bethurum, *Homilies*, 158, lines 28–9.

80 On the generalizing tendency of the third member of a triadic list, or *tricolon abundans*, see Atkinson, *Our Masters' Voices*, 57–8.

81 Scragg, *Vercelli Homilies*, 316, lines 12–13.

82 Describing God, the homily reads "þe geworhte heofonas 7 eorðan 7 ealle gesceafta" [who created the heavens and earth and all of creation] (Scragg, *Vercelli Homilies*, 315, line 2).

83 Scragg, *Vercelli Homilies*, xli–xlii.

The Old English translation of Bede's *Historia ecclesiastica* contains two occurrences of the *ealle gesceafta* version of this triadic phrase, with the second one also containing reference to the *ymbhwyrft*, this time of the earth.[84] That second passage, the one most strikingly similar to *Juliana*, also employs four elements in the list of God's creations, describing God as follows:

> se gescop heofon 7 eorðan 7 monna cyn 7 ealle gesceafta, ond wære toweard to demanne eorðan ymbhwyrft on rihtwisnesse[85]

> He created heaven and earth and humanity and all creation, and will come to judge the entirety of the earth in righteousness.

Here humanity replaces the sea of other versions, but the repetition of key concepts and words – *gescop*, *heofon*, *eorðan*, and *ymbhwyrft* – demonstrates a resonance with *Juliana* or at least the same tradition that informs *Juliana*. Importantly, both of the passages from the Old English *Bede* recount a Christian explaining the faith to a non-Christian. One comes from the account of St Alban, a *passio* like *Juliana*, and the other from the story of King Oswiu converting King Sigeberht and the East Saxons. The phrases specifically constitute portions of the confession of the Christian faith in these two passages, just as in Juliana's speech the phrase forms part of Juliana's description of her faith to her father in response to his urgings to give in to Heliseus's advances. Whether Cynewulf knew Bede's text remains unclear, but the similarities show that at the very least the apparently formulaic description of God the creator was appropriate for a prose, religious discourse. Some variations of this phrase occur in a few poems, also presenting confessions of faith, but the Bedan passages in particular, given their recounting of the conversion of pagans, relate the passage in *Juliana* solidly to the realm of prose discourse, and the prevalence of this formula in later homilies further supports this conclusion. *Juliana* and these prose texts thus coalesce into a speech genre as Bakhtin envisioned, a grouping forged by their sharing various lexical items and features of content in similar contexts, such as confessions of faith.

The later portion of Juliana's speech to her father, however, leaves the religious discourse and returns to the heroic language of treasure,

84 Miller, *Bede's Ecclesiastical History*, 36, lines 20–1, and 224, lines 20–2.

85 Miller, *Bede's Ecclesiastical History*, 224, lines 20–2.

characterizing conjugal love as a possession for Heliseus to seek elsewhere. Juliana discontinues her confession of faith, and immediately two unique compounds appear, and, moreover, *ides* [woman] is generally restricted to poetry.[86] *Holm* [ocean], appearing in the first portion of this passage, is also generally considered poetic, but its use here seems more pragmatic than anything else, since it provides the alliteration in the second half of the line. Juliana's speech, then, divides into two sections: the first invokes a prose, religious mode of speech associated with the confession of faith, and the second returns to the poetic discourse of the rest of the poem.

The two passages in *Juliana* which contain *yfeldæd* also connect with a confessional paradigm, this time not with the confession of faith but of sins.[87] Juliana uses the word to prompt the demon to continue his confession of the torments that he inflicted on previous Christians:

> "Þu scealt ondettan yfeldæda ma,
> hean helle gæst, ær þu heonan mote,
> hwæt þu to teonan þurhtogen hæbbe
> micelra manweorca manna tudre
> deorcum gedwildum."[88]

> You must confess more evil deeds, wretched spirit of hell, before you will be allowed to leave here, what great wicked deeds you have carried out as injuries against the children of men with dark heresies.

The *DOE* lists this occurrence of *ondettan* under sense 6: "to declare, disclose, acknowledge, admit," which is certainly accurate for this occurrence in *Juliana*.[89] Nonetheless, this passage and the lines preceding it contain several echoes of confessional vocabulary which add another layer of religious discourse to the scene. The phrase "ondettan yfeldæda" closely resembles language in Old English penitentials, such as "misdæda andettan" and "dæda andettan" in the Old English *Handbook*, which clearly

86 It is possible that the non-poetic meaning "virgin" is operative in this passage, but that interpretation seems unlikely given the immediate context and the reference to Heliseus seeking out "conjugal love" from such a woman.

87 See also the discussion of *Juliana* and penitential discourse in Frantzen, *Literature of Penance*, 188–90.

88 Woolf, *Juliana*, lines 456–60a.

89 *DOE*, s.v. *andettan*.

employs *ondettan* in the specifically religious sense of confessing one's sins.[90] *Ondettan* is again associated with a *–dæd* compound in the Old English *Bede*:

> Monede se cyning hiene gelomlice, þæt he ondette 7 bote 7 forlete his synna 7 mandæda, ær ðon he mid ofercyme sæmninga deaðes ealle tid hreowe 7 bote forlure.[91]

> The king warned him frequently to confess and atone for and abandon his sins and evil deeds before he should suddenly lose all time for repentance and atonement with the arrival of death.

Here, the king encourages the confession of evil deeds as in the other passages, this time expressed with *mandæd*. This passage also shows the association of *ær* [before] with the *ondettan/dæd* collocation that also occurs in Juliana's comments to the demon. In the Bedan passage, the *ær* clause expresses the negative consequences of procrastination, suggesting the damnation awaiting the non-confessing sinner. Both passages present confession as an act which should be completed quickly before the sinner's release.

The same affliction of torment also awaits the demon in *Juliana*, although in an ironic twist the demon begs for such release; he may dread his reception in hell, but he nonetheless would prefer it to Juliana's interrogation. The demon's dread relates not just to his punishment but also specifically to the shame he will endure for his failure to undermine Juliana's religious conviction.[92] Shame constitutes another important element found in penitential homilies, given the common motif that it is better to undergo the shame of confession while alive than to suffer after death the ultimate shame of a sinner before God.[93] While Juliana does not herself mention shame, the demon does, and the reference cements once again the connection of the

90 Fowler, "Late Old English Handbook," lines 19, 85–6, 87–8, and 89–90. *Ondettan* meaning specifically to confess one's sins is *DOE* sense 1. Although the *Handbook* and other, related penitential works were likely composed later than *Juliana*, they must have drawn upon an existing tradition and did not appear *ex nihilo*. The Handbook is quoted here just as a specific example of this tradition.

91 Miller, *Bede's Ecclesiastical History*, 436, lines 27–9.

92 Woolf, *Juliana*, lines 443–5.

93 Godden, "Penitential Motif."

scene to the discourse of confession. The second occurrence of *yfeldæd* in Juliana maintains this connection, again introducing the concept of shame to Cynewulf's confession in the epilogue.[94] The recurrence of this pairing of *yfeldæd* and shame must not be simply formulaic repetition internal to *Juliana*; the resonance the pairing has with penitentials marks the poem's extrapolation beyond poetic diction into prose discourse. Although the extant penitential works and homilies resembling the language in *Juliana* are presumably later than Cynewulf's texts, it is unlikely that they drew inspiration from *Juliana*. Most likely, both that group of texts and Cynewulf drew upon the same tradition of expressing these concepts, a tradition which was generally found in prose.

The many reminiscences of confession make it clear that this scene in *Juliana* does not simply play on the conceptual relationship between confessor and sinner but also draws upon the actual language of that discourse to shape the characters' dialogue. The demon's dialogue contains some of these elements, but it does not fully emulate the discourse of confession, for the demon remains unrepentant.[95] He also fails to maintain the prose vocabulary, employing almost exclusively poetic compounds for the next fifty lines in his answer to Juliana's confessorial question.[96] Even a subtle reference back to the confessional discourse falls flat when the demon uses *womdæd* [evil deed], which only occurs in poetic texts and thus compares favourably with Juliana's *–dæd* compound, *yfeldæd*. The instances of prose vocabulary in the demon's dialogue help summon the prose discourse, but only Juliana's dialogue maintains a consistent connection with the prose discourse. The demon's failures, in fact, highlight even further his distance from God and Juliana's pure religious character.

A single, isolated word, of course, cannot alone prove Juliana's connection to prose religious discourse, but the pattern demonstrated above is widespread. Poetic compounds are not absent from the saint's dialogue – *Juliana*, after all, remains a poem – but prose discourse is much more present in her words than in any other character's lines. Juliana's affiliation

94 Woolf, *Juliana*, line 713. Also see Rice, "Penitential Motif."

95 Bjork, *Saints' Lives*, 55–61, points out that the demon attempts but fails to emulate other aspects of Juliana's speech as well.

96 For example, *hleoþorcwide* [speech] (Woolf, *Juliana*, line 461) and *þreaned* [punishing affliction] (line 464) occur only in poetic texts. See the *DOEC*.

with a discourse outside of the poem separates her from the other characters, her adversaries, and further distinguishes her as a holy individual. Conversely, the avoidance of unique and rare compounds in Juliana's dialogue maintains her universality as an exemplar of the saintly life. Just as she is set apart from the other characters, her language connects her with a discourse that the poem's audience would certainly have known, either through contact with the religious texts or possibly through the act of confession itself.[97] Although the demon fills the role of confessing sinner, forcing the audience to confront its own sins, Juliana most fully recreates the prose languages of confession, providing an image of the ideal to which Christians should aspire.

The cultural resonance of this stylistic move is difficult to determine, especially since Cynewulf remains an ambiguous figure, the date and location of whose work prove difficult to determine. Claims for the time of composition for the four signed poems – *Juliana*, *Elene*, *Christ II*, and *Fates of the Apostles* – range from the early 800s to c. 1000, with geographical provenance being similarly variable.[98] Making solid conclusions on the connections between Cynewulf's texts and his (uncertain) original context thus becomes difficult and tendentious. More solid footing can be found, however, when one attends to the context of copying rather than attempting to reconstruct compositional context. Arguably, there must have been good reason for a text to have been recorded in a manuscript, whether as a first-ever copy or as a recopying from an earlier exemplar.[99] It is possible that the copying of *Juliana* into the Exeter Book in the late tenth century

97 It is impossible to know with certainty how widespread the practice of confession truly was in Cynewulf's time, but the existence of vernacular translations of penitential texts suggests that the practice was indeed known beyond the restricted circle of those literate in Latin. On this topic, see Meens, "Frequency and Nature," 35–61. For a discussion of penance generally and public penance specifically, see Bedingfield, "Public Penance"; Hamilton, "Remedies for 'Great Transgressions'"; Hamilton, "Rites for Public Penance"; and Thomas, "Meaning, Practice and Context," 221–82.

98 Fulk, "Cynewulf," 3. See also, among others, Cook, *The Christ of Cynewulf*, lxxi–lxxvi; Sisam, "Cynewulf and His Poetry"; Calder, *Cynewulf*; Fulk, *Old English Meter*; and Conner, "On Dating Cynewulf."

99 Drout, *Tradition and Influence*, 136–7, makes a similar argument regarding other poems in the Exeter Book, although he pointedly leaves the Cynewulfian texts in that manuscript out of the discussion. See also the treatment of post-conquest copies of Old English texts in Treharne, *Living through Conquest*.

was roughly contemporary with its composition,[100] but one need not pursue such a strong stance to examine the text's general resonances with the contexts of its copying. Whenever the poem was originally composed, the decision to include it in the Exeter Book reveals an interest in the poem, likely from members of the Benedictine Reform movement.[101] The manuscript was at least probably copied at a centre associated with the Benedictine Reform of the tenth century.[102] It is risky to make overly strong claims about resonances between a text and its time of copying, since a slight possibility exists that the copying may have been accidental or unrelated to the social context (e.g., the text was on hand, and the manuscript had extra space in need of filling).[103] Nonetheless, the fact remains that centres associated with the reform are largely responsible for the preservation of much of the extant Old English poetry,[104] demonstrating that the interest of the movement extended beyond so-called hermeneutic Latin.[105] The presence of *Juliana* in a manuscript associated with the Reform therefore implies some degree of interest in the poem's contents, and one can thus read the poem through the lens of that interest.

The monastic identity produced in the Reform depended on the memorization and performance of texts central to the movement:

> In the most general sense, such an identity is textual in that its corporate performance is driven and judged by a written Rule (a portion of which was recited daily), centred on the voicing of sacred texts in the round of monastic liturgies, and on the reading and hearing of scripture and religious writings.

---

100 This possibility is at least allowed by the dating in Conner, "On Dating Cynewulf," and actively argued in Abraham, "Cynewulf's Recharacterization." On the date of the Exeter Book, see Ker, *Catalogue*, no. 116; Muir, *Exeter Anthology*, 1:1–3; Gneuss, *Handlist*, no. 257; and Gneuss and Lapidge, *Anglo-Saxon Manuscripts*, no. 257.

101 See Drout, *Tradition and Influence*, 135–7.

102 The most likely centres at which the Exeter Book may have been produced are Glastonbury; Christ Church, Canterbury; and Exeter itself. See Conner, *Anglo-Saxon Exeter*, and Gameson, "Origin of the Exeter Book."

103 For further discussion on this point, see Drout, *Tradition and Influence*, 137–8, where, admittedly, Drout decides to eliminate Cynewulf's poems from his consideration due to dating issues.

104 See Letson, "Poetic Content." On the reformers' interest in the vernacular, see Drout, *Tradition and Influence*, 149.

105 On hermeneutic Latin and the Benedictine Reform, see primarily Winterbottom, "Style of Æthelweard"; Lapidge, "Hermeneutic Style"; Lapidge, "Poeticism"; Stephenson, "Ælfric of Eynsham and Hermeneutic Latin," 117–24; and Stephenson, "Scapegoating the Secular Clergy," 107–12.

> The strong distinction between monks and secular clergy, made in the wake of the Benedictine Reform, is that the former were literate, conducted their struggle against the clerics in a variety of ideological texts, and defined themselves and their program through texts in Latin and the vernacular.[106]

Monks were to learn texts, in both Latin and Old English, and recite them frequently, which would forge a community based on the shared knowledge and internalization of those texts.[107] This practice of memorization and internalization would have created great sensitivity to subtle allusions and lexical effects like the invocation of prose discourses in Juliana's dialogue. Recognition of those patterns would have been even more easily induced by the use of compound words, due to their significant cognitive-linguistic weight and the power of their generic resonances. Those resonances would have rendered the occurrences of characteristically prose compounds quite noticeable to an audience already sensitive to textual identities.

Into Juliana's mouth, then, the poem puts discourses that were likely deeply internalized elements of the textually constructed monastic identity during the Benedictine Reform. As shown above, the confessions of sins and of faith coalesce into traditionalized patterns, which must have been familiar to monks of the Reform. Indeed, the *Regularis concordia* prescribes a time each day for monks to make public confession or confession *invicem* [to one another].[108] Although handbooks and manuals often present Latin as the vehicle for confession, the several extant Old English formulae and examples were also employed, and their frequent repetition as stipulated in the *Regularis concordia* would have cemented the association connecting, for example, *ondettan* and *–dæd* compounds with the speech genre. Thus, Juliana's invocation of prose discourses, while probably resonant at other times and places, must have been particularly impactful at the time of the poem's copying during in the late tenth century. Perhaps that resonance explains the choice to include *Juliana* in the Exeter Book. A tenth-century, monastic audience of the manuscript anthology or the

106 O'Brien O'Keeffe, *Stealing Obedience*, 97–8. See also Cubitt, "Tenth-Century Benedictine Reform," 89.

107 See also Stock, *Implications of Literacy*; Coleman, *Ancient and Medieval Memories*; and Cubitt, "Memory and Narrative."

108 Kornexl, *Die "Regularis concordia,"* lines 407–15 and line 562, respectively. See the discussion in Thomas, "Meaning, Practice and Context," 221–82.

poem individually, if it circulated thus, must have at least noted the poem's parallels in diction to what would have been daily, fundamental texts.

In this way, *Juliana* mixes quotidian, perhaps monastic language with the elevated diction of traditional Old English poetry; similarly, the prosimetric version of the Old English *Boethius* alternates between the vocabulary of (probably newly adapted) standard prose and the same elevated, poetic diction. Features such as simple, monomorphemic vocabulary and the presence or absence of metre support the successful creation of these various discourses, but compound words evidently perform the bulk of the work invoking them. The scribal decisions in presenting the versions of the *Boethius* seem to have been most sensitive and responsive to the changes in the generic associations of compounds, with poetic compounds best signalling the change to poetry. For *Juliana*, the compounds create a fundamental difference between Juliana's speech and that of her adversaries. We see, then, these texts using the linguistic weight of compounds, as discussed in chapter 3 above, to do more than create emphasis on a concept or theme. Rather, the texts deploy compounds that have connections to specific speech genres and interlink with non-lexical features; those connections, this interlinking, produce expectations of particular vocabulary, styles, themes, and cultural contexts that accompany the compounds. The texts thus take advantage of the cognitive and linguistic weight of compounds to produce complex discursive effects unachievable through other means.

5 Controlling Pace in Prose: Wulfstan's Old English Homilies[1]

Wulfstan's style, in both his homiletic and his non-homiletic works, shows great concern for the details of language, employing, for example, specific rhythms, sets of vocabulary, and frequent aural punning.[2] His homilies are replete with verbal ornamentation that reveals attention to the sound and shape of words in addition to the overall message, and compounding constitutes a major tool for creating the aural play characteristic of Wulfstan's writing.[3] While compounds that occur individually in Wulfstan's homilies are discussed above (in chapter 3), the majority of the compounds in his homilies occur in clusters, grouped together as rhetorical units. These clustered compounds most frequently participate in echoing parallelism, thus grouping together naturally as a result of the structure of the rhetorical device itself. Wulfstan regularly employs compounds in parallel phrases as an easy source of both repetitive and varied sound: for example, the phrase "wedlogan ne wordlogan" [oath-liars nor word-liars][4] allows Wulfstan to repeat the *–logan* constituent while varying the beginning of the words yet

1 A version of the first sections of this chapter previously appeared in Davis-Secord, "Rhetoric and Politics."

2 Bethurum, *Homilies*, 88–9, goes so far as to suggest that Wulfstan in fact patterned his rhetorical style according to the tenets of Cicero and Augustine, although such claims are unlikely, given what we now know about Anglo-Saxon knowledge of classical rhetoric (see chapter 1 above). Hollowell, "Linguistic Factors," also follows Bethurum's line of argumentation; she takes up Wulfstan's rhythmic tendencies in "Two-Stress Theory," which builds on the work of McIntosh, "Wulfstan's Prose." Dance provides a detailed synthesis of the scholarship on Wulfstan's style in his article "Sound, Fury, and Signifiers."

3 See Chapman, "Stylistic Use."

4 Quoted and translated by Chapman, "Stylistic Use," 1.

still retaining alliteration. But the clustering of compounds occurs beyond even this intra-sentential level of language. Most often, doublets cluster together in large lists, which are generally self-contained. The lists are essentially set pieces in that they are relatively independent within their homily as a whole. They have their own internal organizations, and their content, while not incongruous, does not specifically advance the main argument of their homily. Given these large compound-laden passages, the presence of the compounds registers not just at the level of individual sentences but also at the larger discourse levels of the paragraph and even the entire homily, differentiating the set pieces from the rest of the text. Ultimately, these set pieces retard the pace of the homilies in which they appear, allowing Wulfstan to dwell on a particular point without having to produce any further explanation, argument, or narrative. Thus, the compound structures that make these set pieces of doublets and lists formally possible and coherent allow Wulfstan to control the pace of his prose and force his audience to dwell on the points that he considers most important in fundamental ways unachievable without compounds.

Wulfstan's *Be hæðendome* (Napier LX), on the dangers of paganism, illustrates the features of these set pieces well and fairly succinctly. It opens abruptly, shifting quickly from the short Latin pericope into exhortations against idol worship and in favour of penance:

> *Nemo christianorum paganas superstitiones intendat, sed gentilium inquinamenta omnia omnino contemnat.* eala, mycel is nydþearf manna gehwylcum, þæt he wið deofles larswice warnige symle, and þæt he hæðenscype georne æfre forbuge, þæs þe he gedon mæge. and, gyf hit geweorðe, þæt cristen man æfre heonanforð ahwar heðendom begange oððon ahwar on lande idola weorðige, gebete þæt deope for gode and for worolde; and, se ðe to gelome þæt unriht begange; gylde mid Englum swa wer, swa wite, and on Dena lage lahslite, be ðam ðe seo dæd sy.[5]

> *No Christian should follow the superstitions of the pagans but should entirely condemn all the obscenities of the gentiles.* Now, there is great need for each person always to keep watch against the devil's trickeries, and always zealously to avoid paganism as much as possible. And, if it happens that a Christian person henceforth ever anywhere enters into paganism or worships idols anywhere in this land, let him deeply atone for that before God and before the

5 Napier, *Wulfstan*, 309, lines 11–21, original emphasis.

world; and he who enters into that perversity too often should pay, among the English, the penalty according to social station and, among the Danes, the legal fine according to the nature of the deed.

In this first portion of the homily there are only three compounds. The first two, *nydþearf* [need] and *larswice* [trickery] occur in the same sentence, although they are not linked together through sound play as later compounds in the homily are. Only *lahslite* [fine for a breach of the (Danish) law] participates in sound play (echoing *lage*). The next section, however, contains several groups of compounds nested together and frequently linked through sound play and/or parallelism:

and, gyf wiccean oððe wigelearas, horingas oððe horcwenan, morðwyrhtan oððe mansworan innan þysan earde weorðan agytene, fyse hy man georne ut of þysan earde and clænsige þas þeode oððon on earde forfare hy mid ealle, butan hi geswicon and þe deoppor gebetan. and do man, swa hit þearf is, manfulra dæda on æghwylcan ende styre man swyðe. her syndan on earde godcundnessæ wiðersacan and godes lage oferhogan, manslagan and mægslagan, cyrichatan and sacerdbana, hadbrecan and æwbrecan, myltestran and bearnmyrðran, þeofas and þeodscaðan, ryperas and reaferas, leogeras and liceteras and leodhatan hetele ealles to manege, þe ðurh mansylene barjað þas þeod, and wedlogan and wærlogan and lytle getrywða to wide mid mannum.[6]

And, if witches or wizards, fornicators or adulterers, murderers or perjurers are discovered in this land, people should eagerly banish them from this land and purge this people or completely destroy them in this land, unless they cease and repent the more deeply. And people should do what is necessary: greatly punish evil deeds in every region. Here in this land there are enemies of divinity and people who despise God's law, murderers and kin-killers, church-haters and priest-killers, breakers of holy vows and adulterers, prostitutes and child-murderers, thieves and enemies of the people, plunderers and robbers, hypocrites and liars and people who hate the people all too violently who depopulate this country through slaving, and oath-breakers and traitors and much too little truth among men.

This central section of the homily is classic Wulfstan, presenting a long list of sins or sinners plaguing the land and undermining God's community.

6 Napier, *Wulfstan*, 309, line 21–310, line 6.

Here compounds are frequent and almost always parallel-linked with another word, often another compound, through sound play or conceptual similarity. For example, in the first sentence of this section there is alliteration on *w*, *h*, and *m* in quick succession, with each pair of words unified on a single theme. After a short comment on how these sinners must be dealt with, the homily resumes listing with further alliteration (on *m*, *þ*, *r*, *l*, and *w*) as well as conceptual linkage in several pairs: *cyrichatan* [church-haters] and *sacerdbanan* [priest-killers] are both enemies of the church in some way; *hadbrecan* [breakers of holy vows] and *æwbrecan* [law-breakers] violate the law, sacred and secular respectively; *myltestran* [prostitutes] and *bearnmyrðran* [child-murderers] pervert the natural order of human procreation. Although there are short phrases within this portion of the homily containing no compounds, these are few, and this section is mainly characterized by a rapid succession of compounds paired through various rhetorical devices.

The concluding section of the homily exhibits once again a paucity of compounds:

> and ne byrhð se gesibba hwilan gesibban þe ma, þe ðam fremdan, ne broðor his breðer oþre hwile ne bearn for oft his fæder ne meder. ne na fela manna ne healt his getrywða swa wel, swa he scolde, for gode and for worolde. ac do man, swa hit þearf is, gebete hit georne and clænsige þas þeode, gyf man godes miltse geearnjan wylle.[7]

> And kinsman no longer defends kinsman any more than the foreigner, nor brother his brother at another time, nor the child very often his father or mother. Many people do not keep their promises as well as they should before God and the world. But people should do what is necessary: atone for it eagerly and purify this people if they want to merit God's mercy.

The first sentence of this concluding portion in part continues the list-making of the middle section, but without compound pairs. Rhetorical ornamentation remains in the repetitions of *gesibba* and *broðor*, but it is not deployed in the same rapid-fire manner of the middle section at its height. Instead of stringing together a long list of nouns, the first sentence places the sonic repetitions within somewhat more complex grammatical constructions than a simple list. Unlike the passage concerning

7 Napier, *Wulfstan*, 310, lines 6–12.

oath-breakers and church-haters, it is not mere existence but the kin's foul actions that are emphasized here.

Thus, moving from the breathless list of specific evils plaguing the land to the generalized communal ills of intrafamily strife, the homily concludes as it began, with an exhortation for repentance and cleansing penance. The initial emphasis on paganism, however, has disappeared: there is no mention at all of idols or any form of the words *hæðenscyp* or *heðendom*. It is as though the original topic has been forgotten, replaced by a concern for general social problems. Even with this subtle shift in focus, however, the beginning and the end of the homily remain very similar stylistically, each showing a striking absence of compounds in comparison to the central section. The introductory section does contain three compounds, but they are not employed in sound play as those in the middle section are. In the place of compounds in the introductory and final sections, more time is taken for instructions on how to remedy the evils, while the central section of the homily forms a somewhat self-contained block of text – internally organized as a list of doublets – surrounded by contextualizing material. Moreover, the central, self-contained block shifts the homily's argument from the specific danger of paganism to the problem of general social instability; the generic nature of the set-piece redirects the pointed argument and sets up a more general conclusion.

This phenomenon of compounds concentrated in lists extends beyond this very short homily and is also readily apparent in the *Sermo Lupi ad Anglos*.[8] The first ninety-nine lines of the *Sermo Lupi* contain very few compounds compared to its central section. Compounds appear about three times more frequently in the central section of the homily, comprising lists of the people's sins and the awful results of those sins in lines 129–74.[9] For example, several compounds appear in the following passage containing an extremely long alliteration on *m*:

> Her syndan *m*annslagan 7 *m*ægslagan 7 *m*æsserbanan 7 *m*ynsterhatan; 7 her syndan *m*answoran 7 *m*orþwyrhtan; 7 her syndan *m*yltestran 7 bearn*m*yrðran 7 fule folegene horingas *m*ange.[10]

8 The following quotations are from the third version of the *Sermo Lupi ad Anglos* in Bethurum, *Homilies*, 267–75.

9 Going by Bethurum's lineation, the beginning sections contain about one compound every 3.4 lines, while the central sections contain about one compound every 1.15 lines.

10 Bethurum, *Homilies*, 273, lines 160–4, emphasis added.

> Here there are man-slayers and kin-killers and priest-killers and monastery-persecutors; and here there are perjurers and murderers; and here there are prostitutes and child-murderers and many wicked, fornicating whores.

Another cluster of compounds appears in lines 133–8, detailing again the sins through which the *þeodscip* [community] has become corrupted:

> þurh morðdæda 7 þurh mandæda, þurh gitsunga 7 þurh gifernessa, þurh stala 7 þurh strudunga, þurh mannsylena 7 þurh hæþene unsida, þurh swicdomas 7 þurh searacræftas, þurh lahbrycas 7 þurh æwswicas, þurh mægræssas 7 þurh manslyhtas, þurh hadbrycas 7 þurh æwbrycas, þurh siblegeru 7 þurh mistlice forligru.

> Through murderous deeds and through foul deeds, through greed and through avarice, through thefts and through robberies, through slave-selling and through heathen impurities, through deceptions and through treacheries, through law-breakers and through traitors, through kin-killings and through murders, through breakers of holy vows and through adulterers, through incest and through various fornications.

Similar to the list containing the long alliteration on *m*, this passage also creates internal coherence through rhetorical devices: repetition of *þurh* ties the whole list together, while echoing parallelism and alliteration tie together individual doublets within the list. Each of these two lists acts as a self-contained block of text: the sections connect to the main point of the homily, but loosely and only at the very beginnings and ends of the larger units. Internally, they are governed by the logic of lists, which will be explored in detail below.

A fairly clear compositional pattern emerges when we examine these textual units: they tend to occur centrally in each homily, are relatively independent of the main argument of the homily, and contain a comparatively high number of compound words. This is not to say that their content is incongruous, but that, as lists, they tend to contribute a massive set of examples without necessarily furthering the argument in a logical fashion. The lists are essentially set pieces that can be inserted without affecting the homily's line of explanation or argumentation. This pattern easily applies to Napier LX, a fairly simple homily in terms of organization: as discussed above, it has three main sections consisting of the introduction of the main point, a block of examples rich with compounds, and a conclusion. There is some contextualizing language in the central section, but the core of that section is the long list which contains little logical advancement of the argument. The *Sermo Lupi* is more complex than Napier LX, making several different points throughout and shifting in and out of list-making several times. It remains true, however, that the sections heavy with compounds are lists which could be easily removed from the homily without undermining the logical progression of the argument. In other words, the lists bolster each homily's warnings without being indispensably necessary to its argument. By their very nature, of course, lists do not contain logical argumentation, but I emphasize this point in order to show clearly that each list section is in many ways independent of the homily in which it appears.

These lists are interchangeable. At one level, individual doublets are frequently repeated throughout Wulfstan's corpus, but even groups of doublets and collections of compounds are also repeated. For example, in *De fide catholica* (Bethurum VII), the following passage describes those who are destined for the tortures of hell:

> Đyder sculan mannslagan, 7 ðider sculan manswican; ðider sculan æwbrecan 7 ða fulan forlegenan; ðider sculan mansworan 7 morðwyrhtan; ðider sculan gitseras, ryperas 7 reaferas 7 woruldstruderas; ðider sculon þeofas 7 ðeodscaðan; ðyder sculon wiccan 7 wigleras, 7, hrædest to secganne, ealle þa manfullan þe ær yfel worhton 7 noldon geswican ne wið God þingian.[11]

> There shall go murderers, and there shall go traitors; there shall go oathbreakers and foul fornicators; there shall go perjurers and murderers; there shall go misers, robbers and plunderers and spoliators; there shall go thieves and enemies of the people; there shall go magicians and wizards, and, to put it simply, all the wicked who previously worked evil and did not want to cease nor to pray to God.

The phrase "mansworan 7 morðwyrhtan" is almost perfectly parallel to the phrase "mansworan 7 morþorwyrhtan" in the *Sermo Lupi.*[12] Also, almost immediately after these *m*-alliterating doublets in each homily occurs the phrase "ryperas 7 reaferas 7 woruldstruderas."[13] The two homilies both employ almost identical language to list evils and sins, although in each case the lists are used to underscore somewhat different points. In Bethurum VII, the list of compounds details the types of people who will

11 Bethurum, *Homilies*, 163, lines 128–34.

12 Bethurum, *Homilies*, 163, line 130, and 273, lines 162–3 respectively.

13 Bethurum, *Homilies*, 163, line 131, and 273, line 165.

go to hell; in the *Sermo Lupi*, the list details the kinds of people who have brought the wrath of God down upon the Anglo-Saxons. While those sets of people may ultimately be identical, it remains notable that the list is repeated in different rhetorical contexts to support different points.

Perhaps even more striking are the parallels between this passage from Bethurum VII and the following passage from *Sermo ad populum* (Bethurum XIII), also describing the future denizens of hell:

> Ðyder sculan manslagan, 7 ðider sculan mansworan; þyder sculan æwbrecan 7 ða fulan forlegenan; ðider sculan wiccan 7 bearnmyrðran; ðider sculan þeofas 7 ðeodscaðan, ryperas 7 reaferas, 7, hrædest to secganne, ealle þa manfullan þe God gremiað, butan hy geswican 7 ðe deoppor gebetan.[14]

> There shall go murderers, and there shall go perjurers; there shall go oathbreakers and foul fornicators; there shall go magicians and child murderers; there shall go thieves and enemies of the people, robbers and plunderers, and, to put it simply, all the wicked who revile God unless they cease and repent that much more deeply.

Several of the same compounds are repeated from the other texts: *manslagan*, *mansworan*, *æwbrecan*, *ðeodscaðan*. Several other individual, non-compound words as well as phrases are also repeated, such as *þeofas* (with *ðeodscaðan* again), *fulan forlegenan*, and *ryperas 7 reaferas*. Although not entirely exact, this passage from Bethurum XIII is very close to a verbatim repetition of the passage from Bethurum VII. There are some variations between the two passages, such as pairing *mansworan* with *manslagan* in Bethurum XIII but with *morðwyrhtan* in Bethurum VII. Also, the list in Bethurum VII ends with the idea of beseeching God alone, whereas Bethurum XIII more clearly emphasizes the need for earthly repentance as well. Nonetheless, a significant number of verbal parallels remains between the lists in the two homilies.

A similar passage occurs in *De regula canonicorum* (Bethurum Xa), concerning the conduct of canons:

> Ne beon hi æfre manslagan ne manswican ne mansworan ne morðwyrhtan ne æwbrecan, ac healdan heora riht æwe, þæt is heora mynster. Ne beon hi wordlogan ne weddlogan ne ryperas ne reaferas ...[15]

---

14 Bethurum, *Homilies*, 231, lines 92–7.

15 Bethurum, *Homilies*, 192, lines 11–14.

> They should never be killers nor traitors nor perjurers nor murderers nor unfaithful, but should adhere to their correct rule, that is their church. They should not be liars nor oath breakers nor robbers nor thieves …

This passage is not an exact repetition of the language in the other two homilies, but the same compounds appear in almost the same order as in the other homilies: *manslagan* … *manswican* … *mansworan* … *morðwyrhtan*. Only *æwbrecan* appears in different points in the homilies: after *manswican* in Bethurum VII, after *mansworan* in Bethurum XIII, after *morðwyrhtan* in Bethurum Xa, and absent entirely in *Sermo Lupi*. With very slight adjustment, then, the same matrix of compounds appears in several different circumstances to illustrate different points. Multiple blocks of text from four different homilies make use of the same core vocabulary, particularly the same compounds.

However, this compositional pattern of inserting blocks of formulaic, compound-laden text into the centre of a homily is not universal: not all of Wulfstan's homilies follow this pattern. For example, *Incipiunt sermones Lupi Episcopi* (Bethurum VI) consists of a long, continuous narrative of Christian history without any list-interludes and without many compounds.[16] On the short end of the spectrum, *To folce* (Napier XXV), a brief address prompting the audience to learn the Christian faith, also lacks any central list and contains only a smattering of compounds.[17] Thus, the lists appear only in homilies of a certain type and seem to fulfil a very pointed function. If one separates Wulfstan's homilies into general types based not only on topical content but on rhetorical strategies as well, a few general trends emerge. Specifically, the homilies generally break into the four categories of explanatory, narrative, legal, and exhortatory.[18] The explanatory

16 Bethurum, *Homilies*, 142–56. This text contains twenty-four compounds but, as one of Wulfstan's longest homilies (217 lines in this edition), the relative frequency of compound occurrence is only about one every nine lines.

17 Napier, *Wulfstan*, 122–4. This text contains only three compounds in its thirty-five lines, resulting in a relative frequency of occurrence of roughly one compound per eleven and a half lines.

18 Of course any individual homily often contains elements of all four categories but nonetheless tends to focus on one aspect or another, for the most part fitting into only one category of overarching description. Moreover, although these categories resemble those employed by Bethurum in her edition, namely Eschatological Homilies, The Christian Life, Archiepiscopal Functions, and Evil Days (*Homilies*, 29–36), I do not intend my categories to function as prescriptive classifications but mostly as descriptive aids in organization. I base my categories mainly on the "tone" of each homily and not solely its contents, and there is some significance to the differences in "tone" between the categories, as I discuss below.

homilies expound a topic relevant to Christian life, such as the meaning of baptism. For example, *Dominica IIIa vel quando volueris* (Bethurum VIIIb) explains, ostensibly to catechumens, the spiritual meanings behind the priest's actions during the baptismal rite.[19] The narrative homilies obviously relate biblical stories or general Christian history, as in *Incipiunt Sermones Lupi Episcopi* (Bethurum VI). The legal homilies focus on the actions Christians must or must not take to live rightly and in accordance with church law; for example, *Be mistlican gelimpan* (Napier XXXV) details the specific levels of tithing appropriate for each social class.[20] These homilies should be kept separate from general exhortations, since the legal homilies focus on specific details of particular duties rather than general salvation and social order in a large sense. The fourth category, exhortatory homilies, is the home of the compound-laden lists, in which category I include Bethurum Xa, XIII, XX, and XXI, along with Napier XXVII, L, LIX, LX, and XXIV; Bethurum VII and IX incorporate an exhortatory tone at their closes. The main purpose of these homilies is to call for the audience to take action, normally by turning from sin, repenting, and doing penance before God and the world. For the most part, these are the homilies concerning the disheartening events of the Danish invasions and general social decline.

These categories are by no means hard-line guides, and occasional overlap between types does occur. For example, Bethurum VII generally falls into the explanatory category, parsing the contents of the Creed and the Pater Noster.[21] The explanation continues until line 104, at which point the homily turns to the Day of Judgment, and this description of God's wrath easily shifts into a description of hell and its future denizens. At this point, the homily quickly takes on the tone of exhortation, reminding the audience through an alliterating list of compounds of the various sins which lead to damnation.[22] A call for repentance and penance ends this explanatory homily, perhaps as a reminder to the catechumenate audience of the reason for their presence: education in the correct faith to avoid eternal punishment and gain instead eternal bliss. As Wulfstan says in conclusion:

> Nu ic hæbbe eow areht rihtne geleafan. Se ðe hine aht þisses tweoð 7 his gelyfan nele, ne cymð he æfre to Godes rice gyf he on þam geendað. And

19 Bethurum, *Homilies*, 172–4.
20 Napier, *Wulfstan*, 169–72.
21 Bethurum, *Homilies*, 299.
22 Bethurum, *Homilies*, 163, lines 128–34.

se ðe ðonne rihtne geleafan hæfð 7 his ealles gelyfð þæs ðe ic rehte þæt ðurh God geweard 7 gyt gewurðan sceal, gif he þurhwunað on þam rihtan geleafan 7 God georne lufað 7 his bebodu gehealdeð, he þæs habban sceal ece edlean on Godes rice.[23]

Now I have explained to you the correct faith. Whoever doubts any part of this and does not wish to believe in it will never come to God's kingdom if he ends his life that way. And he who keeps the correct faith and believes completely in what I have explained, namely what has come about and yet will come about through God, if he endures in the correct faith and eagerly loves God and keeps his commandments, he will have as a result an eternal reward in God's kingdom.

Thus, a homily which for the most part maintains an explanatory tone nonetheless contains an exhortatory section near the end and ultimately closes out the lesson in that tone. The exhortation impresses upon the catechumens the importance of the lessons in Christian faith; it does not overwhelm the homily but serves only as a way to underline briefly a general but essential point.

Interestingly, lists involving compounds and the concomitant rhetorical ornamentation were evidently felt to be inappropriate for non-exhortatory tones. In particular, the legal homilies frequently contain lists but lack compounds and much rhetorical ornamentation. For example, *Ðis man gerædde, ða se micela here com to lande* (Napier XXXIX) lists the many steps people should take to ward off further Danish incursions, such as fasting for three days and giving alms according to their social station. This long list, however, lacks the rhetorical force of the compound lists from the exhortatory homilies. It is unadorned and straightforward. For example, the following passage specifies a basic action and the punishment for those who do not carry out that action, but in a very plain manner:

and sceote man æt æghwilcre hide pænig oððe pæniges weorð, and bringe man þæt to cirican and siððan on þreo dæle be scriftes and be tunes gerefan gewitnesse. and, gif hwa þis ne gelæste, ðonne gebete he þæt, swa swa hit gelagod is: bunda mid .xxx. penigan, þræl mid his hide, þegn mid xxx scillingan.[24]

And a man in each hide should pay a penny or a penny's worth, and a man should bring that to church and afterwards divide it into three as witnessed

23 Bethurum, *Homilies*, 164, lines 159–65.
24 Napier, *Wulfstan*, 181, lines 4–10.

by the confessor and the town steward. And, if someone does not discharge this duty, then he should repent for it as it has been decreed: a householder with thirty pennies, a slave with his hide, a thegn with thirty shillings.

The few instances of alliteration in this passage must be accidental and achieve no larger, rhetorical effect similar to what alliterating, echoing compounds achieve elsewhere. The (probably accidental) repetition of *pænig* does not call attention to any special idea as does the repetition of *man* in the phrase "manslagan ne manswican ne mansworan."[25] The latter phrase creates a semantic "centre" on the syllable *man*, causing the triplet to feel unified around a single concept, expressing not three isolated ideas but a connected sphere of ideas. Moreover, there is ambiguity about what that single concept actually is: whether *man* means "person" (*măn*) or "wickedness" (*mān*). Although the vowel length should theoretically have been specified by the pronunciation when spoken aloud, the two words nonetheless remain very similar phonetically, and either one could be active in the three compounds. This ambiguity combines with the basic cognitive demands of processing compounds (see chapter 3 above) to force the audience to decipher this triplet of compounds actively: it could be a list of crimes done against individuals or a list of crimes condemned as foul. Whichever word was ultimately intended, the syllable calls up all of these associations, giving the phrase challenging semantic depth. The legal passage, however, poses no such difficulties and creates no semantic depth: a *pænig* is a *pænig*. The same holds for the apparently accidental alliteration of *þræl* and *þegn*: these words are present only as part of a list of social classes and summon no extra semantic associations through their alliteration.[26] This list, like those in the other legal homilies, clearly avoids the rhetorical devices that Wulfstan uses elsewhere to add semantic depth and aural weight; the legal lists function simply to convey necessary information.

The absence of compounds in the legal lists can thus be explained by the fact that the legal homilies lack an exhortatory tone. As with the passage

25 Bethurum, *Homilies*, homily Xa, 192, lines 11–12.

26 I assume here that *þ–* and *þr–* can alliterate, following analogously from the fact that *sp–*, *st–*, and *sc–* alliterate in Ælfric's corpus. Presumably, the necessity for complete onset alliteration would also have fallen away for Wulfstan. Moreover, full onset alliteration for clusters other than for *sp–*, *st–*, and *sc–* is irregular at best, according to Minkova, *Alliteration and Sound Change*, 241–2. For a discussion of alliteration of these clusters in Ælfric's rhythmical prose, see Pope, *Homilies of Ælfric*, 1:128–9, and Bredehoft, *Early English Metre*, 83.

quoted above, they consist mainly of unadorned lists presenting what seems almost to be technical information. The only gestures resembling exhortation come briefly at the beginning or end of these homilies. For example, the end of Napier XXXIX reads:

> and æghwilce geare heononforð gelæste man godes gerihta huru rihtlice, wið ðam þe us god ælmihtig gemiltsige and us geunne, þæt we ure fynd ofercuman motan. god ure helpe. amen.[27]

> And indeed each year afterward let people perform their duties to God so that God almighty might take mercy on us and grant us that we may overcome our enemy. God help us. Amen.

As far as Wulfstan's exhortations go, this is a very weak and subdued example. It does contain some sound play between *gerihta* and *rihtlice* and perhaps even between *ælmihtig* and *gemiltsige*. These bits of adornment, however, add little to the passage. In contrast, the ending of *Sermo Lupi ad Anglos* clearly has more force and energy:

> Ac nu on Godes naman uton don, swa us neod is, beorgan us silfum swa we geornost magon, þi læs we ætgædere ealle forweorðan ... And utan gelome understandan þone micclan dom þe we ealle to sculon, 7 beorgan us georne wið þone weallendan bryne helle wites, 7 geearnian us ða mærða 7 þa myrhða þe God hæfð gegearwod þam þe his willan on worlde gewyrcað. God ure helpe, amen.[28]

> But now let us do in God's name what we must: defend ourselves as earnestly as we can lest we all be destroyed together ... And let us continually understand the great judgment to which we shall all go and defend ourselves against the raging heat of hell's torture and attain for ourselves the glory and joy which God has prepared for those who do his will in the world. God help us, amen.

Although this passage contains no more ornamentation in terms of sound play than the end of Napier XXXIX, it clearly pushes its point more forcefully. It repeats the imperative to do what is necessary and spells out the

27 Napier, *Wulfstan*, 181, lines 30–3.
28 Bethurum, *Homilies*, 265–6, lines 163–78.

horrible fate awaiting those who fail to listen. Moreover, the passage from *Sermo Lupi* employs more of the emphatic words so common in Wulfstan's homilies: *georne*, *geornost*, *gelome*. These words amplify the basic sense of the passage and communicate further urgency. In comparison, the ending for Napier XXXIX seems bare and unemphatic, but there would be no need for extra emphasis or exhortation in a list of semi-technical information.

This emphatic tone of exhortation in several of Wulfstan's homilies, then, licenses and perhaps even encourages the use of the rhetorically flamboyant compound lists. These exhortations do nothing to explain a particular rite, tell a biblical story, or hand down a specific set of penitential actions to be taken; their focus is more general. Although it is likely that Wulfstan chose the individual elements of his lists with an eye to the particular situations in his communities, their specific contents necessarily balance with the function which they perform as large units of discourse in each homily as a whole. On the one hand, one could argue that the repetition of the lists in several homilies reveals only Wulfstan's concern for the individual sins named. This argument, however, loses potency in light of the apparent ease with which these blocks of texts were adapted and inserted into different homilies without incongruity. If the specific details of each list were the only significant point, it is likely that they would be presented in a manner similar to the unadorned lists in the legal homilies, wherein the content clearly takes precedence over any possible rhetorical flourishes. Instead, the rhetorical flourishes made available by compounds highlight the list form itself through prolonged alliteration and echoing. These multiple internal references tie each list together aurally beyond the syntactic links, thus reinforcing the impression of the lists as self-contained and internally cohesive units of discourse. Moreover, the alliteration, echoing, polyptoton, paranomasia, etc. that characterize these passages maintain the audience's interest while underlining the perniciousness of sin in general. What could have been a monotonous and lacklustre list instead retains attention through its style, adding weight to a short exhortation to repent while avoiding monotony. These functions of filling in and energizing a homily build upon the specific contents of a particular list; the individual members of each list are certainly not superfluous, but the full impact of a list comes out of its balance between form and content.

The organizing form of lists and that form's concomitant effects, then, must have been important factors in Wulfstan's choice of this manner of exhortation. Although lists were not the optimum "didactic strategy" in comparison to catalogues,[29] they must have suited Wulfstan's purposes quite well, considering their frequent appearance in his homilies. Catalogue entries each present detailed and often lengthy explanation, whereas individual members of a list are generally limited to a single sentence or even word.[30] Lists are therefore excellent aids for memory but insufficient as a method for packaging detailed information; specifically, a list is fundamentally "a naming form" and the catalogue fundamentally "a describing form."[31] The list only fails as a didactic form, however, if the underlying intention is to present a large amount of information. If the intent is instead to create order without going into much detail, to create a pattern of thinking without a full account of information, then lists are exactly right for the job. Lists can indeed teach quite well, just with a somewhat different emphasis than that of catalogues. Moreover, Wulfstan's lists are not only didactic; they provide memorable rhetorical weight, giving the audience a specific instance in an address to remember.[32] Lists can perform this function of creating memorable moments without overwhelming the rest of the text. Whereas a catalogue normally determines the structure of an entire work, a list can be inserted into a text to add rhetorical weight without overly influencing the structure of the text. Lists are thus more flexible than catalogues.

Lists often emphasize their mode of presentation over their content and, by doing so, create a sense of authority through their very existence. The decontextualized regnal lists of the *Anglo-Saxon Chronicle*, for example, do not so much present individual pieces of information as construct a larger image of "England" as an intellectual category with various connotations.[33] As suggested by the scribal errors present in these lists, the kings and abbots of the lists lost importance as individuals, contributing instead to the overarching concept of "England" as a construct. The very act of listing a line of kings and abbots, or of reproducing such a list, creates and defines the category itself. Lists can thus be acts of creation in and of themselves, not simply a reaction to pre-existing modes of thought.[34] Unlike the

29 Howe, *Old English Catalogue Poems*, 20–1.

30 Howe, *Old English Catalogue Poems*, 21.

31 Howe, *Old English Catalogue Poems*, 22.

32 For example, three-part lists tend to be especially memorable for modern English speakers. See Atkinson, "Two Devices," 223.

33 Stodnick, "Documentary Lists."

34 Goody, *Written Tradition*, 146.

regnal lists, which often become decontextualized, Wulfstan's lists retain their homiletic context; as shown above, however, that context is often nearly irrelevant, thus placing them in a position and function similar to the regnal lists. The interchangeability of Wulfstan's lists and the reuse of a single matrix of compounds in multiple contexts show that the lists maintain their authority separately from any individual homily. The form itself performs the work of authorizing the ideas contained within them.

Wulfstan's concern for form and list structure itself is clear in the following passage from Bethurum VII, discussed above but quoted again here with emphasis on formal repetition:

> *Ðyder sculan* mannslagan, 7 *ðider sculan* manswican; *ðider sculan* æwbrecan 7 ða fulan forlegenan; *ðider sculan* mansworan 7 morðwyrhtan; *ðider sculan* gitseras, ryperas 7 reaferas 7 woruldstruderas; *ðider sculon* þeofas 7 ðeodscaðan; *ðyder sculon* wiccan 7 wigleras, 7, hrædest to secganne, ealle þa manfullan þe ær yfel worhton 7 noldon geswican ne wið God þingian.[35]

> *There shall go* murderers, and *there shall go* traitors; *there shall go* oathbreakers and foul fornicators; *there shall go* perjurers and murderers; *there shall go* misers, robbers and plunderers and spoliators; *there shall go* thieves and enemies of the people; *there shall go* magicians and wizards, and, to put it simply, all the wicked who previously worked evil and did not want to cease nor pray to God.

This list displays a clear shape involving several standard list devices.[36] Specifically, the phrase *ðider sculon* accompanies both items in the first pair of the list; then one *ðider sculon* for each of the next two pairs. The central portion of the lists employs only one *ðider sculon* for four items before returning to one *ðider sculon* per pair for the next two pairs. The final element of the list changes the pattern, signalling the close of the list cycle. Moreover, the final item constitutes an all-purpose phrase covering all the sins left unmentioned, a standard strategy for ending lists with a sense of completeness.[37] The patterned repetition of the phrase *ðider sculon* telescopes from individual elements of the list to a large group of elements

35 Bethurum, *Homilies*, 163, lines 128–34, emphasis added.

36 For a discussion on standard features of lists, see Jackson, "'Not Simply Lists.'"

37 Atkinson, *Our Masters' Voices*, 57–8.

and back again, giving the list a sense of order and completeness. This telescoping also changes the tempo of the list, with more elements coming in quicker succession in the central section, because of the absence of a *ðider sculon* for each, than in the first section, which interjects *ðider sculon* more frequently. This variation of tempo combines with sound play involving compounds, such as alliteration and word-initial off-rhyme (*þeofas* with *ðeodscaðan*), and together they break up any possible monotony in the list. Given these features, the passage is clearly constructed with an interest in the characteristics and integrity of a well-formed list.

A similar emphasis on form is apparent in the formulaic nature of the lists, which, although obviously repetitive, do not exemplify any of the standard types of repetition discussed by scholars of Oral Theory. These Wulfstanian passages somewhat resemble, but do not perfectly match, the structure of repetition termed "clusters," which are groups of morphemes repeatedly associated with an idea or action.[38] Wulfstan's exhortatory lists clearly display a repeated cluster of compounds, but clusters in Oral Theory are not dependent on verbatim repetition of the specific morphemes, sometimes depending instead on synonymic repetition – repetition of the idea using a different word.[39] The Wulfstanian lists depend to a very large degree on verbatim repetition; synonymic repetition is not apparent, and only minor variations occur, such as the difference between *morðwyrhtan* and *morþorwyrhtan*. The sounds of the words govern the passages so fully that synonymic instead of phonological repetition would destroy the parallels. Also, the arrangement of the repeated words remains almost unchanged in the Wulfstanian passages, suggesting that the order of repetition plays an important role, unlike in Oral Theory's clusters.[40] Finally, the underlying concept of the repeated lists differs in key details: the lists in Bethurum VII and XIII, for example, describe those people destined for hell, whereas the list in Bethurum Xa describes sins to be avoided by canons. The same

38 Foley, *Traditional Oral Epic*, 206. Foley gives the example of the repetition of *niht* [night], *eall* [all], *sceadu* [shadow], and *scriðan* [to go, glide] in expressions of the "onset of darkness and all of the terror and ravaging that it poetically connotes" (211–12).

39 For example, Foley, *Traditional Oral Epic*, 226, gives the example of the cluster associating the invasion of Grendel in *Beowulf* and of Andrew in *Andreas*: the morpheme *-hran* (from *hrinan* [to seize]) is repeated, but the *folmum* [with hands] of the *Beowulf* passage is echoed only by its synonym *hand* [hand] in *Andreas*.

40 Foley's examples of the "onset of darkness" cluster vary the order of the repeated morphemes, apparently with no effect on the nature of the cluster's traditional repetition (*Traditional Oral Epic*, 211–12).

matrix of compounds appears in all three, but the motivation for the lists and the specific topics vary. All three deal with sin in some way, but the details differ.

This type of repetition instead most closely resembles that of formulaic binomials, but on a large scale. Formulaic binomials, essentially the doublets that Wulfstan is so fond of, are normally fixed, with the words repeated in the same order in each occurrence and phonetically connected through devices such as alliteration, rhyme, or echoic repetition.[41] A common use for these doublets is the creation of merisms, phrases which metonymically represent a whole larger than the individual parts, for example the phrase "grain and barley" denoting all cereal crops.[42] Wulfstan clearly employs these types of phrases individually throughout his homilies, but his repeated lists group multiple instances of binomials together, linking several at a time through aural devices. One list in *Sermo Lupi*, for example, contains two merisms linked together in multiple ways: "Her syndan *m*annslagan 7 *m*ægslagan 7 *m*æsserbanan 7 *m*ynsterhatan" [Here there are man-slayers and kin-slayers and priest-killers and monastery-persecutors].[43] The first binomial alliterates and repeats *slagan*, while the second continues the alliteration while introducing synonymic repetition between *slagan* and *banan* and a close semantic relation between *mæsser* and *mynster*, which two constituents also participate in a sort of off-rhyme or off-echo. The two merisms link together into a single, larger list member, and similar linkage continues through the rest of the list. The repetition of such lists, with the extended phonetic connections and the order of the compounds essentially fixed, clearly emulates the behaviour of formulaic binomials. As a result of this idiosyncratic type of repetition, the form of the passages comes to be as important as the content – not structure *without* content but structure *and* content, as in Jakobson's poetic function.[44] Beyond the mnemonic ease which repetition provides, this emphasis on the list structure itself accords with the assertion that lists as a form wield an authority separate from their content. That attention to form reifies the

41 Southern, "Formulaic Binomials." Also see the discussion of bipartite noun-phrases in Watkins, *How to Kill a Dragon*, 43–9.

42 Watkins, *How to Kill a Dragon*, 45. Other types of possible binomial combinations include an argument plus its synonym, for example "safe and sound" (Southern, "Formulaic Binomials," 261, and Watkins, *How to Kill a Dragon*, 44), or an argument plus its negation, for example "seen and unseen."

43 Bethurum, *Homilies*, 273, lines 161–2, emphases added.

44 See the discussion in chapter 3 above.

contents, and Wulfstan's lists of sins thus solidify the reality of those sins and recast them as "concept-objects."[45]

Moreover, lists emulating and borrowing the characteristics of formulaic binomials also take on the expressive force of binomials, specifically the impact and intensity added to the expression through the creation of iconicity.[46] Iconicity refers to the "mapping of the semantic level onto the level of the expressive forms," that is, the reflection in a word or phrase's form of the meaning of that word or phrase.[47] For a formulaic binomial merism, the tight phonetic and syntactic connections iconically reflect the phrase's expression of a single, unified concept; the surface form of the phrase imitates its semantic underpinnings.[48] For example, the fact that the two members of the phrase "seen and unseen" tie together semantically to denote "all of creation" is reflected by the repetition of the constituent "seen" tying the words together phonetically. The presence of this structural reflection of meaning lends formulaic binomials increased expressive force compared to simplices or phrases which are not similarly linked on multiple linguistic levels. Wulfstan's lists, by stretching the formal linkages characteristic of formulaic binomials throughout a large discourse unit, tap into this iconically expressive force, further unifying and intensifying the lists and increasing yet again the sense of them as objects. Just as binomials can express concepts beyond their individual parts, so also do Wulfstan's lists serve as large-scale merisms denoting sin in all its forms. The expressive force of binomials, essentially using the added "weight" of increased syllables, aural effects, and syntactic and semantic relations to intensify a concept, extends to these lists. Again, form adds to content, not obscuring but amplifying it.

This combination of form and content depends ultimately on the complex structures of compound words, especially because Wulfstan clearly valued sound play so highly. The individual elements of binomial merisms are not always linked formally, for example, "grain and barley," which plays on semantic rather than formal linkage. Some binomials formally link together through sound play without employing compound structures, but such instances nonetheless require some sort of repetition with the variation

---

45 See again Stodnick, "Documentary Lists," and Goody, *Written Tradition*.

46 Southern, "Formulaic Binomials," 255, lists "iteration/intensity or immediacy" among the most common functions of binomials.

47 Russo, "Iconicity and Productivity," 166.

48 Southern, "Formulaic Binomials," 260.

often coming in the form of a prefix, for example, "seen and unseen." That type of construction is thus rather limited, being mainly populated by merisms depending on negation. Wulfstan's employment of compound words significantly expands the options for formal repetition and linkage. With compounds, many kinds of repetition become possible: the first constituents of the compounds, the second constituents, alliteration of the initial sound, or even internal rhyme, all of which appear in Wulfstan's lists. All of these types of repetition nonetheless do not become *repetitive*, since compound structures are so complex that variation still comes into play. The example from the *Sermo Lupi* discussed above again provides good illustration: "Her syndan *m*annslagan 7 *m*ægslagan 7 *m*æsserbanan 7 *m*ynsterhatan" [Here there are man-slayers and kin-slayers and priest-killers and monastery-persecutors].[49] Only through the use of compounds does the passage incorporate alliterative repetition (*m*), verbal repetition (*slagan*), and homoeoteleuton (the several /a/ sounds in the second constituents) alongside both synonymic variation (*slagan* and *banan*) and general variation of the first constituents. The passage thus combines variation and repetition in a way that avoids monotony while retaining formal repetition, and it does so through the opportunities made available by the inclusion of compounds. Indeed, compounding lays the foundation for all the different elements that combine to make Wulfstan's lists coherent and rhetorically powerful.

The augmentation of argument through rhetorical flourishes is of course nothing new,[50] and the Anglo-Saxons themselves studied rhetorical strategies in order to interpret and understand the scriptures and other Christian texts, as discussed in chapter 1 above. Wulfstan's compound lists, however, go beyond the normal practices of emphasis and ornamentation, which, according to Anglo-Saxon treatises, generally involve individual rhetorical devices and, bluntly, fewer words.[51] The devices not discussed by but clearly employed by Anglo-Saxons, such as apposition and envelope patterns, are also smaller in scale than these lists.[52] In contrast to those

49 Bethurum, *Homilies*, 273, line 161–2, emphases added.

50 Classical rhetorical handbooks, such as the *Rhetorica ad Herennium*, which was popular in the Middle Ages due in part to its erroneous attribution to Cicero, provide guidance on how best to deploy rhetorical devices in persuasion; see Caplan, *Rhetorica ad Herennium*.

51 See, for example, the explanation of individual rhetorical devices in Bede's treatises, the exemplary passages for which are generally rather short: Kendall, *De schematibus et tropis*.

52 See, among many others, the discussion of formal techniques in Foley, *Traditional Oral Epic*. Type-scenes perhaps compare to Wulfstan's lists in their size and incorporation of individual, smaller rhetorical effects, but type-scenes neither rely as fundamentally on those effects nor are as self-contained as the lists.

individualized, often small-scale devices, Wulfstan weaves together multiple formal effects at once in the lists and extends them through very long passages. Moreover, Wulfstan's lists are not part of a persuasive argument per se. As discussed above, the lists are self-contained units that slot into several different argumentative contexts. At one level, then, a Wulfstanian list, as made possible by compound words, becomes a single, coherent rhetorical device, albeit one made up of various smaller rhetorical effects on a more detailed level. While those smaller rhetorical effects function at the discursive levels of word, phrase, and sentence, the lists function at the level of discourse units, affecting the pattern and progression of the argument in a literally different but analogously similar manner. In this macroscopic view of discourse units, the lists analogously compare to dramatic pauses or effects that displace a sentence's focus to the end, making the audience wait for resolution. In other words, while "standard" rhetorical effects can delay the syntactical resolution of a sentence, the lists discursively delay the resolution of the entire argument or exhortation.

Wulfstan's manipulation of the pace of his arguments in this way is surprisingly complex. Assessing pace in narrative texts is relatively straightforward, consisting of comparing the duration of events in the plot to the duration of their expression in the telling.[53] Issues of analepsis (flashback), prolepsis (foreshadowing), extended description, and various other manipulations of narrative make sense in a dyadic system linking a sequence of events (the plot) with their description. In non-narrative texts such as Wulfstan's homilies, however, pace is difficult to evaluate rigorously, since recounting a plot is not their main concern. As discussed above, some homilies present narratives, generally along with explanation, but many, especially the exhortatory ones, are bereft of an organizing plot. While Wulfstan's exhortatory homilies sometimes refer to historical events, such as the Danish invasions, they seek not to narrate those events but rather react to them and appeal to the audience in some manner. In this view, they are akin to oration as conceived of by Aristotle, Cicero, and innumberable rhetoricians since, including those studying modern political discourse. It is indeed no surprise that scholars have applied classical models to Wulfstan's works,[54] even though his knowledge of those models is highly unlikely.[55] Nonetheless, although he almost certainly did not

53 Pace in narrative discourse, specifically *Beowulf*, is considered in detail below in chapter 6.

54 For example, Bethurum, *Homilies*, 88–9, and Hollowell, "Linguistic Factors."

55 See the discussion in chapter 1 above.

learn classical rhetoric per se, his homilies employ basic rhetorical patterns that are described by classical treatises, and methods of analysing modern discourse also fit them quite well. Those classical and modern models therefore become useful not as evidence of Wulfstan's actual knowledge and methods but as tools for describing and analysing his homiletic performances, since his homilies employ the rhetorical pose of proving a point and convincing their audiences of a particular view. Through an analysis within the framework of argumentation, the complexities of controlling non-narrative pace become clear.

The pose of argumentation in Wulfstan's case is somewhat misleading, since, although they seem to seek to persuade their audience, homilies actually present a one-sided argument, to which no real reply is expected. The audience of a homily, which was likely to have been an audience of at least nominal Christians, would not have been likely to disagree with the homilist. In other words, Wulfstan's homilies preach to the proverbial choir as their imagined audience. To the contrary, these elements, which seem to subvert the pose of argumentation, are in fact common elements of non-agonistic argument, in which conversations take the form of an argument, even when all participants in fact agree with each other. For example, the following excerpt from a conversation about Parisian traffic law employs several elements of argumentation, although there are overt expressions of agreement:

> CO: Au fait, qu'est-ce que vous en pensez, de la loi, euh ... on parlait justement sur euh ... cette loi, là, qui a été votée, là, qu'on a respecté la loi, vous savez la ... pair/impair, pour les voitures
>
> CLF: Ecoutez, moi je vais vous dire mon sentiment, pour Paris, on devrait faire ça tous les jours
>
> CO: [*En écho*] Tous les jours
>
> CLH: Voilà. Ben nous sommes tous d'accord
>
> CLF: Moi je trouve que c'est formidable. D'abord parce que finalement, tous les jours, y a déjà un maximum de gens qui pourraient arriver à s'organiser ... Tout le monde a pas besoin de sa voiture tous les jours!

> CO: Actually, what do you think of the law, er ... we were actually talking about er ... this law, there, that was just voted, that is in effect, you know, the law about traffic restriction for odd-even numbered license plates for the cars.
>
> CLF: Listen, I will tell you what I think, for Paris, we should be doing this all the time.

CO: All the time.
CLH: Exactly. We all agree then.
CLF: I find this a great idea. First of all because at last, every day, there is already a maximum number of people who could find a way to organize their transportation ... People do not need their car all the days![56]

In this portion of the conversation, the hortatory "Ecoutez" [Listen] and the continued explanation of the speaker's point of view fit the pattern of an argument between disagreeing parties. The pattern holds in later portions of the conversation with demands of "Attendez!" [Wait!] and several responses beginning with "Non" [No]. The response of "Voilà. Ben nous sommes tous d'accord" [Exactly. We all agree then], however, clearly and directly undercuts any sense of disagreement, but the conversation nonetheless continues in the form of an argument. Rather than argue against each other, the participants in this type of conversation together argue against an unrepresented opposition; they may mention or subtly connote opposing arguments, adducing them, however, only to demonstrate an awareness of them and not to engage substantively with them.[57] For example, the Parisian-traffic-law argument continues with a reference to opposition to the law and several pieces of evidence refuting that opposition. In these ways, even with clear and frequent expressions of agreement between the speakers, the conversation mimics a "true" argument in which the parties involved try to convince each other of opposed points of view. From one perspective, a "true" argument requires that there be real doubt about the claim in question,[58] while non-agonistic arguments presuppose the absence of doubt among the actual participants, entertaining the possibility of doubt only due to the form of argumentation. Thus, a conversation or discourse between like-minded parties may employ standard features of argument without in fact being an argument.

Wulfstan's exhortatory homilies fit this description quite well in several places, for example in *Her is gyt rihtlic warnung 7 soðlic myngung ðeode to ðearfe* (Bethurum XXI):

And þa hyt wæs on þeode for Gode 7 for worolde wislic 7 weorðlic, þa man riht lufode 7 unriht ascunode. Ac nu þincð þe wærra 7 mycele þe snotera se

56 Text and translation from Doury, "Preaching to the Converted," 112 and 101, respectively; original emphasis.
57 Doury, "Preaching to the Converted," 106–7.
58 Pinto, "Argumentation," 284, and Pinto, "Uses of Argument," 230.

> ðe can mid leasungan wæwerdlice werian 7 mid unsoðe soð oferswiðan. Ac wa him þæs wærscipes 7 ealles þæs weorðscipes, butan he geswice. La, riht is þæt we lufian þa þe God lufian 7 hetelice ascunian þa þe God græmian …[59]

> And at that time things were wise and honourable throughout the nation before God and the world, when people loved justice and rejected injustice. But now the one who knows how to successfully obstruct truth with lies and overcome truth with untruth seems to be more prudent and much wiser. But woe will befall him because of that cunning and all that glory, unless he ceases. Indeed, it is just that we love what God loves and fiercely shun what God reviles.[60]

This passage nostalgically recalls the justice of past days before introducing the contemporary valuation of unjust cunning over just wisdom. This allusively introduces an opposition to Wulfstan's argument, but he barely engages with it, instead simply asserting without any evidence or explanation that ruin will come to unjustly cunning people and that justice requires aligning oneself with God's likes and dislikes. There is no call to engage directly with the implied opposition, for example, the Antichrist; they simply cannot be convinced of the error of their ways. The homily's concern is thus not any actual opposition. The allusion to an opposition simply justifies the homily's argumentative tone, since it implies that Wulfstan must indeed make an argument for his exhortations rather than recognize that his audience most likely already shared his point of view, at least to some extent.

That "to some extent" underlies Wulfstan's employment of an argumentative pose in the exhortatory homilies: while his audiences likely did not disagree with him, they perhaps agreed only tepidly. Non-agonistic argument, in the absence of the need to make the other party accept a particular point of view, serves several non-persuasive purposes; indeed, there must be ends other than overt persuasion to which argumentation can be put, if people in agreement can "argue."[61] Rather than convince, Wulfstan's homiletic arguments strengthen his audiences' dedication to his view of Christianity and Anglo-Saxon society. They define the homilist's

---

59 Bethurum, *Homilies*, 277, lines 21–7.

60 Some of my choices in translating this passage are informed by Pons-Sanz, *Norse-Derived Vocabulary*, 103–4.

61 See recently Goodwin, "Argument Has No Function"; Micheli, "Arguing without Trying to Persuade?"; and Doury, "Preaching to the Converted."

positions and by extension the audiences', and that definition then creates a particular Christian identity. The creation of that identity depends initially on the fact that argumentation requires the participants to express opinions, for which they must then take responsibility as representative of their beliefs.[62] Opinions often coalesce or concretize only in the moment of their expression in argument,[63] making argumentation a powerful vehicle for the formation of opinion and belief. As performative acts, such expression and concretization ultimately become constitutive of a self or subject.[64] The audience of a homily may not have been meant to respond verbally in the moment, but that expectation of consensual silence also implicates them in the identity constructed through the homily. As a result, a homilist performs a particular Christian identity, and the audience is to accept that performance as their own. Moreover, as discussed above, non-agonistic argumentation alludes to opposing viewpoints in order to justify its argumentative form, but those allusions also, in fact, create and reify the concept of the opposition. The presence of opposition of course contributes further to the construction of identity by providing an other, against which to define the self.[65] Wulfstan's exhortatory homilies take advantage of all these features of argument to perform for their audiences a specific, zealous Christian identity and draft them into that identity. The homilies presume not the audience's disagreement or lack of Christian faith but a need to strengthen that agreement and Christian identity, and argumentation provides an excellent means for accomplishing that strengthening.

Argumentation of course does not automatically imply compound words or even lists, but several features of Wulfstan's compound-laden lists become clear within its framework, especially their effect on pace. Regardless of the critical or rhetorical tradition, assuming the pose of argumentation invokes a set of expectations for the text's form and rhetorical tactics.[66] One basic and fairly obvious tactic expected of an argumentative text is the

62 Doury, "Preaching to the Converted," 109, and Garver, "Comments," 307.

63 Doury, "Preaching to the Converted," 108–9, and Nonnon, "Activités argumentatives."

64 Among many other discussions of the formation of subjects through performative acts and texts, see Butler, *Gender Trouble*, and O'Brien O'Keeffe, *Stealing Obedience*.

65 Anderson, *Imagined Communities*, 6, and Heng, *Empire of Magic*, 99.

66 Classical and modern rhetorical models all share a baseline concept of argumentation having standard features necessary for success. *Rhetorica ad Herennium*, for example, describes useful rhetorical devices and gives positive examples of orations in different styles alongside failed examples. For modern perspectives, see, for example, Killingsworth, *Appeals in Modern Rhetoric*, and Innocenti, "Normative Pragmatic Model."

presentation of evidence in support of an appeal. This move serves several purposes, particularly in instances of "fear appeals," such as Wulfstan's warnings of dire consequences for failing to repent adequately. Beyond simply justifying such warnings, presenting evidence creates rhetorical force.[67] In particular, rhetorically well-crafted presentations of evidence can convince and co-opt an audience where spare appeals or even strong evidence presented clumsily would fail.[68] Of particular interest in light of Wulfstan's rhetorical preferences is the concept that "evidence works best in quantity"; in such situations of appeal, brevity is not a virtue.[69] Increasing the amount of evidence thus intrinsically increases an appeal's rhetorical impact, in a way nearly regardless of the actual nature of the evidence. Audiences simply expect arguments to present evidence, and the better crafted and more prodigious that presentation, the more powerful the argument. Wulfstan's compound-laden lists fulfil all of these features: they provide the evidence expected by any audience of an argument, they do so copiously, and they do so in a rhetorically well-crafted manner. The lists are thus not simply an idiosyncratic stylistic tic on Wulfstan's part; they perform rhetorical work on several different planes.

The manipulation of pace in non-narrative discourse – to return to the main point – and Wulfstan's lists are thus tied up with these issues of argumentation. The presentation of evidence is not fundamentally an advancement of an argument in terms of taking logical steps. Evidence in one sense explains a logical claim, but it is not another step in, say, a syllogistic chain leading to a *demonstrandum*. One might thus evaluate the pace of an argument in relation to logical landmarks rather than plot landmarks, as one does for narrative texts. The less time or page space, depending on the point of reference, given to each logical step, the quicker the pace of the argument. An argument's audience expects a certain pace that does not rush through the logical points but rather takes the time to support those claims with evidence.[70] In Wulfstan's case, evidence is in a sense not necessary, since his audience likely already shared his basic

---

67 See Killingsworth, *Appeals in Modern Rhetoric*; Innocenti Manolescu, "Norms of Presentational Force"; and Innocenti, "Normative Pragmatic Model."

68 See Innocenti, "Normative Pragmatic Model," 285–6.

69 Killingsworth, *Appeals in Modern Rhetoric*, 14, and Innocenti Manolescu, "Norms of Presentational Force," 148.

70 Such expectation would certainly change depending on the venue; the expectations of evidence in, say, modern political interviews are much less than in speeches, which are much less again than in official policy papers.

beliefs; the pose of argumentation nonetheless imposes the expectation, which his lists fulfil. Once that expectation is invoked, scanty evidence would be less acceptable than abundant support, thus partially explaining the large chunks of texts dedicated to providing copious examples in the lists. The interest in reifying the danger posed by the various threats that Wulfstan discusses aligns with the need to introduce an opposition within the argumentation form, thus further motivating the large size of the lists. The superior effectiveness of rhetorically well-formed presentations of evidence then partially motivates the presence in the lists of compound words, the complex structures of which allow the aural play characteristic of Wulfstan and indicative of rhetorical polish.[71] Those complex structures also in and of themselves provide greater rhetorical impact than simplices, thereby adding additional weight to the evidence. These features of the compound-laden lists – intrinsic rhetorical impact, aural play, reification of an opposition – harmonize to slow the progression of argumentation in support of the exhortatory homilies' poses as arguments. The compounds and lists delay the movement to the next logical step in the argument in a way that fulfils multiple expectations about the argument, demonstrating that such slowing is essential to the argumentative pose; in other words, it makes the argument work and work well. Wulfstan's homilies thus carefully deploy compound words to create formal features that control their pace of argumentation, all in order to best achieve their exhortatory ends, again in a way unachievable without compounds.

71 This concept also helps to explain the difference between Wulfstan's legal and exhortatory lists: the legal lists are statements or declarations rather than arguments, and the expecations of rhetorical polish are therefore absent.

6 Controlling Pace in Poetry: *Beowulf*

After becoming the sole king of the Geats, Beowulf rules in peace for fifty years, about which time the poem tells us effectively nothing. In the course of only eleven lines, the poem moves quickly from the rewards that Beowulf receives upon his return to Geatland, through the deaths of Hygelac and Heardred and Beowulf's fifty years of peaceful rule, and on to the first appearance of the dragon. Those fifty years themselves occupy only two half-lines: "he geheold tela / fiftig wintra" [he ruled well for fifty winters].[1] Earlier in the poem, in a barely less compressed manner, the twelve years of Grendel's reign of terror in Heorot pass in only a few half-lines.[2] These two interludes capture little of the poem's interest, perhaps because they involve consistent states of affairs: constant terror and death in Grendel's reign, and constant peace in Beowulf's. The significant action – the beginnings and endings, the instances of *edhwyrft* [reversal] that so interest the poem – occurs outside these periods of continuity, and the poem therefore races to them. At other times, however, the pace of action slows nearly to a standstill, with lines upon lines filling up with description or variation, but no development of the plot. This manipulation of pace comprises a pervasive and important feature of *Beowulf*. Variation plays a prominent role in this narrative slowing, and compound words constitute primary building blocks that allow variation to succeed by providing several degrees of freedom in manipulating initial sounds for alliteration, in repeating second elements, and in filling half-lines.[3] Moreover, beyond even

1 Fulk, Bjork, and Niles, *Klaeber's Beowulf*, lines 2208b–9a.

2 Fulk, Bjork, and Niles, *Klaeber's Beowulf*, lines 146b–9a.

3 See the discussion of the importance of compound words to oral-traditional style in chapter 1 above.

their utility in producing variation, the very structure of compounding creates a degree of linguistic weight that in and of itself slows the narrative. Chapter 5 explored this phenomenon in the prose of Wulfstan's Old English homilies, and this chapter explores it in *Beowulf*, showing that clusters of compounds appear in moments of important violence in the poem in a way that undercuts the celebrations of heroism and highlights instead the complicated social meaning and consequences of violence.

Pace is much easier to assess in narrative texts such as *Beowulf* than in non-narrative texts such as Wulfstan's homilies, largely due to Gérard Genette's rigorous theorization of narrative discourse.[4] The difficulty in analysing Wulfstan's manipulations of pace lies in the absence of an external frame of reference provided by a series of events to be described in the text. Instead of such an account of events, Wulfstan presents arguments and explanations, which invoke a different set of expectations for pace. Narrative texts, on the other hand, pair a series of events (historical or fictional) with its linguistic description. That description is necessarily governed by its own internal rules, with any seemingly natural correlation between the events themselves and their narration – i.e., realism – being an illusion. Genette signals this fundamental distinction with the terms "story time" denoting the duration of events and "narrative time" denoting the duration of their description.[5] Especially important for an application of this framework to medieval literature is Genette's assertion that one can assess a narrative's duration whether it be written or oral. Audiences of Old English poetry could have either listened to or read the texts, but that difference does not affect Genette's concept of duration. An oral narrative produces a clear "temporality" in that it must be "consumed" through its performance or recitation, which is necessarily a time-bound action.[6] Written text, as Genette observes, is more complicated than oral performance in this regard because a reader can theoretically skip between parts and consume the text in a nonlinear fashion.[7] Reading a written text nonetheless requires time, and most written texts at the very least implicitly assume that a reader will proceed linearly through the text (regardless of the order of events as presented in the text), thus creating narrative duration in a manner quite similar to oral performance. This expectation was especially

4 Genette, *Narrative Discourse*. For an application of Genette's theories to *Beowulf*, see Lapidge, "*Beowulf* and Perception."

5 Genette, *Narrative Discourse*, 33.

6 Genette, *Narrative Discourse*, 33–4.

7 Genette, *Narrative Discourse*, 34.

correct for medieval readers, since subvocalizing while reading was the norm, and speed-reading probably unheard of.[8] The narrative duration of written text thus relates directly to the space it takes on a page or the number of lines dedicated to narrating a particular story event in a poem, allowing Genette's framework to apply to either oral or written narrative.[9] Extending a narrative moment over several or even many lines, regardless of whether they were read or heard, thus affects the narrative's duration and delays the narrative's movement to the next story event.

One tactic that *Beowulf* uses to delay the resolution of action is to digress from the main narrative, providing additional background or an analogue to that narrative moment. For example, as Beowulf prepares to enter the mere to pursue Grendel's mother, the poem provides a great deal of information about his war-gear. In particular, the origin of his helmet takes centre stage for several lines:

ac se hwita helm hafelan werede,
se þe meregrundas mengan scolde,
secan sundgebland since geweroðad,
befongen freawrasnum, swa hine fyrndagum
worhte wæpna smið, wundrum teode,
besette swinlicum, þæt hine syðþan no
brond ne beadomecas bitan ne meahton.[10]

But the shining helmet protected his head – he who had to stir up the bottom of the mere, seek the surging water glorified by treasure – encircled by splendid chains, just as the weaponsmith created it in ancient days, wondrously formed it, decorated it with boar-images, so that afterward no sword or battle-blade could cut it [*or* him].

The "backstory" of the helmet, including the artistry of its decoration and skill of its smith, breaks into the main narrative here, interrupting Beowulf's progress towards battle. This digressive move, however, is less a manipulation of pace – Genette's *duration* – than an example of his *anachrony*, a reorganization of the order of events. The account of the helmet's creation comprises an analeptic moment in which the past interrupts the "present"

8 See Chaytor, "Medieval Reader," and O'Brien O'Keeffe, *Visible Song*, 14–21.
9 Genette, *Narrative Discourse*, 34.
10 Fulk, Bjork, and Niles, *Klaeber's Beowulf*, lines 1448–54.

of the main narrative. Thus, the poem produces here a nonlinear relationship between "the temporal *order* of succession of the events in the story and the pseudo-temporal order of their arrangment in the narrative,"[11] such that the narration of an early element of the story is presented in the midst of the narration of a later part. This reordering of chronology indeed delays the narration of Beowulf entering the mere, but not by slowing down the pace of describing his preparation. The digression, rather than extending the passage's focus on Beowulf's preparation without creating any progress, briefly distracts, as it were, from that moment by focusing on a different moment.

The few past discussions of manipulations of actual duration in *Beowulf* have rightfully identified variation as a powerful tool to retard narrative progression.[12] Variation, the basis of the poem's "appositive style" and effectively ubiquitous in Old English poetry, consists of "syntactically parallel words or word-groups which share a common referent and which occur within a single clause."[13] In other words, variation is the addition of words or phrases that restate a previous part of a sentence. Restatement by definition prevents the progress of narrative events; it pauses the progress of the narrative on one moment. While the variation inherent in the appositive style may highlight different facets of a moment with each apposed phrase or word, the narrative remains frozen in time. *Cædmon's Hymn* provides classic examples of this stylistic tool, significantly expanding its two sentences through extensive use of variation:

> Nu sculon herigean heofonrices weard,
> meotodes meahte ond his modgeþanc,
> weorc wuldorfæder, swa he wundra gehwæs,
> ece drihten, or onstealde.
> He ærest sceop eorðan bearnum
> heofon to hrofe, halig scyppend;

11 Genette, *Narrative Discourse*, 35, original emphasis. See also the discussion in Lapidge, "*Beowulf* and Perception," 72–4.

12 Many studies of the style of *Beowulf* discuss variation; for discussions of variation with attention to narrative pace specifically, see Engelhardt, "Study in Dilatation"; Brodeur, *Art of "Beowulf,"* 39 and 51; Harris, "Techniques of Pacing"; and Mize, *Traditional Subjectivities*, 60. See also O'Brien O'Keeffe, "Diction, Variation, the Formula," 95: "This [variation] is not a narrative style for the impatient."

13 Robinson, "Two Aspects of Variation," and Robinson, *Appositive Style*, 3.

þa middangeard moncynnes weard,
ece drihten, æfter teode
firum foldan, frea ælmihtig.[14]

Now we ought to praise the guardian of heaven, the measurer's might and his mind, the work of the glory-father, since he, the eternal lord, established the origin of every wonder. He, the holy shaper, first created heaven as a covering for earth's children; then the guardian of mankind, the eternal lord, the almighty master, later constructed the world for the men of earth.

In these nine lines appear five different epithets for God, with "ece drihten" [eternal lord] occurring twice, even though God only fulfils two grammatical functions – a genitive possessor initially and later a subject. Moreover, the products to be praised – the *meaht* [might] and *modgeþanc* [mind] – are rephrased as "weorc wuldorfæder" [the work of the glory-father].

The apposition employed in the last two sentences of the preceding paragraph demonstrates one valuable function of such variation, which is to provide additional, often increasingly specific information that explains the original formulation. The poetic implications of variation, however, go beyond such pragmatic uses, and the side-by-side placement of appositive phrases can produce additional, associative meanings.[15] For example, irony or condemnation may be present in the description of Beowulf's retainers' decision not to support him in the battle against the dragon: "Nealles him on heape handgesteallan, / æðelinga bearn ymbe gestodon" [His comrades, sons of noblemen, did not stand about him as a troop].[16] At the most basic level, *æðelinga bearn* [sons of noblemen] simply provides additional information about the *handgesteallan* [comrades]. The appositive relationship, however, may also be concessive, implying a failure to live up to expectations that can be paraphrased in this way: "although they were sons of noblemen, nonetheless they failed to stand by him."[17] Without overtly criticizing the retainers, the poem subtly introduces doubt about their quality through its style. Variation thus proves to be not simply aesthetically pleasing or pragmatically useful

14 Dobbie, *Anglo-Saxon Minor Poems*, 106.
15 See also the discussion of associative, connotative meaning in Beechy, *Poetics of Old English*, 1–20.
16 Fulk, Bjork, and Niles, *Klaeber's Beowulf*, lines 2596–7.
17 See the discussion of these lines in Robinson, *Appositive Style*, 4.

but also subtextually expressive, and therefore fundamentally important to understanding Old English poetry.[18]

The phrase *æðelinga bearn* is technically the apposed element in those two lines from *Beowulf*, but the ironic or condemnatory implication is first activated by the compound *handgesteallan*. More than simply "comrades," the *hand*– constituent denotes proximity: the comrades should be close *at hand*.[19] That they are not, a failure already made clear by the negation (*nealles*) that begins the line, comprises the first indication of their failure to live up to their oaths. The poem's appositive style promotes associative reading and thus supports the production of that meaning even before the appearance of the verb that *nealles* technically negates. Taking the text as it unfolds – whether as read or heard – allows *nealles* to associatively, if not necessarily grammatically, negate *handgesteallan*. This interpretation depends also on the proximity with which the poem groups the various elements of the sentence: the "pieces" need to be relatively close by for the associative implications to activate. The compound nature of *handgesteallan* therefore becomes essential, because it allows the word to fill a single half-line as the balance to the half-line containing *nealles*. Being contained entirely in the b-line first allows the textual proximity necessary for associative meaning and, second, puts a degree of emphasis on the word itself purely due to its metrical isolation. While a simplex could attain similar textual proximity, it would lack both the emphasis on the retainers' physical proximity created by the *hand*– constituent and the general emphasis created by the metrical isolation. Thus, without using compound structures there would be no way to produce the same combination of textual proximity, grammatical and metrical isolation, and semantic emphasis that *handgesteallan* provides. As a result primarily of that compound structure, the associative implications produced by the apposition of *æðelinga bearn* are therefore already present before the variation appears.

Variation, of course, can occur without compound words, since its basic rhetorical form depends only on grammatical parallelism, not word-internal compound structures. Nonetheless, variation without compounds is highly rare, and compounds also produce a form of micro-apposition internally through the "juxtaposing of independent elements, with the reader or audience being left to infer the relationship of the two and their

18 See also Trilling, *Aesthetics of Nostalgia*, 8–10.

19 Robinson, *Appositive Style*, 4 and 84n5, citing BT.

composite meaning."[20] Ultimately, given the frequent collocation of the two features, variation at the lexical and phrasal levels are effectively inseparable from compounds. The standard conception of the relationship between the two features is unilateral: variation is the dominant feature, with Anglo-Saxon authors using compounds simply to create variation.[21] Drout's concept of "feature interlink," however, posits a bilateral connection, in which both features create their own discursive effects that happen to cooperate and resonate with each other.[22] Variation, according to this paradigm, is simply more effective and powerful with compounds than without. One reason must be that compounds act, as it were, as middle men, linking the lexical and phrasal features of variation to the "noun-heavy" metrical preferences of Old English verse.[23] Variation is not intrinsically metrical, as it can occur at any level of discourse, such as that of the word, the phrase, the clause, and even the paragraph. Compounds, so important for the oral-traditional style of Old English verse in so many ways, therefore ground variation in the metrical building blocks of the poetry.[24]

The bilateral relationship of feature interlink, moreover, establishes that compounds remain useful in and of themselves, not simply enabling variation but also enabled by it. More than simply allowing for variation, in other words, the presence of compounds produces rhetorical effects, such as the influencing of narrative pace, on its own. This recognition reintroduces to the analysis the cognitive effects unique to compound words, specifically the demands of processing and constructing their meanings. As shown in chapter 3 above, processing an individual compound word often occurs paradoxically faster than processing a simple word, due to the facilitative links connecting the entries for the individual constituents in the mental lexicon with the compound's whole-word entry. Nonetheless, processing an individual compound in isolation is verifiably different than processing a compound as part of parsing an entire sentence; indeed, experimental data show that the two levels of processing interact, as already suggested by the theory of feature interlink.[25] According to these studies, contextual

20 Robinson, *Appositive Style*, 14.
21 See, for example, Niles, "Compound Diction."
22 Drout, *Tradition and Influence*, 5–6 and 105–10.
23 See Brodeur, *Art of Beowulf*, 7, and Robinson, *Appositive Style*, 17.
24 See the discussion of the roles of compounds in oral-traditional style in chapter 1 above.
25 Morita and Tamaoka, "Semantic Involvement"; Gagné, Spalding, and Gorrie, "Sentential Context"; Brusnighan and Folk, "Combining Contextual and Morphemic Cues"; and Juhasz, "Sentence Context."

information influences the processing even of a well-known, common compound; for example, the competition among possible different relationships between a compound's constituents is influenced by their probability within the larger sentential context.[26] This understanding of the interaction of context and meaning depends on the recognition of two different levels of mental action: processing and parsing.[27] By *processing*, I mean the activation of entries in the mental lexicon and the construction of a relationship between the constituents of a compound. On the other hand, I use *parsing* here to refer to the assemblage of individual words' meanings into grammatical relationships with each other within a larger, sentential meaning. Due to the interaction of these two levels, parsing can force, for example, the re-processing of a polysemous word to disambiguate competing meanings when the sentential context indicates that the less likely meaning must be active.[28] This re-processing should be especially applicable for compound words, given the multiple possible relationships between each compound's constituents. Moreover, a cluster of several compounds occurring in close proximity would cause the processing demands to accumulate and build on one another, which in turn would interfere with the swift parsing of the sentence in which the cluster appears. Thus, the simple presence, in and of itself, of a cluster of compounds can slow narrative pace, and any interaction with devices such as variation or drawn-out description amplify this effect.

An additional factor that becomes particularly germane in discussions of *Beowulf* is that compounds that are unique or rare in the corpus lack the facilitative links that speed the processing of high-frequency, well-known compounds. Unique compounds, presumably newly coined *for the nones*, cannot have lexicalized to any degree, and rare compounds are highly unlikely to have done so.[29] Thus, there are no links between the lexical entries for the individual constituents of these compounds and those of the entire compounds themselves, which would be necessary for their comparatively swift processing. Any reader or listener would have necessarily decomposed rare or unique compounds into their constituents and constructed meanings on the fly, as it were. The processing of unique and rare compounds thus holds

---

26 Gagné, Spalding, and Gorrie, "Sentential Context," 216–17.

27 Several theories of sentence parsing currently compete, since current experimental designs are unable to distinguish perfectly between effects of lexical access and those of syntactic and semantic assessment. See Kennison, "Different Time Courses."

28 See, for example, Hagoort and Brown, "Brain Response to Lexical Ambiguity," 45–80.

29 See the discussion of lexicalization and of the validity of trusting the corpus as it stands, respectively in chapters 2 and 3 above.

no speed advantage over that of monomorphemic words on an individual basis, and in fact, in a sentence context, unfamiliar words can induce momentary pauses for additional assessment, at least in reading.[30] We can therefore conclude that clusters of low-frequency (rare) compound words exacerbate further the delays in parsing compared to clusters of common compounds.[31]

Clusters of compounds, often both producing and produced by variation, should therefore attract special attention, just as they did in the analysis of Wulfstan's homilies in the previous chapter. Given the slowing effects of variation and compounds, such clusters are especially likely to participate in slowing the poem's narrative pace in some manner, even without entirely suspending the text's progress as do Wulfstan's lists. The clusters of compounds in Wulfstan's works were easy to identify, since they so obviously collect in the lists of sins and sinners, and rarely elsewhere. What counts as a cluster of compounds in *Beowulf*, however, is much less clear, since the poem contains such a high number of compounds.[32] With such a large data set, patterns rarely present themselves obviously, and one cannot rely solely on intuition or basic levels of observation. Rather, statistical analysis must underlie any conclusions about the patterns of compound occurrence in *Beowulf*. Indeed, while a passage may initially seem to contain a large number of compounds, that group may not be statistically significant in comparison to the rest of the poem. For example, the description of the Danes' paganism contains more compounds than the basic average predicts:

> Hwilum hie geheton   æt hærgtrafum
> wigweorþunga,   wordum bædon
> þæt him gastbona   geoce gefremede
> wið þeodþreaum.[33]

> Sometimes they offered sacrifices at heathen temples, asked with words that the spirit-slayer would provide help for them against the kingdom's calamity.

This collection of compounds seems to form a significant cluster, and the importance of this moment in the narrative seems to qualify it for rhetorical

30 Chaffin, Morris, and Seely, "Learning New Word Meanings."

31 Not all clusters slow pace equally: a cluster of compounds without significant variation would be less effective at slowing pace than a cluster combined with variation.

32 According to my count, *Beowulf* contains approximately one compound every 2.17 lines, effectively one every other line.

33 Fulk, Bjork, and Niles, *Klaeber's Beowulf*, lines 175–8a.

emphasis, which compounds provide, as discussed in chapter 3 above. Nonetheless, this cluster fails to reach statistical significance in comparison to the pattern of compound occurrence in the poem overall.[34] Of course, one must not follow statistics blindly but rather use this method as a guide for identifying passages that may be important within this particular paradigm of the patterns of compound occurrence. Slavishly following a decontextualized count of compounds can erroneously flag a passage as significant, and each flagged passage must therefore be fully analysed to determine its relevance and the validity of its designation as significant. For this reason, this chapter's analysis of passages with significant clusters of compounds is not simply a mechanical product directed by statistics. Rather, I apply the standards and thresholds put forth above as a hopefully objective means to confirm the statistical importance of compound clusters within their textual contexts and ensuring that I am not simply going with my "gut" in claiming that any given passage has an important cluster of compounds.

Given the links between style and content, one expects clusters of compounds in scenes traditional to poetry, such as descriptions of battles and sea-voyages, a phenomenon found, for example, in the description of Beowulf's return to Geatland, which is presented in the traditional terms of the sea-voyage type-scene.[35] Beyond the preparations for the voyage, the time on the water itself receives fairly lengthy attention:

Gewat him on naca
drefan deop wæter, Dena land ofgeaf.
Þa wæs be mæste merehrægla sum,
segl sale fæst; sundwudu þunede;

34 I calculate the average number of compounds per five lines in *Beowulf* to be 2.30, with a standard deviation of 1.28. Those numbers mean that, on average, any given five-line passage of the poem should contain between 1.02 (one standard deviation below the average) and 3.58 (one standard deviation above the average) compounds. Any passage slightly more than one standard deviation beyond the average may be abnormal, but true statistical significance is generally reserved for two standard deviations beyond the average. By this analysis, a five-line passage in *Beowulf* contains a statistically significant number of compounds only if it contains five or more compounds. The choice to analyse the poem in terms of five-line passages allows for a balanced "resolution" in sample size – neither too small nor too large. For an analogous discussion of sample size, see Drout et al., "Of Dendrogrammatology," 313–14.

35 On type-scenes as elements of oral-traditional literature, see the discussions and notes in chapters 2 and 4 above. For discussions specifically of sea-voyage type-scenes, see Diamond, "Theme as Ornament"; Ramsey, "Sea Voyages in *Beowulf*"; and Foley, *Traditional Oral Epic*, 329–58.

no þær wegflotan wind ofer yðum
siðes getwæfde; sægenga for,
fleat famigheals forð ofer yðe,
bundenstefna ofer brimstreamas,
þæt hie Geata clifu ongitan meahton,
cuþe næssas; ceol up geþrang,
lyftgeswenced on lande stod.[36]

The ship travelled on to stir up the deep water; it left the land of the Danes. Then a sea-garment, a sail, was [fastened] firmly to the mast with rope; the sea-craft creaked; no wind over the waves kept the way-floater from its journey; the sea-goer went forth, floated foamy-necked over the waves, the bound-prowed [ship] over the sea-current, so that they could see the cliffs of the Geats, the known nesses; the keel drove up, the weather-beaten [ship] stood on land.

The scene's opening and closing, three half-lines each, express rather directly the ship's departure and its arrival; both contain variation, but the appositions are fairly straightforward and pose little difficulty in parsing the grammar. The intervening lines, however, present more variation and a cluster of compounds that work together to slow the narrative progress. For example, the predicate for the copulative *wæs* in line 1905 is not completed until the next line with *fæst* [firm], delayed by the compound *merehrægl* [sea-garment] and the variation of *segl* [sail]. Most germane to the current discussion, lines 1905 through 1910 contain a cluster of seven compounds, which, even if the two in line 1910 are ignored to limit the sample to five lines, meets the requirements for significance. The lines already consist largely of description of relatively constant features of the voyage, such as the lack of a headwind, and repetition of the ship's motion, which together provide little narrative advancement. The most salient events of the sea voyage could be dispensed with through the opening and closing alone; the other seven-and-a-half lines are technically unnecessary to convey the bare essentials and thus delay the narration of the ship's arrival. In other words, although the ship is said to make consistent progress, the images themselves are static, and the addition of the compounds weighs them down even further.

36 Fulk, Bjork, and Niles, *Klaeber's Beowulf*, lines 1903b–13.

A situation similar to Beowulf's sea voyage obtains in the lines describing the Geats' first approach to Heorot, already discussed in chapter 3 above in relation to the rhetorical emphasis created by clusters of compounds. That emphasis created by the compounds for war-gear also contributes to a slowing of the narrative pace, this time with a land voyage:

> Stræt was stanfah, stig wisode
> gumum ætgædere. Guðbyrne scan
> heard hondlocen; hringiren scir
> song in searwum. Þa hie to sele furðum
> in hyra gryregeatwum gangan cwomon,
> setton sæmeþe side scyldas,
> rondas regnhearde wið þæs recedes weal;
> bugon þa to bence. Byrnan hringdon,
> guðsearo gumena; garas stodon,
> sæmanna searo samod ætgædere,
> æscholt ufan græg; wæs se irenþreat
> wæpnum gewurþad.[37]

> The street was stone-paved; the path guided the warriors together. The hard, hand-linked battle-byrnie shone, the bright iron-ring of the armour resounded, when they set out first for the hall in their awe-inspiring armour. The sea-weary men set down their wide shields, those exceptionally hard rounds, against the wall of the building; they bent down onto the bench – the byrnies, the warriors' war-gear, rang; the spears stood, the gear of the sea-men gathered together, an ash-grove topped with gray; the armed troop was honoured by the weapons.

Including the eight compounds denoting or describing war-gear, this passage contains eleven compounds in total in its eleven-and-a-half lines. Even adjusting for comparison to the statistics for five-line samples, this cluster remains significant. The repetition created by the variation, which again restrains the narrative from moving to the next event in "story time," combines with the linguistic weight of the compounds to create a significant narrative pause. One major element contributing to the linguistic weight of this cluster of compounds in particular is the frequency of the compounds: as noted in chapter 3, almost all of them are unique, and the rest are rare

37 Fulk, Bjork, and Niles, *Klaeber's Beowulf*, lines 320–31a.

throughout the corpus.[38] These compounds thus make the greatest cognitive demands possible on the reader/listener, requiring decomposition into constituents in processing and complicating the parsing of the passage as a whole. Thus again, the compounds contribute importantly to the dilatation of the narrative speed beyond simply participating in variation.

The narrative utility for slowing the pace in these two passages surfaces in several ways. First of all, the presence of a cluster of compounds fulfils the stylistic expectations produced by the connections between type-scene and diction: the narration of a sea journey "should" contain a large number of compounds. Beyond motivations purely of style, an additional need for a slow pace in narrating the sea voyage seems fairly clear: the voyage would lose all sense of consequence otherwise. Making only the opening and closing few half-lines the entirety of the journey's narration would minimize the supposed duration of the actual journey. The slow narrative pace on one level comprises an attempt to represent story time somewhat realistically in narrative time. While true realism would be impossible, the slow narration at least gestures at the actual duration of the journey. A short description of the journey would also minimize the general danger of taking to the water and Beowulf's surmounting of an obstacle in coming to Hrothgar's aid. The slow pace retains those elements, thus building up Beowulf's deeds and character.

In the Geats' approach to Heorot, the linguistic weight of compound structures can emphasize the Geats' war-gear all by itself, as discussed in chapter 3 above, but the manipulation of the passage's narrative pace plays into that emphasis as well. The warriors do indeed reach Heorot and begin to set aside their weapons, but, in a sense, they have not truly completed their journey, since they aim for an audience with Hrothgar, not simply arrival outside his hall. More importantly, the focus on war-gear persists throughout the passage, and the achievement of narrative progress is almost hidden by it: the byrnies continue to ring after their arrival, just as they did on the approach. The moments of and after arrival effectively continue the most salient features of the approach, in that the foci of description and emphasis remain the same. The repetition of the ringing of the byrnies also continues the invocation of the traditional language of the approach-to-battle type-scene, retaining at the end of the passage the same mood with

38 Outside of *Beowulf*, *guðsearo* [war-gear] appears only in *Andreas*, *æscholt* [ash-grove (spear)] in *Battle of Maldon*, and *guðbil* [war sword] in *Waldere B*. See the *DOEC*.

which it began.[39] The passage thus draws out this moment of ambiguous approach, subtly playing up the suggestion of imminent violence through a slower-than-necessary description. Without this extension of narrative time focusing on the war-gear, that suggestion would likely fall flat. A brief account of the Geats' journey to Heorot would not allow for the development of ambiguity for two reasons. First, mechanically, approach-to-battle type-scenes commonly involve repetition and slow narrative progress; a passing reference to war-gear – in a poem replete with such references – would not have successfully invoked the type-scene. Second, without the space (or perhaps time) provided by the slow narrative progress, an audience would pragmatically have difficulty noting the ambiguity since one event would pass quickly to another without a chance to develop ambiguous connotations.

Violence in some way also features in all of the other passages in *Beowulf* that contain the most significant clusters of compounds. From the standpoint of emphasis, such clustering makes good sense: in a poem largely about violence, rhetorical strategies for creating emphasis should naturally converge on moments of important violence. Also naturally, several of these passages involve Grendel, either as aggressor or victim. First is Hrothgar's description of life during Grendel's attacks:

"Ful oft gebeotedon beore druncne
ofer ealowæge oretmecgas
þæt hie in beorsele bidan woldon
Grendles guþe mid gryrum ecga.
Đonne wæs þeos medoheal on morgentid,
drihtsele dreorfah þonne dæg lixte,
eal bencþelu blode bestymed,
heall heorudreore; ahte ic holdra þy læs,
deorre duguðe, þe þa deað fornam.
Site nu to symle ond onsæl meoto,
sigehreð secgum, swa þin sefa hwette."[40]

"Very often did warriors, having taken beer, vow over the ale-cup that they would wait in the beer-hall with the terror of swords for Grendel's attack.

39 See the full discussion of this passage as an approach-to-battle type-scene in chapter 3 above.
40 Fulk, Bjork, and Niles, *Klaeber's Beowulf*, lines 480–90.

Then, in the morning, this mead-hall, this lordly house, was stained with gore; when daylight shone, all the bench-planks, the hall, were drenched with blood, battle-gore; I had thus fewer loyal men, valued veterans, whom death had taken. Now sit down to the feast and reveal your thoughts, your glory of victory, to the men, as your mind urges."

The compounds in this passage emphasize the bloody aftermath of Grendel's nightly aggression, reiterating several times the spray of blood settling over the entire hall. Combining masterfully with the instances of variation, the compounds impede swift progress through the description. For example, the oscillations between the nominatives (*medoheal*, *drihtsele*, *bencþelu*) and the temporal phrases ("on morgentid" and "þonne dæg lixte") restrain the grammar from fully resolving immediately. While *dreorfah* could be taken as a predicate adjective completing *wæs* as a copulative in line 485, *wæs* ultimately resolves as an auxiliary paired with *bestymed*. That delayed resolution also slows down the narrative pace, since the full grammatical situation becomes clear very slowly. In this slow context, the compounds and instances of variation intervening between *wæs* and *bestymed* rhetorically produce a slow-motion narrative forcing the audience to linger over the aftermath of Grendel's violent attack.

Grendel's engagement with Beowulf also merits a significant cluster of compounds:

Þæt wæs geocor sið
þæt se hearmscaþa to Heorute ateah.
Dryhtsele dynede; Denum eallum wearð,
ceasterbuendum, cenra gehwylcum,
eorlum ealuscerwen. Yrre wæron begen,
reþe renweardas. Reced hlynsode.
Þa wæs wundor micel þæt se winsele
wiðhæfde heaþodeorum, þæt he on hrusan ne feol,
fæger foldbold; ac he þæs fæste wæs
innan ond utan irenbendum
searoþoncum besmiþod.[41]

That was a sad journey that the malicious enemy took to Heorot. The lord-hall resounded; grave terror befell all the Danes, the fortress-dwellers, each

41 Fulk, Bjork, and Niles, *Klaeber's Beowulf*, lines 765b–75a.

> of the keen ones, the earls. Both were enraged, the fierce house-guards. The hall reverberated. It was a great wonder then that the wine-hall withstood the battle-beasts, that it did not crumble to the ground, the beautiful building; but it was so firmly fastened skilfully inside and out with iron fetters.

This passage marks the beginning of the end, as it were, for Grendel, with the admission that this attack was in fact sad (*geocor*) for him, unlike all his previous visits. It also marks the beginning of the fight's crescendo. The opening lines narrating the scene set up Grendel's initiation of the night's hostilities, Beowulf's assessment of his adversary, and the first direct clash between the two. Immediately before this passage, the poem recounts Grendel's reaction to finally encountering a worthy foe, but this passage moves the narration to the next level, describing the fight at its height. Finally, after Beowulf initially seeming slow to commit to the fight, both combatants are equally engaged, as expressed by grouping the two together in "Yrre wæron begen" [Both were enraged] and referring to both as *renweardas* [house-guards]. Moreover, the violent clash reaches such a pitch that it threatens the hall itself and strikes fear into the observers.

Several rhetorical features cooperate to keep the narration in this passage lingering on this moment. Variation leads to three different ways of re-expressing the watching Danes: "ceasterbuendum" [fortress-dwellers], "cenra gehwylcum" [each of the keen ones], and "eorlum" [earls]. The fact of the hall producing sound like a musical instrument is repeated, with it first resounding ("dynede") and then reverberating ("hlynsode") a few lines later. Of course, a large number of compounds fill the lines as well, with nine compounds appearing in the final ten of the quotation's eleven lines. None of these compounds occur commonly in the extant corpus, and only one can be considered even uncommon in the corpus; in fact, seven of the nine are unique to *Beowulf*, of which five are even *hapax legomena*.[42] These compounds again impose the maximum possible cognitive demands on the audience. The inherent effects created by the compound structures and the rarity of these particular words interlace with the other narrative techniques to extend the fight's crescendo and keep the audience in that moment of intensification.

42 The seven are *hearmscaþa*, *dryhtsele*, *ceasterbuendum*, *ealuscerwen*, *renweardas*, *heaþodeorum*, and *foldbold*; only *drihtsele* and *heaþodeor* occur elsewhere in the poem.

The next passage containing a significant cluster of compounds arrives quickly, during the climax of the fight:

Licsar gebad
atol æglæca; him on eaxle wearð
syndolh sweotol, seonowe onsprungon,
burston banlocan. Beowulfe wearð
guðhreð gyfeþe. Scolde Grendel þonan
feorhseoc fleon under fenhleoðu,
secean wynleas wic; wiste þe geornor
þæt his aldres wæs ende gegongen,
dogera dægrim.[43]

The terrible combatant suffered a body-wound; a clear, terrible injury appeared on his shoulder, sinews snapped asunder, joints burst. War-glory was granted to Beowulf. Grendel was forced to flee, mortally wounded, from there under the fen-slope, to seek the joyless dwelling; he knew very clearly that the end of his life had arrived, the final count of his days.

Here Beowulf ends Grendel's reign of terror by mortally wounding him, and the poem matches the narrative importance of this moment with another rhetorical concatenation. Variation again features prominently with, for example, several different expressions of Grendel's wound: he endures a body-wound, a terrible injury appears, sinews snap, and joints burst. Without advancing the action in any notable way, the passage also oscillates from Grendel's perspective to Beowulf's and back to Grendel's, creating the impression of narrative change without allowing any true progression. The compounds in this passage, seven in the sixteen half-lines, again exceed the theshold for statistical significance and add their weight as well.[44] *Hapax legomena* make up a smaller proportion of this cluster than the one above, but they nonetheless create cognitive demands as did those in the passage from earlier in the fight.[45] As a result of these features

43 Fulk, Bjork, and Niles, *Klaeber's Beowulf*, lines 815b–23a.

44 I prefer to err on the side of caution and omit *æglæca* [fierce opponent] as a compound here, because the derivation of the *æg-* component is unclear and the component denoting "opponent" seems not to occur independently; see BT and *DOE*, s.v. *æglæca* and *aglæca*.

45 The *hapax legomena* in this passage are *syndolh*, *guðhreð*, *feorhseoc*, and *fenhleoðu*.

collecting together, the eight line passage produces little narrative movement after its first line. While details and alternative perspectives enter the text, the basic event expressed by "Licsar gebad" remains the only real event of the passage.

The violence of Grendel's wound is in some ways an apex of *Beowulf*, one of the most important and memorable moments in the entire poem, and as such it certainly seems fitting that it should receive heightened treatment stylistically. Violence, of course, is central to *Beowulf*, with actual violence or the threat of it suffusing the text. Slowing the pace at particularly important moments of actual or possible violence emphasizes them by expanding their narrative presence. That expansion fits well with an interpretation of the poem as a celebration of the heroic past, since it gives violence great prominence within the text. Peter Baker argues that violence plays an integral role in the culture depicted in *Beowulf* as part of what he terms "the Economy of Honour," which is "organized around the possession of treasure as a sign of one's prowess in battle and the overlapping and conventional roles of various participants in this system."[46] In Baker's view, violence is not indicative of the breakdown of *Beowulf*'s societies but rather is necessary for their correct functioning: "Violence is a social practice, and every violent act is a social transaction."[47] Without acts of violence, the economy of exchange would break down, leading to Baker's deeper conclusion that violence in *Beowulf* is in fact positive and beneficial, with any negative interpretations of it being the product of the application of anachronous, modern aversion.[48] Celebration of violence in *Beowulf*, in this paradigm, is thus a celebration of the culture in general and a normal trope in vernacular, medieval texts.

Slow narrative pace initially seems to support this celebration by allowing an audience more time to savour the violence, but in fact it undercuts the celebration of violence qua violence. A useful analogue for understanding the effect of slow-motion narrative in *Beowulf* is the employment of slow motion in film, a visual form of narrative but a narrative nonetheless. A fight scene in a film – constructed and therefore narrated through various choices in choreography, framing, and editing – can evoke in its audience echoes of the physical moves it sees on screen, a kind of "muscular

46 Baker, *Honour, Exchange and Violence*, 240.
47 Baker, *Honour, Exchange and Violence*, 7.
48 Baker, *Honour, Exchange and Violence*, 201–2.

sympathy."[49] Through this "kinesthetic imagination,"[50] an audience member experiences in miniature a reproduction of what he or she sees acted out and thereby can experience a type of catharsis. Slow-motion effects, however, reduce any opportunities for "muscular sympathy," since the supposed reality of the depicted movements is revealed as the construct it truly is. The seeming verisimilitude of film is shattered by the departure from "real time" movement, calling attention to the medium interposed between the audience and the depicted events and thus to the style of the narrative itself.[51] An extreme example of this shattering is the "bullet time" special effect, first used in the 1999 film *The Matrix*. Mainly in the movie's fight scenes, the pace of action slows almost to a stop, with the camera seeming to sweep around the antagonists and bullets nearly frozen in mid-air (hence the "bullet time" moniker). As a result, fights become less violent clashes than stylized dances that lose a good deal of the visceral, physical impact, pushing the audience to focus on the constructedness and performance of the moments, both within the narrative as a representation of the movie's premise and extradiegetically as a reminder of the fact that it is a movie and not reality.[52] Sam Peckinpah's scenes of violence produce a similar effect, interspersing "normal" motion with slow-motion effects:

> Peckinpah incorporated the brief slow-motion interlude into his more complex montage sequences because the dynamic oscillation between normal and decelerated time demands a continuing perceptual reorientation from viewers. He apparently hoped the stylistic artifice would alternately immerse viewers in the spectacle on screen and then realign their perspective through the nonrealistic slow-motion insertions. These perceptual realignments he hoped would re-establish a new, less complacent and passive relationship between viewers and the screen spectacle, would, as he put it, wake viewers up to what violence is really all about.[53]

---

49 Martin, *Modern Dance*, 12. This point is discussed with further application to film in Bordwell, "Aesthetics in Action"; Anderson, "Kinesthesia in Martial Arts Films"; and Anderson, "Violent Dances."

50 Roach, *Cities of the Dead*, 26–7.

51 Sontag, "Imagination of Disaster"; Prince, *Savage Cinema*, especially 62–7; Bruder, "Aestheticizing Violence"; and Jung, *Narrating Violence*, especially 96–7.

52 In *The Matrix*, the "bullet time" effect dramatizes the conceit that human experience is a virtual-reality construct and that the laws of physics are therefore highly manipulable by certain characters.

53 Prince, *Savage Cinema*, 66.

Peckinpah used slow-motion to shock viewers out of complacent enjoyment of violent spectacles and, by making them notice the artificiality of the montage, push them to attend to the reality of violence and pain in life rather than in the constructed narrative. Slow-motion representations of violence in film, then, deny the audience visceral pleasure and instead emphasize the abstract interpretations – and sometimes the problems – of violence.

While these arguments on the effect of slow motion come from film theory, the basic framework for understanding narrative pace in film remains Genette's *Narrative Discourse*.[54] Especially given Genette's concern to apply his theories to both the aural and visual consumption of verbal narrative, as discussed above, the differences between visual and verbal discourses are less problematic when examining pace. One can analyse both film and text broadly as narrative by attending specifically to the effects created by varying the pace of the presentation of events, whether visually or verbally. In both mediums, slow motion calls attention to the form and style. The passages from *Beowulf* discussed above amass rhetorical effects as part of slowing narrative pace, filling lines not with plot advancement but with description, variation, compound words, etc. This practice produces an effect perfectly analagous to Peckinpah's slow-motion interludes: the artificiality and constructedness of the poetic discourse overshadows or at least rivals the actual events and interrupts any appearance of verisimilitude. Indeed, the alternation in pace in *Beowulf* parallels those in Peckinpah's montages. For example, to begin his final raid of Heorot, Grendel devours a warrior with great speed, and the narration of that event moves swiftly. Immediately afterward, however, comes the very slow-paced narrations of the fight's crescendo and climax, discussed above. That juxtaposition achieves a reorientation similar to that of Peckinpah's montages, demonstrating a fundamental similarity between verbal and visual art on a narrative level. Applying this understanding of slow motion to *Beowulf* then problematizes our interpretation of the passages discussed above. Within Baker's framework of violence as a positive element in the "Economy of Honour," the narration of fights should be to a large degree celebratory. The slow narrative pace nonetheless acts against any such celebratory effect by preventing any savouring of the violence. The form and style of the poem assert themselves and distract from the violence itself.

---

54 Gunning, "Narrative Discourse," discusses the debt to Genette explicitly and in detail.

Beyond the denial of pleasure in the slow-motion passages, the effect of that distraction remains unclear in Baker's framework, in part because he avoids situating *Beowulf* in any specific cultural context.[55] That move is problematic, since so much of a narrative's meaning stems from its interaction with its contexts. At the very least, form – as a conception of genre – is historically determined, being produced over time and as a product of cultural influences.[56] For example, the slow-motion effects in *The Matrix* display the post-modern concern for the constructedness of reality prevalent around the turn of the millenium, while those in Peckinpah's films react to an apparent numbing of the population to acts of violence in the 1960s and 1970s. The styles of these works produce meaning through necessary and unavoidable conversation with their respective milieux, and those meanings are different because of their different contexts. Thus, although Old English poetic form was crafted to seem timeless,[57] that form is necessarily historically contingent because the same stylistic features will be interpretted differently in different times and contexts. The effects of the slow-motion scenes in *Beowulf* then can only be fully understood when the poem is placed within a particular context.

Contextualizing *Beowulf*, of course, is a fraught and dangerous pursuit. Scholars have posited various dates for the poem's composition spanning the entire Anglo-Saxon period.[58] Recent work, drawing on several different elements and methodologies, supports an early date for the composition of the poem, i.e., at least before 900, although those claims have not gone uncontested.[59] Nonetheless, regardless of the accuracy of any of the claims for *Beowulf*'s date of original composition, it would be difficult to contextualize the poem in any milieu other than that of its surviving

55 Baker, *Honour, Exchange and Violence*, 33–4.

56 See Cohen, "History and Genre," and Cohen, Introduction, in *Shakespeare and Historical Formalism*, especially 14–16.

57 Tyler, *Old English Poetics*, 2.

58 For several of the most prominent arguments put forward before 2000, see Chase, *The Dating of "Beowulf*," and Bjork and Obermeier, "Date, Provenance, Author, Audiences," 13–34.

59 Lapidge, "Archetype of *Beowulf*," posits a written form of the poem before 800; Fulk, "On Argumentation in Old English Philology," reiterates a metrical argument for an early date; and Davis, "An Ethnic Dating of *Beowulf*," supports a date of copying, if not composition, in the 890s. Find responses to these early daters in Stanley, "Paleographical and Textual Deep Water"; Frank, "A Scandal in Toronto"; and the newest argument for a very late date of composition in Damico, *Beowulf and the Grendel-kin*. By no means do these represent the full array of recent publications on the date of *Beowulf*.

manuscript copy. The poem may well have existed in some form before the year 700, but we are unlikely to be able to reconstruct that form. Perhaps, using paleographic patterns to identify additions to the text, certain passages could be excised from the poem's current form in an attempt to determine what the earlier form contained. Nonetheless, there would be no way to verify the accuracy of that reconstruction, especially considering the scribal practice of altering Old English poetry during copying.[60] Sadly, the only solid context that we currently have is that of the poem's copying into London, British Library, Cotton Vitellius A. xv.[61] We can therefore analyse *Beowulf* in terms of its resonances in early-eleventh century England, even while acknowledging the poem's much earlier original composition.[62] As with the similar arguments in the chapters above, contextualization based on the time of copying, limited though it may be, can nonetheless be extremely useful, especially since we have much more documentation from later periods of Anglo-Saxon England than earlier ones.

Especially germane to the present discussion, the early-eleventh century witnessed a significant change in Anglo-Saxon conceptions of violence.[63] As Katherine O'Brien O'Keeffe demonstrates, between c. 970 and 1035 the meaning of mutilation and the results of violence changed in Anglo-Saxon England.[64] Rather than demonstrating the overwhelming power of a ruler as it had in prior periods, violence came to produce knowledge of an individual's guilt or innocence:

> Unlike Foucault's liturgy of punishment elaborated in *Discipline and Punish*, where the spectacle resides in the community's watching the criminal body being destroyed and thus witnessing both the docility of the body and

60 See O'Brien O'Keeffe, *Visible Song*, and Liuzza, "On the Dating of *Beowulf*"; see the response to Liuzza's claims in Fulk, "On Argumentation in Old English Philology."

61 Kiernan, *"Beowulf" and the Beowulf Manuscript*, argues that the poem was composed as it was copied. I do not subscribe to that point of view.

62 On the date of Cotton Vitellius A.xv, see Ker, *Catalogue*, no. 216; Dumville, "Beowulf Come Lately"; Gneuss, *Handlist of Anglo-Saxon Manuscripts*, no. 399; Fulk, Bjork, and Niles, *Klaeber's Beowulf*, xxvii and clxii; and Gneuss and Lapidge, *Anglo-Saxon Manuscripts*, no. 399. Attempting to reconcile the mostly positive treatment of the Danes in *Beowulf* with the Danish attacks during this time is beyond the scope of this discussion.

63 For a reading analogous to mine in terms of the connection between violence, war-gear, and changes in royal succession, see Biggs, "*Beowulf* and Some Fictions," and Biggs, "Politics of Succession in *Beowulf*."

64 O'Brien O'Keeffe, "Body and Law."

> the prince's power, the spectacle, as Wulfstan defines it, resides in the show of the altered body itself. Such spectacle is designed to produce *post factum* knowledge about the body of the criminal as well as remind the onlooker of the king's punishment and his power. As Wulfstan implies, sight of those mutilations reveals all that need be known about the bodies that suffered it. They are marked, punished, guilty.[65]

Violence produces wounds and mutilation, which acted for Anglo-Saxons around the year 1000 as evidence of guilt, not simply punishment for that guilt. This transformation of violence from a source of power in and of itself to a means of producing evidence problematizes violence in reality and in texts from the period. For example, O'Brien O'Keeffe finds outrage at undeserved violent mutilation in the entry in the *Anglo-Saxon Chronicle* C-text for 1036, which describes the murder of Alfred ætheling and the subsequent mutilation of his men. The text decries that mutilation because it acts as evidence of their guilt, which the *Chronicle* denies.[66] The text's outrage demonstrates that, in the new understanding of violence, the punishment implies a spiritual guilt in a way that it would not have a century earlier.

A similar but subtler unease with violence appears in *Beowulf*, when read through this lens. For example, Hrothgar's description of the aftermath of Grendel's attack, discussed above, is problematic in that the slaughtered warriors would not have "deserved" their fate. They did nothing overtly aggressive to arouse Grendel's ire, and they in fact followed the social norms of their world by drinking and boasting of their dedication to defending their lord and his hall. Grendel's initial attack on Heorot may have been a reaction to human behaviour, but the poem gives no explanation for his subsequent, sustained depredations and suggests no guilt on the part of the Danes. Their deaths, then, especially combined with the impossibility of acquiring compensation from Grendel, represent challenges to the entire heroic social structure. The interest in the propriety of the warriors' actions before battle and the dwelling on the bloody aftermath reveal unease over Grendel's violence. Lingering over the splattered blood of one's thanes is no celebration. This situation, of course, is the crux of the first third of *Beowulf*, which celebrates the imagined society of Germanic pre-history and casts Grendel as the foil that threatens to destabilize the entire system.

---

65 O'Brien O'Keeffe, "Body and Law," 228.

66 O'Brien O'Keeffe, "Body and Law," 214–15.

Especially if *meoto* indeed refers to mead in the passage,[67] perhaps at least punningly implying it, the final two lines are not simply a jarring change of topic: "Site nu to symle ond onsæl meoto, / sigehreð secgum, swa þin sefa hwette" [Now sit down to the feast and reveal your thoughts, your glory of victory, to the men, as your mind urges].[68] Rather, these lines produce one of the many appositional juxtapositions so important to the poem, creating a connection between, on the one hand, the now-dead retainers drinking beer before their slaughter and, on the other hand, Beowulf about to sit down, drink, and boast in the same manner. The violence thus becomes doubly problematic. Violent ends befit neither the earlier Danes nor the great hero Beowulf but would instead mark them as the criminals, rather than Grendel. The possibility that Beowulf would suffer the same gory fate and thereby be metaphorically branded as spiritually guilty must have discomfited the poem's early-eleventh century audience.

This unease appears in the other passages discussed above as well, most easily discernable in the poem's interest in differing perspectives and especially in the point of view of victims.[69] When the meadhall resounds in reaction to Beowulf and Grendel's fight, the attention to Heorot distracts from the visceral details of that fight. The hall's sounds in one sense provide the noise associated with the traditional diction of battle scenes, but they also abstract the narration from the physical combat, allowing the audience for a moment to view the clash from a distant perspective. The move briefly spares the audience from the blood. This change is analogous to Peckinpah's jump cuts between normal- and slow-motion footage, which again undercut the physicality of the moment. The manipulation of pace thus removes the audience from the physicality of the violence and forces a confrontation with the meaning of that violence in abstract, possibly spiritual terms. Nonetheless, *Beowulf*'s audience is not ultimately shielded from witnessing Grendel's wound: the poem quickly focalizes through Grendel's perspective,[70] noting that he must flee mortally wounded and knowing that the end of his life had arrived. While Beowulf's triumph receives a moment of celebration ("Beowulfe wearð / guðhreð gyfeþe" [War-glory was granted to Beowulf]),[71] much more attention is given to

67 Fulk, Bjork, and Niles, *Klaeber's Beowulf*, 147–8, commentary to lines 489bff.

68 Fulk, Bjork, and Niles, *Klaeber's Beowulf*, lines 489–90.

69 See Lapidge, "*Beowulf* and Perception," and Orchard, *Critical Companion*, 169–202.

70 On focalization, see Genette, *Narrative Discourse*, 185–98.

71 Fulk, Bjork, and Niles, *Klaeber's Beowulf*, lines 818b–19a.

Grendel's state of mind. The loser and victim hold more interest for the poem, undercutting that celebration of Beowulf's victory. This attention fits well with, for example, the prominent place given to Hildeburh's suffering in the midst of the Danes' own celebration of Grendel's defeat.[72] Routinely, joy at the outcome of violence is marred and problematized by attention on the victim.

This understanding of violence, arising from the style of its narration, complicates the entire poem. If, as Baker argues, Beowulf's victory over the dragon is a positive result in the Economy of Honour, why then do its dire consequences dominate the rest of the poem? Why do mourning and impending doom fill the subsequent several hundred lines? The Economy of Honour certainly explains much of the poem's presentation of violence, but not all; the positive, celebratory view of violence appears at points in the poem, but it is not alone. Given the effect of clustered compounds in passages narrating moments of important violence, that celebratory view is undercut by slow-motion narration that forces an ultimately negative reckoning of the meaning and results of violence. *Beowulf*, unsurprisingly, is thus not simple; it is not one-sided in its presentation of violence. Rather than allow a dualistic, zero-sum-game view of violence, the poem incorporates both seemingly irreconcilable views of violence: it is both positive and negative. The poem clearly displays a desire for the supposed simplicity of the past, when men performed violent, heroic acts as beneficial elements of society, but the poem also recognizes how dangerous that paradigm is, both in a Christian context of sin and guilt and also in a simply human context, wherein the loss of a powerful king leads to his people's destruction. Perhaps this confliction partially explains the motivation for copying *Beowulf* into Cotton Vitellius A. xv: the poem exhibits the same concern over the changing meaning of violence as found in the 1036 entry in the *Chronicle* C-text. The poem's conflicted attitude toward violence, discernible especially in its deployment of clusters of compound words, resonates in important ways with the early-eleventh century. *Beowulf* thus demonstrates the power of compound words not just to fulfil traditional stylistic expectations but also to subtly affect the meaning of a text and connect to a specific cultural context, showing again that compounds are one of the most flexible and important linguistic features of Old English literature within Anglo-Saxon theories of vernacular verbal art.

72 See Orchard, *Critical Companion*, 179–83.

7 Conclusion: Ubi Est Ælfric?

This book began with Ælfric and comments from his bilingual grammar of Latin, but he has been absent – perhaps notably – since then. His absence has not resulted from exclusion but rather necessity: Ælfric simply uses few compound words. Given his awareness of the unique linguistic nature of compounds demonstrated in the *Grammar*, Ælfric's homilies might seem particularly well positioned to provide evidence of the centrality of compound words in Old English literature and theories of verbal art. The avoidance of compounds becomes all the more remarkable in light of the recognition of the poetic – or at least alliterative and rhythmical – nature of Ælfric's vernacular works and the "poetic" flavour of many compounds. Nonetheless, the joinings made possible by compounds and discussed in the previous chapters seem to have held little interest for Ælfric. That disinterest stems most immediately from Ælfric's twin focus instead on clarity and on incorporating Anglo-Saxon England within the historically transcendent Church – the purportedly atemporal traditions and beliefs of Christianity as an institution abstracted from specific cultural contexts. A nuanced understanding of these causes, however, ultimately reveals the fundamental significance of compound words as primary sites of linguistic-literary-cultural joinings in the Anglo-Saxon theory of vernacular verbal art posited and applied throughout this book.

Ælfric's vernacular style is not an unchanging monolith.[1] He evidently developed his unique alliterative, rhythmical style later in his career, using it in some narratives and conclusions in the second series of the *Catholic Homilies* and then adopting it as his standard in the *Lives of Saints* and later writings.[2] The

1 See, however, Corona, "Ælfric's (Un)Changing Style."

2 Clemoes, "Chronology of Ælfric's Works," 222–3, and Godden, *Introduction*, xxxvi–xxxvii.

exact character of that later style remains somewhat under debate, since, after early scholars pointed to discontinuities between it and Old English poetic practices,[3] some recent scholars have championed its various poetic features,[4] but its non-poetic features still retain attention.[5] While the differences between Ælfric's rhythms and those of classical Old English poetry rightly draw the most attention in this debate, Ælfric's lexicon also features prominently, since he rarely employs poetic vocabulary.[6] Compounds, frequently recognized as a fixture of Old English poetic diction, therefore comprise one element that could shed light on Ælfric's move from his early, non-rhythmical style to his later, perhaps poetic practices. To assess Ælfric's use of compounds, I present here a brief analysis of representative texts for each style: an early sermon for a midlent Sunday from the first series of the *Catholic Homilies* (*CH* I.12) does not employ the rhythmical style; the adaptation of Bede's metrical *Vita Cuthberti* (*CH* II.10), it has been argued, may contain some poetic diction as a result of its source; a homily for a midlent Sunday from the second series of *Catholic Homilies* (*CH* II.12) employs the style in its second half; and the life of Eugenia (*LS* 2) displays the style throughout.[7]

First of all, no overtly poetic compounds – that is, compounds that solely or almost solely appear in metrical texts – appear in any of the four homilies, not even *CH* II.10, the adaptation of the metrical *Vita Cuthberti*. *CH* II.10 may contain some other elements of poetic diction, but the absence specifically of poetic compounds suggests that Ælfric did not want to create a hybrid discourse in terms of lexicon, as discussed in chapter 4 above. Some of the compounds occur almost solely in Ælfric's texts, but they occur very frequently within several of his homilies or are related to other words that occur commonly.[8] Ælfric is thus not inventing new compounds in the way Wulfstan does with the *þeod–* compounds discussed in chapter 3 above, although *CH* II.10 does contain some rare prose words.[9] Most of the less common compounds are simply derivatives

3 Pope, *Homilies of Ælfric*, 1:105–36, and Clemoes, "Ælfric," 203.

4 Bredehoft, *Early English Metre*, 70–98, and Beechy, *Poetics of Old English*, 31–8.

5 Mitchell, "Relation between Old English Alliterative Verse." See also Momma, *Composition of Old English Poetry*, 12–14.

6 Godden, *Introduction*, xxxvii, and Mitchell, "Relation between Old English Alliterative Verse," 350–1.

7 Godden, *Introduction*, xxxvi–xxxvii.

8 For example, *uðwitegung* [philosophy] is unique to Ælfric's writings, but *uðwita* [philosopher] is not. See the *DOEC*.

9 For example, *cyfesboren* [base-born] and *holdrædene* [loyalty]. I find one *hapax legomenon*, *nedbricum* [requirement]. See the *DOEC*.

of other, common compounds.[10] Lastly, I find no difference in the presence of compounds between the rhythmical and non-rhythmical sections: comparatively very few compounds appear in either type of section, demonstrating that at no point did they play a significant role in Ælfric's diction. Regardless of the fact that Ælfric changed and honed his style over time, he evidently never changed his general avoidance of compound words.

Ælfric's avoidance of compounds initially seems to comprise a reaction against the difficult lexicon of so-called hermeneutic Latin, the dominant Latin style of his contemporaries in tenth-century Winchester. The defining element of this style is the employment of elevated or poetic registers even in prose, including notably difficult vocabulary but also certain features of syntax, rhyme, and rhythm.[11] Ælfric's prose seems to be an ill fit with this style,[12] but, as I argue elsewhere, Ælfric in fact falls in line with the fundamental strategy of hermeneutic Latin, if not its specific tactics, with his attention to rhythm and metre in otherwise prose compositions.[13] Ælfric himself identifies metre as the feature distinguishing poetry from prose, and Bede characterizes rhythmic verse as analagous to quantitative metrical verse.[14] These two assertions lay the groundwork for an application of rhythmic metre – or at least patterns reminiscent of rhythmic metre – as a poetic element in prose.[15] The milieu in reformed Winchester would have further encouraged a focus on rhythm and metre, given Wulfstan Cantor's mastery of Latin quantitative metre,[16] Lantfred's interest in *cursus*

10 For example, *foreðingere* [intercessor] is uncommon, but *foreðingian* [to intercede] is not; similarly with *wacmodnys* [moral weakness] and *wacmod* [morally weak]. See the *DOEC*.

11 See Winterbottom, "Style of Æthelweard"; Lapidge, "Hermeneutic Style"; Lapidge, "Poeticism"; Stephenson, "Ælfric of Eynsham and Hermeneutic Latin," 117–24; and Stephenson, "Scapegoating the Secular Clergy," 107–12.

12 Lapidge, "Hermeneutic Style," 139; Jones, "*Meatim sed et rustica*"; and Stephenson, "Ælfric of Eynsham and Hermeneutic Latin." See also Stephenson, *Politics of Language*.

13 Davis-Secord, "Sequences and Intellectual Identity."

14 Zupitza, *Ælfrics Grammatik*, 295–6, and Kendall, *De arte metrica*, in *Bedae Venerabilis Opera, Pars I*, 138.

15 On the possibility of Ælfric importing Latin style into Old English, see Gerould, "Abbot Ælfric's Rhythmic Prose"; Bethurum, "Form of Ælfric's *Lives of Saints*"; Pope, *Homilies of Ælfric*, 1:108–12; and Nichols, "Ælfric and the Brief Style," 10–12.

16 Lapidge, *Cult of St Swithun*, 343–64; specifically, Lapidge comments that Wulfstan Cantor was "a Latin poet of outstanding calibre whose verse bears comparison with that of any early medieval Latin poet or even, in some small ways, with the poets of classical antiquity" (364).

(i.e., the patterns of stressed and unstressed syllables ending a clause or sentence),[17] and the intertwining of melody and rhythm in many sequences in the Winchester Tropers.[18] Ælfric's rhythmical style, with its resonances of poetic metre, fits this pattern well and thus makes good sense as consonant with the interest in "poeticizing" prose texts that is characteristic of tenth-century Winchester.

Ælfric's interest in joining prose and poetry on the rhythmic level then makes all the more striking his avoidance of compound words, since, as discussed in chapters 2 and 4 above, they can easily and powerfully invoke poetic discourse in Old English literature. His careful exclusion of compounds must therefore instead be a product of his insistence on clarity. In his Latin prefaces, Ælfric discusses his rhetorical approach, describing his desire to write "non garrula verbositate aut ignotis sermonibus, sed puris et apertis verbis" [not with garrulous verbosity or unknown diction, but with unadorned and plain words].[19] He cultivated an "unadorned and plain" vocabulary in both Latin and Old English in order to avoid losing his lay and less-educated audiences.[20] Keeping his audience engaged was essential in preventing misinterpretation, which could lead to misunderstanding the Bible and even heresy, both of which Ælfric greatly feared.[21] The multiple levels of meaning – *lichamlice* [literal] and *gastlice* [spiritual] – that Ælfric finds in scripture require careful interpretation without the interference of confusing or showy vocabulary.[22] Thus, Ælfric reveals an interest specifically in vocabulary as either a source of confusion or a means of promoting clarity.

Compound words interfere with clarity. As demonstrated in chapters 2 and 3 above, the semantic precision made possible by compound structure was not their most valuable characteristic for Anglo-Saxon authors. Rather, the cognitive weight and rhetorical emphasis afforded by that structure, which comes from the indeterminancy of a compound's meaning, are by

17 Lapidge, *Cult of St Swithun*, 224–32, analyses Lantfred's prose style in detail.

18 Davis-Secord, "Sequences and Intellectual Identity." The Winchester Tropers are Cambridge, Corpus Christi College, 473, and Oxford, Bodleian Library, Bodley 775; CCCC 473 is available in facsimile in Rankin, *Winchester Troper*.

19 Wilcox, *Ælfric's Prefaces*, 111; cited and discussed in Stephenson, "Ælfric of Eynsham and Hermeneutic Latin," 113.

20 See also Nichols, "Ælfric and the Brief Style"; Gatch, *Preaching and Theology*; and Davis, "Boredom."

21 See Lees, *Tradition and Belief*, 57.

22 See the discussion of *Dominica in Media Quadragesima* (*CH* I.12) in chapter 1 above.

far the preferred features. The cognitive work that produces that rhetorical weight is precisely the work that Ælfric did not want his audiences to do. He sought to "eliminate variables" so that his explications could not be confused.[23] He wanted each word to be clearly and easily understood in exactly the way he intended, whereas compounds put the onus of understanding on the audience as interpreters of the relationship between a compound's constituents internally and between the compound and the sentential context externally. On a cognitive level, then, compounds go directly against Ælfric's stated aims. On a stylistic level, compounds powerfully invoke and fulfil specific expectations, as demonstrated in chapters 2 and 4 above, directing the audience's attention to a text's form. For Ælfric, attention should be on the clear content without the distraction of formal flourishes, specifically lexical flourishes. His rhythmical prose style, rather than creating distraction, was engineered to enhance the efficacy of his homilies. Compounds thus create imprecision in meaning and push attention to form over meaning, both of which undermine Ælfric's prized clarity.

Connected with clarity is the issue of pace: too much variation of pace would again interfere with the explication of meaning that Ælfric pursued. Chapters 5 and 6 demonstrate the ways in which the simple presence of compounds slows pace in both narrative and non-narrative texts. Brevity, for Ælfric, is conducive to clarity, for brevity fends off boredom. In his homily of Job (*CH* II.30), he notes that excessive length would bore an unlearned audience and thereby undermine the homily's pedagogical value.[24] Any significant presence of compounds would nullify Ælfric's construction of swift-paced, or at least even-paced, brevity. Wulfstan's homilies and *Beowulf* slow their paces at particular points to produce targeted stylistic effects that support their meanings within specific contexts. They do not aim at the same type of clarity: Wulfstan's homilies relied on a slow pace in argumentation, and *Beowulf* similarly in moments of important violence. In contrast, Ælfric, endeavouring to produce clear, pragmatic prose in both narrative and non-narrative modes, needed to

23 Davis, "Boredom," 333.

24 Godden, *Second Series*, 260, lines 4–6: "Man sceal læwedum mannum secgan be heora andgites mæðe. swa þæt hi ne beon ðurh ða deopnysse æmode. ne ðurh ða langsumnysse geæðrytte" [One must speak to laymen according to the capacity of their understanding, so that they will not be discouraged by the depth nor wearied by the length]. See the discussion of this passage in Davis, "Boredom," 328–9.

avoid most compounds, lest they bog down his pace and mar his audience's understanding.

Ælfric's interest in placing England within the tradition of the universal Church provides the final motivation behind the lack of compound words in his writings. As a reformer, Ælfric was committed to adhering to the best ideals of traditional Christianity, which he saw embodied in a "chain of authority" extending back through Carolingian and patristic writers.[25] His choice of writing in Old English instead of Latin complicates, but does not completely invalidate, his place in that chain.[26] Ælfric adheres to the traditions of homiletic writing in other features of style and content and thereby creates the appearance of continuity and suppresses moments of discontinuity.[27] Compounds would have undermined essential elements of that appearance of continuity. As each chapter above demonstrates, the full impact of compounds in any given text only becomes clear within a particular cultural context. *Beowulf*'s conflicted interest in violence makes the most sense within the context of its copying in the early 1000s; Wulfstan's concern with social order is clearly of a particular moment; the issue of a translation's acceptability for the Old English *Boethius* and Cynewulf's texts coincides with Alfred's promotion of English and the concerns of the Benedictine Reform, respectively; and the valences of poetry and prose in those same texts become most prominent in the context of those same periods. To be sure, any element of a text becomes more meaningful in context, but compounds carry an especially "Old English" connotation because of their participation in particular forms of discourse. Moreover, the cognitive weight involved in processing and parsing them puts an onus on the individual audience member, which detracts from the sense that a text delivers timeless material that has lived unchanged in the tradition for centuries. Ælfric's homilies cultivate that sense and therefore must avoid any feature that reveals the constructed nature of "tradition," especially compounds because of their intrinsically contextualized nature.[28]

Due to the connections of compounds to the different levels of grammar, style, and culture, an analysis of Ælfric's avoidance of compound words within the paradigm set forth in this book reveals the importance of

25 Hill, "Translating the Tradition," 62. See also Lees, *Tradition and Belief*; Jones, "Ælfric and the Limits"; and Davis, "Boredom," 323–5.

26 See Lees, *Tradition and Belief*, 32–5.

27 See Lees, *Tradition and Belief*, 35.

28 On the construction of tradition, see Lees, *Tradition and Belief*, 1–45.

compound words to Old English literature generally at those three levels and also their centrality in Anglo-Saxon theories of vernacular verbal art. On a pragmatic level, compound words produce cognitive and stylistic effects that would have interfered with Ælfric's pedagogical goals, and on an abstract level he also avoided compounds in an attempt to make his writing transcend specificity and contextualized expectations. The absence of compounds in Ælfric's homilies demonstrates their different uses and effects just as effectively as the presence of compounds in the Old English *Boethius*, *Juliana* and *Elene*, *The Seafarer* and *The Wanderer*, Wulfstan's Old English homilies, and *Beowulf*. Compound words – themselves the products of a type of joining – cut across supposed divides between basic word formation, rhetorical patterns, and cultural practices to produce a type of joining that provided unique literary options in Old English and which the Anglo-Saxons considered essential for the composition and fully contextualized understanding of Old English literature.

Bibliography

Abraham, Lenore MacGaffey. "Cynewulf's *Juliana*: A Case at Law." *Allegorica* 3, no. 1 (1978): 172–89.

– "Cynewulf's Recharacterization of the *Vita sanctae Julianae* and the Tenth Century Benedictine Revival in England." *American Benedictine Review* 62, no. 1 (2011): 67–83.

Abrams, Lesley. "King Edgar and the Men of the Danelaw." In *Edgar: King of the English, 959–975*, edited by Donald Scragg, 171–91. Woodbridge: Boydell Press, 2008.

Amodio, Mark C. "Res(is)ting the Singer: Towards a Non-Performative Anglo-Saxon Oral Poetics." In *New Directions in Oral Theory*, edited by Mark C. Amodio, 179–208. Tempe: Arizona Center for Medieval and Renaissance Studies, 2005.

– *Writing the Oral Tradition: Oral Poetics and Literate Culture in Medieval England*. Notre Dame, IN: University of Notre Dame Press, 2004.

Anderson, Aaron. "Kinesthesia in Martial Arts Films." *Jump Cut: A Review of Contemporary Media* 42 (1998): 1–11.

– "Violent Dances in Martial Arts Films." *Jump Cut: A Review of Contemporary Media* 44 (2001): online.

Anderson, Benedict. *Imagined Communities: Reflections on the Origin and Spread of Nationalism*. New ed. New York: Verso, 2006.

Andrews, Sally. "Morphological Influences on Lexical Access: Lexical or Nonlexical Effects?" *Journal of Memory and Language* 25, no. 6 (1986): 726–40.

Andrews, Sally, Brett Miller, and Keith Rayner. "Eye Movements and Morphological Segmentation of Compound Words: There is a Mouse in the Mousetrap." *European Journal of Cognitive Psychology* 16 (2004): 285–311.

Anlezark, Daniel. "Three Notes on the Old English *Meters of Boethius*." *Notes and Queries* 51 (2004): 10–15.

Arndt-Lappe, Sabine. "Towards an Exemplar-Based Model of Stress in English Noun-Noun Compounds." *Journal of Linguistics* 47, no. 3 (2011): 549–85.

Atkinson, Max. *Our Masters' Voices: The Language and Body Language of Politics*. London: Routledge, 1984.

– "Two Devices for Generating Audience Approval: A Comparative Study of Public Discourse and Texts." In *Connectedness in Sentence, Discourse and Text*, edited by K. Ehlich and H. Van Riensdijk, 199–235. Tilburg: Tilburg University Press, 1983.

Auerbach, Eric. "Figura." In *Scenes from the Drama of European Literature*, 11–76. Gloucester, MA: Peter Smith, 1973.

Bai, Chen, Ina Bornkessel-Schlesewsky, Luming Wang, Yu-Chen Hung, Matthias Schlesewsky, and Petra Burkhardt. "Semantic Composition Engenders an N400: Evidence from Chinese Compounds." *NeuroReport* 19, no. 6 (2008): 695–9.

Baker, Peter S. *Honour, Exchange and Violence in "Beowulf."* Anglo-Saxon Studies 20. Cambridge: D.S. Brewer, 2013.

Baker, Peter, and Michael Lapidge, eds. *Byrhtferth's Enchiridion*. EETS ss 15. Oxford: Oxford University Press, 1995.

Bakhtin, Mikhail. "Discourse in the Novel." In *Dialogic Imagination: Four Essays*, edited by Michael Holquist, translated by Caryl Emerson and Michael Holquist, 259–422. Austin: University of Texas Press, 1981.

– "The Problem of Speech Genres." In *Speech Genres and Other Late Essays*, translated by Vern W. McGee, edited by Caryl Emerson and Michael Holquist, 60–102. Austin: University of Texas Press, 1986.

Bartlett, A.C. *The Larger Rhetorical Patterns in Anglo-Saxon Poetry*. Columbia University Studies in English and Comparative Literature 122. New York: Columbia University Press, 1935.

Bately, Janet. "The Alfredian Canon Revisited: One Hundred Years On." In *Alfred the Great: Papers from the Eleventh-Centenary Conferences*, edited by Timothy Reuter, 107–20. Aldershot, UK: Ashgate, 2003.

– "Book Divisions and Chapter Headings in the Translations of the Alfredian Period." In *Early Medieval English Texts and Interpretations: Studies Presented to Donald G. Scragg*, edited by Elaine Treharne and Susan Rosser, 151–66. Arizona Medieval and Renaissance Texts and Studies. Tempe: Arizona Center for Medieval and Renaissance Studies, 2002.

– "Did King Alfred Actually Translate Anything? The Integrity of the Alfredian Canon Revisited." *Medium Ævum* 78, no. 2 (2009): 189–215.

– *The Literary Prose of King Alfred's Reign: Translation or Transformation?* Old English Newsletter Subsidia 10. 1980; reprinted Kalamazoo, MI: Medieval Institute Publications, 1984.

– ed. *The Old English Orosius.* EETS ss 6. London: Oxford University Press, 1980.

Battles, Horst Richard Paul. "The Art of the Scop: Traditional Poetics in the Old English *Genesis A.*" PhD diss., University of Illinois at Urbana-Champaign, 1998.

Beaty, John O. "The Echo-Word in *Beowulf* with a Note on the *Finnsburg Fragment.*" *PMLA* 49 (1934): 365–73.

Bedingfield, Brad. "Public Penance in Anglo-Saxon England." *ASE* 31 (2002): 223–55.

Beechy, Tiffany. *The Poetics of Old English.* Farnham, UK: Ashgate, 2010.

Bell, Melanie J., and Ingo Plag. "Informativeness is a Determinant of Compound Stress in English." *Journal of Linguistics* 48, no. 3 (2012): 485–520.

Benczes, Réka. *Creative Compounding in English: The Semantics of Metaphorical and Metonymical Noun-Noun Combinations.* Amsterdam: John Benjamins, 2006.

Benediktsson, Hrein, ed. *The First Grammatical Treatise.* University of Iceland Publications in Linguistics 1. Reykjavik: Institute of Nordic Linguistics, 1972.

Benson, D. Frank, and Alfredo Ardila. *Aphasia: A Clinical Perspective.* Oxford: Oxford University Press, 1996.

Benson, Larry D. "The Literary Character of Anglo-Saxon Formulaic Poetry." *PMLA* 81 (1966): 334–41.

Bergsten, Nils. "A Study of Compound Substantives in English." PhD diss., Uppsala University, 1911.

Bertram, Raymond, and Jukka Hyönä. "The Role of Hyphens at the Constituent Boundary in Compound Word Identification: Facilitative for Long, Detrimental for Short Compound Words." *Experimental Psychology* 60, no. 3 (2013): 157–63.

Bethurum, Dorothy. "The Form of Ælfric's *Lives of Saints.*" *Studies in Philology* 29 (1932): 515–33.

– ed. *The Homilies of Wulfstan.* Oxford: Clarendon Press, 1957.

Bethurum Loomis, Dorothy. "*Regnum* and *sacerdotium* in the Early Eleventh Century." In *England before the Conquest: Studies in Primary Sources Presented to Dorothy Whitelock*, edited by Peter Clemoes and Kathleen Hughes, 129–45. Cambridge: Cambridge University Press, 1971.

Bi, Yanchao, Zaizhu Han, and Hua Shu. "Compound Frequency Effect in Word Production: Evidence from Anomia." *Brain and Language* 103 (2007): 55–6.

El-Bialy, Rowan, Chrstina L. Gagné, and Thomas L. Spalding. "Processing of English Compounds Is Sensitive to the Constituent's Semantic Transparency." *The Mental Lexicon* 8, no. 1 (2013): 75–95.

Bieler, Ludwig, ed. *Anicii Manlii Severni Boethii Philosophiae Consolatio*. CCSL 94. Turnhout: Brepols, 1957.

Biggs, Frederick M. "*Beowulf* and Some Fictions of the Geatish Succession." *ASE* 32 (2003): 55–77.

– "The Politics of Succession in *Beowulf* and Anglo-Saxon England." *Speculum* 80 (2005): 709–41.

Birner, Betty J. *Introduction to Pragmatics*. Malden, MA: Wiley-Blackwell, 2013.

Bjork, Robert E., ed. *Cynewulf: Basic Readings*. New York: Garland, 1996.

– "Digressions and Episodes." In *A "Beowulf" Handbook*, edited by Robert E. Bjork and John D. Niles, 193–212. Lincoln: University of Nebraska Press, 1997.

– *The Old English Verse Saints' Lives: A Study in Direct Discourse and the Iconography of Style*. McMaster Old English Studies and Texts 4. Toronto: University of Toronto Press, 1985.

– "Speech as Gift in *Beowulf*." *Speculum* 69 (1994): 993–1022.

Bjork, Robert E., and Anita Obermeier. "Date, Provenance, Author, Audiences." In *A "Beowulf" Handbook*, edited by Robert E. Bjork and John D. Niles, 13–34. Lincoln: University of Nebraska Press, 1997.

Bliss, Alan. *An Introduction to Old English Metre*. Oxford: Blackwell, 1962.

– *The Metre of "Beowulf*." Rev. ed. Oxford: Blackwell, 1967.

Bordwell, David. "Aesthetics in Action: Kung Fu, Gunplay, and Cinematic Expressivity." In *Fifty Years of Electric Shadows*, edited by Law Kar, 81–9. Hong Kong: Urban Council, 1997.

Borges, Jorge Luis. "Pierre Menard, Author of the *Quixote*." In *Collected Fictions*, translated by Andrew Hurley, 88–95. New York: Penguin, 1999.

Bosworth, Joseph. *An Anglo-Saxon Dictionary*. Edited and enlarged by T. Northcote Toller. Oxford, 1898; Oxford: Oxford University Press, 1973.

Brady, Caroline. "Synonyms for 'Sea' in *Beowulf*." In *Studies in Honor of Albert Morey Sturtevant*, 22–46. Humanistic Studies 29. Lawrence: University of Kansas Publications, 1952.

– "'Warriors' in *Beowulf*: An Analysis of the Nominal Compounds and an Evaluation of the Poet's Use of Them." *ASE* 11 (1983): 199–246.

– "'Weapons' in *Beowulf*: An Analysis of the Nominal Compounds and an Evaluation of the Poet's Use of Them." *ASE* 8 (1979): 79–141.

Bredehoft, Thomas A. *Early English Metre*. Toronto: University of Toronto Press, 2005.

– "Secondary Stress in Compound Germanic Names in Old English Verse." *Journal of English Linguistics* 31 (2003): 199–220.

Brekle, Herbert E. "Reflections on the Conditions for the Coining, Use and Understanding of Nominal Compounds." In *Proceedings of the 12th*

International Congress of Linguists, edited by Wolfgang U. Dressler and Wolfgang Meid, 68–77. Innsbruck: Institut für Sprachwissenschaft der Universität Innsbruck, 1978.

Brodeur, Arthur Gilchrist. *The Art of "Beowulf."* Berkeley: University of California Press, 1959.

Bronckart, Jean-Paul, and Cristian Bota. *Bakhtine démasqué: Histoire d'un menteur, d'une escroquerie et d'un délire collectif*. Titre courant 45. Geneva: Librairie Droz, 2011.

Bruder, Margaret Ervin. "Aestheticizing Violence, or How to Do Things with Style." PhD diss., Indiana University, 2003.

Brusnighan, Stephen M., and Jocelyn R. Folk. "Combining Contextual and Morphemic Cues is Beneficial during Incidental Vocabulary Acquisition: Semantic Transparency in Novel Compound Word Processing." *Reading Research Quarterly* 47 (2012): 172–90.

Bryan, William Frank. "Epithetic Compound Folk-Names in *Beowulf*." In *Studies in English Philology: A Miscellany in Honor of Frederick Klaeber*, edited by Kemp Malone and Martin B. Ruud, 120–34. Minneapolis: University of Minnesota Press, 1929.

Butler, Judith. *Gender Trouble: Feminism and the Subversion of Identity*. 2nd ed. London: Routledge, 2006.

Butterworth, Brian. "Lexical Representation." *Language Production* 2 (1983): 257–94.

Cable, Thomas. *The Meter and Melody of "Beowulf."* Urbana: University of Illinois Press, 1974.

– "The Meter and Musical Implications of Old English Poetry." In *The Union of Words and Music in Medieval Poetry*, edited by Rebecca A. Baltzer, Thomas Cable, and James I. Wimsatt, 49–71. Austin: University of Texas Press, 1991.

Calder, Daniel G. *Cynewulf*. Boston: Twayne, 1981.

Campbell, A. *Old English Grammar*. 3rd ed. Oxford: Oxford University Press, 1983.

Caplan, Harry, ed. and trans. *Cicero: Rhetorica ad Herennium*. Loeb Classical Library 403. Cambridge, MA: Harvard University Press, 1954.

Carnicelli, Thomas A., ed. *King Alfred's Version of St. Augustine's Soliloquies*. Cambridge, MA: Harvard University Press, 1969.

Carr, Charles T. *Nominal Compounds in Germanic*. St Andrews Publications 41. London: Oxford University Press, 1939.

Chaffin, Roger, Robin K. Morris, and Rachel E. Seely. "Learning New Word Meanings from Context: A Study of Eye Movements." *Journal of Experimental Psychology: Learning, Memory, and Cognition* 27 (2001): 225–35.

Chapman, Don. "Composing and Joining: How the Anglo-Saxons Talked about Compounding." In *Verbal Encounters: Anglo-Saxon and Old Norse Studies for Roberta Frank*, edited by Antonina Harbus and Russell Poole, 39–54. Toronto: University of Toronto Press, 2004.

– "Germanic Tradition and Latin Learning in Wulfstan's Echoic Compounds." *JEGP* 101 (2002): 1–18.

– "Motivation for Producing and Analyzing Compounds in Wulfstan's Sermons." In *Advances in English Historical Linguistics* (1996), edited by Jacek Fisiak and Marcin Krygier, 15–21. Trends in Linguistics, Studies and Monographs 112. Berlin: Mouton de Gruyter, 1998.

– "Poetic Compounding in the Vercelli, Blickling, and Wulfstan Homilies." *NM* 103, no. 4 (2002): 409–21.

– "Pragmatics of Analyzing Compounds in Wulfstan's Sermons." *The Twenty-Third LACUS Forum*, edited by Alan K. Melby, 575–84. Chapel Hill: University of North Carolina Press, 1997.

– "Stylistic Use of Nominal Compounds in Wulfstan's Sermons." PhD diss., University of Toronto, 1995.

– "Uterque Lingua / Ægðer Gereord: Ælfric's Grammatical Vocabulary and the Winchester Tradition." *JEGP* 109, no. 4 (2010): 421–45.

Chapman, Don, and Ryan Christensen. "Noun-Adjective Compounds as a Poetic Type in Old English." *English Studies* 88, no. 4 (2007): 447–64.

Chase, Colin, ed. *The Dating of "Beowulf."* Toronto: University of Toronto Press, 1981. Reprinted 1997.

Chaytor, H.J. "The Medieval Reader and Textual Criticism." *Bulletin of the John Rylands Library* 26 (1941–2): 49–56.

Chiarelli, V., R. El Yagoubi, S. Mondini, M. Danieli, G. Perrone, and C. Semenza. "The Electrophysiological Correlates of Noun-Noun Compounds." *Brain and Language* 103 (2007): 248–9.

Chinca, Mark, and Stephen Young, eds. *Orality and Literacy in the Middle Ages: Essays on a Conjunction and Its Consequences in Honour of D.H. Green*. Turnhout: Brepols, 2005.

Clemoes, Peter. "Ælfric." In *Continuations and Beginnings: Studies in Old English Literature*, edited by E.G. Stanley, 176–209. London: Thomas Nelson and Sons, 1966.

– ed. *Ælfric's Catholic Homilies: The First Series*. EETS ss 17. Oxford: Oxford University Press, 1997.

– "The Chronology of Ælfric's Works." In *The Anglo-Saxons: Studies in Some Aspects of Their History and Culture Presented to Bruce Dickens*, edited by Peter Clemoes, 212–47. London: Bowes and Bowes, 1959.

– *Interactions of Thought and Language in Old English Poetry*. Cambridge: Cambridge University Press, 1995.

– "*Mens absentia cogitans* in *The Seafarer* and *The Wanderer*." In *Medieval Literature and Civilization: Studies in Memory of G.N. Garmonsway*, edited by D.A. Pearsall and R.A. Waldron, 62–77. London: Athlone Press, 1969.

Clover, Carol J. "The Germanic Context of the Unferþ Episode." *Speculum* 55 (1980): 444–68.

Clunies Ross, Margaret. *A History of Old Norse Poetry and Poetics*. Cambridge: D.S. Brewer, 2005.

– *Skáldskaparmál: Snorri Sturluson's "Ars poetica" and Medieval Theories of Language*. Odense: Odense University Press, 1987.

Cohen, Ralph. "History and Genre." *Neohelicon* 13, no. 2 (1986): 87–105.

Cohen, Stephen. Introduction. In *Shakespeare and Historical Formalism*, edited by Stephen Cohen, 1–27. Aldershot, UK: Ashgate, 2007.

Coleman, Janet. *Ancient and Medieval Memories: Studies in the Reconstruction of the Past*. Cambridge: Cambridge University Press, 1992.

Colgrave, Bertram, and R.A.B. Mynors, eds. *Bede's Ecclesiastical History of the English People.* Oxford Medieval Texts. Oxford: Clarendon Press, 1979.

Conner, Patrick W. *Anglo-Saxon Exeter: A Tenth-Century Cultural History*. Woodbridge: Boydell Press, 1993.

– "On Dating Cynewulf." In *Cynewulf: Basic Readings*, edited by Robert E. Bjork, 23–56. New York: Garland, 1996.

Cook, Albert S. *The Christ of Cynewulf: A Poem in Three Parts*. 1900; reprinted Freeport, NY: Books for Libraries Press, 1970.

Cook, Kimberly K. "Philosophy's Metamorphosis into Wisdom: An Exploration of King Alfred's Re-Creation of the Central Symbol in the *Consolation of Philosophy*." *Journal of Evolutionary Psychology* 17, no. 3–4 (1996): 177–85.

Coolen, Riet, Henk J. van Jaarsveld, and Robert Schreuder. "The Interpretation of Isolated Novel Nominal Compounds." *Memory & Cognition* 19, no. 4 (1991): 341–52.

Copeland, Rita. "Rhetoric and the Politics of the Literal Sense in Medieval Literary Theory: Aquinas, Wyclif, and the Lollards." In *Rhetoric and Hermeneutics in Our Time*, edited by Walter Jost and Michael J. Hyde, 335–57. New Haven: Yale University Press, 1997.

– *Rhetoric, Hermeneutics, and Translation in the Middle Ages: Academic Traditions and Vernacular Texts*. Cambridge Studies in Medieval Literature 11. Cambridge: Cambridge University Press, 1991.

Copeland, Rita, and Ineke Sluiter, eds. *Medieval Grammar and Rhetoric: Language Arts and Literary Theory, AD 300–1475*. Oxford: Oxford University Press, 2009.

Corona, Gabriella. "Ælfric's (Un)Changing Style: Continuity of Patterns from the *Catholic Homilies* to the *Lives of Saints*." *JEGP* 107, no. 2 (2008): 169–89.

Crocker, Richard L. "*Musica rhythmica* and *musica metrica* in Antique and Medieval Theory." *Journal of Music Theory* 2, no. 1 (1958): 2–23.

Cross, J.E. "*De Ordine Creaturarum Liber* in Old English Prose." *Anglia* 90 (1972): 132–40.

Crowley, Tony. "Bakhtin and the History of the Language." In *Bakhtin and Cultural Theory*, edited by Ken Hirschkop and David Shepherd, 68–90. Manchester: Manchester University Press, 1989.

Crowne, David. "The Hero on the Beach: An Example of Composition by Theme in Anglo-Saxon Poetry." *NM* 61 (1960): 362–72.

Cubitt, Catherine. "Memory and Narrative in the Cult of Early Anglo-Saxon Saints." In *The Uses of the Past in the Early Middle Ages*, edited by Yitzhak Hen and Matthew Innes, 29–66. Cambridge: Cambridge University Press, 2000.

– "The Tenth-Century Benedictine Reform in England." *Early Medieval Europe* 6 (1997): 77–94.

Curtius, Ernst Robert. *European Literature and the Latin Middle Ages*. Translated by Willard R. Trask. Princeton: Princeton University Press, 1990.

Damico, Helen. *Beowulf and the Grendel-kin: Politics and Poetry in the Eleventh Century*. Morgantown: West Virginia University Press, 2015.

Dance, Richard. "The Old English Language and the Alliterative Tradition." In *A Companion to Medieval Poetry*, edited by Corinne Saunders, 34–50. Malden, MA: Wiley-Blackwell, 2010.

– "Sound, Fury, and Signifiers: Of Wulfstan's Language." In *Wulfstan, Archbishop of York: The Proceedings of the Second Alcuin Conference*, edited by Matthew Townend, 29–61. Turnhout: Brepols, 2004.

Davis, Craig. "An Ethnic Dating of *Beowulf*." *ASE* 35 (2006): 111–29.

Davis, Kathleen. "Boredom, Brevity, and Last Things: Ælfric's Style and the Politics of Time." In *A Companion to Ælfric*, edited by Hugh Magennis and Mary Swan, 321–44. Leiden: Brill, 2009.

Davis-Secord, Jonathan. "Rhetoric and Politics in Archbishop Wulfstan's Old English Homilies." *Anglia* 126, no. 1 (2008): 65–96. Reprinted in *Classical and Medieval Literary Criticism*, vol. 135, edited by Lawrence J. Trudeau, 319–34. Detroit: Gale Cengage, 2012.

– "Scribal Interpretations of Genre in the Old English *Boethius*." *Carmina Philosophiae: Journal of the International Boethius Society* 19 (2010): 1–23. Reprinted in *Vernacular Traditions of Boethius's "De consolatione philosophiae,"* edited by Noel Harold Kaylor, Jr and Philip Edward Phillips. Forthcoming.

– "Sequences and Intellectual Identity in Winchester." In "Latinity and Identity in Anglo-Saxon England," edited by Emily Thornbury and Rebecca Stephenson. Forthcoming.

Derrida, Jacques. "The Laws of Genre." Translated by Avita Ronell. *Critical Inquiry* 7, no. 1 (1980): 55–81.

Diamond, Robert E. "Theme as Ornament in Anglo-Saxon Poetry." *PMLA* 76 (1961): 461–8.

Dictionary of Old English: A to G. Edited by Angus Cameron, Ashley Crandall Amos, and Antonette diPaolo Healey. Toronto: University of Toronto Press, 2007.

Dictionary of Old English Corpus on the World Wide Web. Compiled by Antonette diPaolo Healey with John Price Wilkin and Xin Xiang. Toronto: Dictionary of Old English Project, 2009.

Discenza, Nicole Guenther. "The Influence of Gregory the Great on the Alfredian Social Imaginary." In *Rome and the North: The Early Reception of Gregory the Great in Germanic Europe*, edited by Rolf H. Bremmer Jr, Kees Dekker, and David F. Johnson, 67–81. Paris: Peeters, 2001.

– *The King's English: Strategies of Translation in the Old English "Boethius."* New York: State University of New York Press, 2005.

– "Power, Skill, and Virtue in the Old English *Boethius*." *ASE* 26 (1997): 81–108.

– "Symbolic Capital in the Translations of Alfred the Great." *Exemplaria* 13 (2001): 433–67.

Doane, A.N., and Carol Braun Pasternack, eds. *Vox Intexta: Orality and Textuality in the Middle Ages*. Madison: University of Wisconsin Press, 1991.

Dobbie, Elliott Van Kirk, ed. *The Anglo-Saxon Minor Poems*. ASPR 6. New York: Columbia University Press, 1942.

Donahue, Charles J. "Potlatch and Charity: Notes on the Heroic in *Beowulf*." In *Anglo-Saxon Poetry: Essays in Appreciation for John C. McGalliard*, edited by Lewis E. Nicholson and Dolores W. Frese, 23–40. Notre Dame, IN: University of Notre Dame Press, 1975.

Donovan, Leslie A. "*Þyle* as Fool: Revisiting *Beowulf*'s Hunferth." In *Poetry, Place, and Gender: Studies in Medieval Culture in Honor of Helen Damico*, edited by Catherine E. Karkov, 75–97. Kalamazoo, MI: Medieval Institute Publications, 2009.

Doury, Marianne. "Preaching to the Converted: Why Argue When Everyone Agrees?" *Argumentation* 26 (2012): 99–114.

Downing, Pamela. "On the Creation and Use of English Compound Nouns." *Language* 53, no. 4 (1977): 810–42.

Dressler, Wolfgang U. "Compound Types." In *Representation and Processing of Compound Words*, edited by Gary Libben and Gonia Jarema, 23–44. Oxford: Oxford University Press, 2006.

Drieghe, Denis, Alexander Pollatsek, Barbara J. Juhasz, and Keith Rayner. "Parafoveal Processing during Reading Is Reduced across a Morphological Boundary." *Cognition* 116 (2010): 136–42.

Dronke, Peter. *Fabula: Explorations into the Uses of Myth in Medieval Platonism.* Leiden: Brill, 1974.

Drout, Michael D.C. *Tradition and Influence in Anglo-Saxon Literature: An Evolutionary, Cognitivist Approach.* New York: Palgrave Macmillan, 2013.

Drout, Michael D.C., Michael Kahn, Mark LeBlanc, Amos Jones, Neil Kathok, and Christina Nelson. "Lexomics for Anglo-Saxon Literature." *Old English Newsletter* 42 (2010): 1–7.

Drout, Michael D.C., Michael J. Kahn, Mark D. LeBlanc, and Christina Nelson. "Of Dendrogrammatology: Lexomic Methods for Analyzing Relationships among Old English Poems." *JEGP* 110, no. 3 (2011): 301–36.

Dumitrescu, Irina. "Bede's Liberation Philology: Releasing the English Tongue." *PMLA* 128, no. 1 (2013): 40–56.

Dumville, David. "Beowulf Come Lately: Some Notes on the Paleography of the Nowell Codex." *Archiv für das Studium der neueren Sprachen und Literaturen* 225 (1988): 49–63.

Duñabeitia, Jon Andoni, Manuel Perea, and Manuel Carreiras. "The Role of Frequency of Constituents in Compound Words: Evidence from Basque and Spanish." *Psychonomic Bulletin & Review* 14, no. 6 (2007): 1171–6.

Duncan, Thomas G. "'Quid Hinieldus cum Christo?': The Secular Expression of the Sacred in Old and Middle English Lyrics." In *Sacred and Secular in Medieval and Early Modern Cultures: New Essays*, edited by Lawrence Besserman, 29–46. New York: Palgrave MacMillan, 2006.

Eiesland, Eli Anne, and Marianne Lind. "Compound Nouns in Spoken Language Production by Speakers with Aphasia Compared to Neurologically Healthy Speakers: An Exploratory Study." *Clinical Linguistics & Phonetics* 26, no. 3 (2012): 232–54.

Einarsson, Stefán. "*Kyning-Wuldor* and *Mann-Skratti*." *Modern Language Notes* 75 (1960): 193–4.

Engelhardt, George J. "*Beowulf*: A Study in Dilatation." *PMLA* 70 (1955): 825–52.

Enright, Michael. "Lady with a Mead-Cup: Ritual, Group Cohesion and Hierarchy in the Germanic Warband." *Frühmittelalterliche Studien* 22 (1988): 170–203.

– "The Warband Context of the Unferth Episode." *Speculum* 73 (1998): 297–337.

Erussard, Laurence. "Language, Power, and Holiness in Cynewulf's *Elene*." *Medievalia et Humanistica* ns 34 (2008): 23–41.

Estes, Zachary. "Attributive and Relational Processes in Nominal Combination." *Journal of Memory and Language* 48 (2003): 304–19.

Estes, Zachary, and Lara L. Jones. "Priming via Relational Similarity: A COPPER HORSE is Faster when Seen through a GLASS EYE." *Journal of Memory and Language* 55 (2006): 89–101.

Fabb, Nigel. "Compounding." In *The Handbook of Morphology*, edited by Andrew Spencer and Arnold M. Zwicky, 66–83. Blackwell Handbooks in Linguistics. Malden, MA: Blackwell, 1998.

Fassler, Margot E. "Accent, Meter, and Rhythm in Medieval Treatises 'De rithmis.'" *The Journal of Musicology* 5, no. 2 (1987): 164–90.

Faulkes, Anthony, ed. *Edda: Háttatal.* 2nd ed. London: Viking Society for Northern Research, 2007.

– ed. *Edda: Prologue and Gylfaginning*. 2nd ed. London: Viking Society for Northern Research, 2005.

– ed. *Edda: Skáldskaparmál 1: Introduction, Text and Notes*. London: Viking Society for Northern Research, 1998; reprinted with minor corrections 2007.

– *Poetical Inspiration in Old Norse and Old English Poetry*. London: Viking Society for Northern Research, 1997.

Fehringer, Carol. "The Lexical Representation of Compound Words in English: Evidence from Aphasia." *Language Sciences* 34 (2012): 65–75.

Fillmore, Charles J. "The Case for Case." In *Universals in Linguistic Theory*, edited by Emmon Bach and Robert T. Harms, 1–88. New York: Holt, Rinehart and Winston, 1968.

Finnegan, Ruth. *Oral Poetry: Its Nature, Significance, and Social Context.* Cambridge: Cambridge University Press, 1977; reprinted Bloomington: Indiana University Press, 1992.

Fiorentino, R., and D. Poeppel. "Compound Words and Structure in the Lexicon." *Language and Cognitive Processes* 22 (2007): 953–1000.

– "Processing of Compound Words: An MEG Study." *Brain and Language* 103 (2007): 18–19.

Foley, John Miles. "How Genres Leak in Traditional Verse." In *Unlocking the Wordhord: Anglo-Saxon Studies in Memory of Edward B. Irving, Jr.*, edited by Mark C. Amodio and Katherine O'Brien O'Keeffe, 76–109. Toronto: University of Toronto Press, 2003.

– *How to Read an Oral Poem*. Urbana: University of Illinois Press, 2002.

– *Immanent Art: From Structure to Meaning in Traditional Oral Epic.* Bloomington: Indiana University Press, 1991.

– *The Singer of Tales in Performance*. Bloomington: Indiana University Press, 1995.

– *Traditional Oral Epic: "The Odyssey," "Beowulf," and the Serbo-Croation Return Song*. Berkeley: University of California Press, 1990.

Foley, John Miles, and Peter Ramey. "Oral Theory and Medieval Literature." In *Medieval Oral Literature*, edited by Karl Reichl, 71–102. Berlin: De Gruyter, 2012.

Fontes Anglo-Saxonici Project, ed. *Fontes Anglo-Saxonici: World Wide Web Register*. http://fontes.english.ox.ac.uk/.

Forster, Kenneth I., and Chris Davis. "Repetition Priming and Frequency Attentuation in Lexical Access." *Journal of Experimental Psychology: Learning, Memory and Cognition* 10 (1984): 680–98.

Fowler, Roger. "A Late Old English Handbook for the Use of a Confessor." *Anglia* 83 (1965): 1–34.

Frank, Roberta. "Did Anglo-Saxon Audiences Have a Skaldic Tooth?" *Scandinavian Studies* 59, no. 3 (1987): 338–55.

– "Poetic Words in Late Old English Prose." In *From Anglo-Saxon to Early Middle English: Studies Presented to E.G. Stanley*, edited by Malcolm Godden, Terry Hoad, and Douglas Gray, 87–107. Oxford: Clarendon Press, 1994.

– "A Scandal in Toronto: *The Dating of "Beowulf"* a Quarter Century On." *Speculum* 82 (2007): 843–64.

– "The Search for the Anglo-Saxon Oral Poet." *Bulletin of the John Rylands University Library of Manchester* 75 (1993): 11–36.

– "Terminally Hip and Incredibly Cool: Carol, Vikings, and Anglo-Scandinavian England." *Representations* 100, no. 1 (2007): 23–33.

Franklin, Carmela Vircillo. "Grammar and Exegesis: Bede's *Liber de schematibus et tropis*." In *Latin Grammar and Rhetoric: From Classical Theory to Medieval Practice*, edited by Carol Dana Lanham, 63–91. London: Continuum, 2002.

Frantzen, Allen J. *The Literature of Penance in Anglo-Saxon England*. New Brunswick, NJ: Rutgers University Press, 1983.

Frederick, Jill. "Warring with Words: Cynewulf's *Juliana*." In *Readings in Medieval Texts: Interpreting Old and Middle English Literature*, edited by David F. Johnson and Elaine Treharne, 60–74. Oxford: Oxford University Press, 2005.

Friesen, Bill. "The *Opus Geminatum* and Anglo-Saxon Literature." *Neophilologus* 95 (2011): 123–44.

Frisson, Steven, Elizabeth Niswander-Klement, and Alexander Pollatsek. "The Role of Semantic Transparency in the Processing of English Compound Words." *British Journal of Psychology* 99 (2008): 87–107.

Fry, Donald K. "Old English Formulas and Systems." *English Studies* 48 (1967): 193–204.

– "Themes and Type-Scenes in *Elene* 1–113." *Speculum* 44 (1969): 35–45.

– "Variation and Economy in *Beowulf*." *Modern Philology* 65, no. 4 (1968): 353–6.

Fulk, R.D. "Cynewulf: Canon, Dialect, and Date." In *Cynewulf: Basic Readings*, edited by Robert E. Bjork, 3–22. New York: Garland, 1996.

– *A History of Old English Meter*. Philadelphia: University of Pennsylvania Press, 1992.

– "On Argumentation in Old English Philology, with Particular Reference to the Editing and Dating of *Beowulf*." *ASE* 32 (2003): 1–26.

Fulk, R.D., Robert E. Bjork, and John D. Niles, eds. *Klaeber's Beowulf and the Fight at Finnsburg*. 4th ed. Toronto: University of Toronto Press, 2008.

Gagné, Christina L. "Lexical and Relational Influences on the Processing of Novel Compounds." *Brain and Language* 81 (2002): 732–5.

– "Psycholinguistic Perspectives." In *The Oxford Handbook of Compounding*, edited by Rochelle Lieber and Pavol Štekauer, 255–71. Oxford: Oxford University Press, 2009.

– "Relation and Lexical Priming during the Interpretation of Noun-Noun Combinations." *Journal of Experimental Psychology: Learning, Memory, and Cognition* 27 (2001): 236–54.

Gagné, Christina L., and Edward J. Shoben. "Priming Relations in Ambiguous Noun-Noun Combinations." *Memory & Cognition* 30, no. 4 (2002): 637–46.

Gagné, Christina L., and Thomas L. Spalding. "Constituent Integration during the Processing of Compound Words: Does It Involve Relational Structures?" *Journal of Memory and Language* 60 (2009): 20–35.

– "Effect of Relation Availability on the Interpretation and Access of Familiar Noun-Noun Compounds." *Brain and Language* 90 (2004): 478–86.

Gagné, Christina L., Thomas L. Spalding, and Melissa C. Gorrie. "Sentential Context and the Interpretation of Familiar Open-Compounds and Novel Modifier-Noun Phrases." *Language and Speech* 48 (2005): 203–21.

Gameson, Richard. "The Origin of the Exeter Book of Old English Poetry." *ASE* 25 (1996): 135–85.

Gardner, Thomas. "The Old English Kenning: A Characteristic Feature of Germanic Poetical Diction?" *Modern Philology* 67, no. 2 (1969): 109–17.

– "Semantic Patterns in Old English Substantival Compounds." PhD diss., Ruprecht-Karl-Universität, Hamburg, 1968.

Garnett, James M. "The Latin and the Anglo-Saxon *Juliana*." *PMLA* 14, no. 3 (1899): 279–98.

Garver, Eugene. "Comments on 'Rhetorical Analysis within a Pragma-Dialectical Framework, The Case of R.J. Reynolds.'" *Argumentation* 14, no. 3 (2000): 307–14.

Gatch, Milton McC. *Preaching and Theology in Anglo-Saxon England: Ælfric and Wulfstan*. Toronto: University of Toronto Press, 1977.

Genette, Gérard. *Narrative Discourse: An Essay in Method*. Translated by Jane E. Lewin. Ithaca, NY: Cornell University Press, 1980.

Gerould, G.H. "Abbot Ælfric's Rhythmic Prose." *Modern Philology* 22 (1925): 353–66.

Gneuss, Helmut. "*Anglicae linguae interpretatio*: Language Contact, Lexical Borrowing and Glossing in Anglo-Saxon England." *Proceedings of the British Academy* 82 (1993): 107–48.

– *Handlist of Anglo-Saxon Manuscripts: A List of Manuscripts and Manuscript Fragments Written or Owned in England up to 1100*. Tempe: Arizona Center for Medieval and Renaissance Studies, 2001.

– *Hymnar und Hymnen im englischen Mittelalter*. Tübingen: Max Niemeyer Press, 1968.

– "The Origin of Standard Old English and Æthelwold's School at Winchester." *ASE* 1 (1972): 63–83.

– "The Study of Language in Anglo-Saxon England." *Bulletin of the John Rylands Library of Manchester* 72 (1990): 3–32. Reprinted with a postscript in *Textual and Material Culture in Anglo-Saxon England: Thomas Northcote Toller and the Toller Memorial Lectures*, edited by Donald Scragg, 75–105. Cambridge: D.S. Brewer, 2003.

Gneuss, Helmut, and Michael Lapidge. *Anglo-Saxon Manuscripts: A Bibliographical Handlist of Manuscripts and Manuscript Fragments Written or Owned in England up to 1100*. Toronto: University of Toronto Press, 2014.

Godden, Malcolm. "Anglo-Saxons on the Mind." In *Learning and Literature in Anglo-Saxon England: Studies Presented to Peter Clemoes on the Occasion of His Sixty-Fifth Birthday*, edited by Michael Lapidge and Helmut Gneuss, 271–98. Cambridge: Cambridge University Press, 1985.

– *Ælfric's Catholic Homilies: Introduction, Commentary and Glossary*. EETS ss 18. Oxford: Oxford University Press, 2000.

– ed. *Ælfric's Catholic Homilies: The Second Series*. EETS ss 5. Oxford: Oxford University Press, 1979.

– "Did King Alfred Write Anything?" *Medium Ævum* 76, no. 1 (2007): 1–23.

– "Literary Language." In *The Cambridge History of The English Language*. Volume 1, *The Beginnings to 1066*, edited by Richard M. Hogg, 490–535. Cambridge: Cambridge University Press, 1992.

– "An Old English Penitential Motif." *ASE* 2 (1973): 221–39.

– "The Player King: Identification and Self-Representation in King Alfred's Writings." In *Alfred the Great: Papers from the Eleventh-Centenary Conferences*, edited by Timothy Reuter, 137–50. Aldershot, UK: Ashgate, 2003.

Godden, Malcolm, and Susan Irvine, eds. *The Old English Boethius: An Edition of the Old English Versions of Boethius's "De Consolatione Philosophiae."* 2 vols. Oxford: Oxford University Press, 2009.

Godlove, Shannon Nycole. "Apostolic Discourse and Christian Identity in Anglo-Saxon Literature." PhD diss., University of Illinois at Urbana-Champaign, 2010.

Godman, Peter. "The Anglo-Latin *Opus Geminatum*: From Aldhelm to Alcuin." *Medium Ævum* 50 (1981): 215–29.

Goodwin, Jean. "Argument Has No Function." *Informal Logic* 27, no. 1 (2007): 69–90.

Goody, Jack. *The Power of the Written Tradition*. Washington: Smithsonian Institute Publications, 2000.

Gordon, Terrence. "*Langue* and *Parole*." In *The Cambridge Companion to Saussure*, edited by Carol Sanders, 76–87. Cambridge: Cambridge University Press, 2004.

Gradon, P.O.E., ed. *Cynewulf's "Elene."* Rev. ed. Exeter: University of Exeter Press, 1977.

Greenfield, Stanley B. *The Interpretation of Old English Poems*. London: Routledge & Kegan Paul, 1972.

Gretsch, Mechthild. "Ælfric, Language and Winchester." In *A Companion to Ælfric*, edited by Hugh Magennis and Mary Swan, 109–38. Leiden: Brill, 2009.

– *The Intellectual Foundations of the English Benedictine Reform*. CSASE 25. Cambridge: Cambridge University Press, 1999.

Griffith, Mark. "The Composition of the Metres." In *The Old English Boethius*, edited by Malcolm Godden and Susan Irvine, 1:80–134. 2 vols. Oxford: Oxford University Press, 2009.

– "Old English Poetic Diction Not in Old English Verse or Prose – and the Curious Case of Aldhelm's Five Athletes." *ASE* 43 (2014): 99–131.

– "Poetic Language and the Paris Psalter: The Decay of the Old English Tradition." *ASE* 20 (1991): 167–86.

Griffiths, Bill, ed. *Alfred's Metres of Boethius*. Rev. ed. Pinner, UK: Anglo-Saxon Books, 1994.

Grundy, Lynne. "Ælfric's Grammatical Theology and Theological Grammar." In *Essays on Anglo-Saxon and Related Themes in Memory of Lynne Grundy*, edited by Jane Roberts and Janet Nelson, 1–14. King's College London Medieval Studies 17. London: King's College London, Centre for Late Antique & Medieval Studies, 2000.

Gunning, Tom. "Narrative Discourse and the Narrator System." In *Film Theory and Criticism: Introductory Readings*, 6th ed., edited by Leo Braudy and Marshall Cohen, 470–81. Oxford: Oxford University Press, 1999.

Hadley, D.M. "Viking and Native: Re-Thinking Identity in the Danelaw." *Early Medieval Europe* 11, no. 1 (2002): 45–70.

Hagoort, Peter, and Colin Brown. "Brain Response to Lexical Ambiguity Resolution and Parsing." In *Perspectives on Sentence Processing*, edited by Charles Clifton, Jr, Lyn Frazier, and Keith Rayner, 45–80. Hillsdale, NJ: Lawrence Erlbaum Associates, 1994.

Häikiö, Tuomo, Raymond Bertram, and Jukka Hyönä. "The Development of Whole-Word Representations in Compound Word Processing: Evidence from Eye Fixation Patterns of Elementary School Children." *Applied Psycholinguistics* 32 (2011): 533–51.

Hall, Thomas N. "Wulfstan's Latin Sermons." In *Wulfstan, Archbishop of York: The Proceedings of the Second Alcuin Conference*, edited by Matthew Townend, 93–139. Turnhout: Brepols, 2004.

Hamilton, Sarah. "Remedies for 'Great Transgressions': Penance and Excommunication in Late Anglo-Saxon England." In *Pastoral Care in Late Anglo-Saxon England*, edited by Francesca Tinto, 83–105. Woodbridge: Boydell Press, 2005.

– "Rites for Public Penance in Late Anglo-Saxon England." In *The Liturgy of the Late Anglo-Saxon Church*, edited by Helen Gittos and M. Bradford Bedingfield, 65–103. Woodbridge: Boydell and Brewer, 2005.

Hanson, Kristin, and Paul Kiparsky. "The Nature of Verse and Its Consequences for the Mixed Form." In *Prosimetrum: Cross-Cultural Perspectives on Narrative in Prose and Verse*, edited by Joseph Harris and Karl Reichl, 17–44. Cambridge: D.S. Brewer, 1997.

Harbus, Antonina. "Articulate Contact in *Juliana*." In *Verbal Encounters: Anglo-Saxon and Old Norse Studies for Roberta Frank*, edited by Antonina Harbus and Russell Poole, 183–200. Toronto: University of Toronto Press, 2005.

– *Life of the Mind in Old English Poetry*. Costerus ns 143. Amsterdam: Rodopi, 2002.

– "The Medieval Concept of the Self in Anglo-Saxon England." *Self and Identity* 1 (2002): 77–97.

Harris, A. Leslie. "Techniques of Pacing in *Beowulf*." *English Studies* 63 (1982): 97–108.

Harris, Joseph. "Older Germanic Poetry." In *Medieval Oral Literature*, edited by Karl Reichl, 253–78. Berlin: Walter de Gruyter, 2012.

Hartman, Megan E. "A Drawn-Out Beheading: Style, Theme, and Hypermetricity in the Old English *Judith*." *JEGP* 110, no. 4 (2011): 421–40.

– "Stressed and Spaced Out: Manuscript-Evidence for Beowulfian Prosody." *Anglo-Saxon* 1 (2007): 201–20.

Heikkinen, Seppo. "The Christianisation of Latin Metre: A Study of Bede's *De arte metrica*." PhD diss., University of Helsinki, 2012.

Heng, Geraldine. *Empire of Magic: Medieval Romance and the Politics of Cultural Fantasy*. New York: Columbia University Press, 2003.

Heusler, Andreas. *Die altgermanische Dichtung*. 2nd rev. ed. Potsdam: Athenaion, 1943.

Heyvaert, Liesbet. "Compounding in Cognitive Linguistics." In *The Oxford Handbook of Compounding*, edited by Rochelle Lieber and Pavol Štekauer, 233–54. Oxford: Oxford University Press, 2009.

Hill, John M. "Beowulf and the Danish Succession: Gift Giving as an Occasion for Complex Gesture." *Medievalia et Humanistica* 11 (1982): 177–97.

– *The Cultural World in "Beowulf."* Toronto: University of Toronto Press, 1994.

Hill, Joyce. "Learning Latin in Anglo-Saxon England: Traditions, Texts and Techniques." In *Learning and Literacy in Medieval England and Abroad*, edited by Sarah Rees Jones, 7–29. Turnhout: Brepols, 2003.

– "Translating the Tradition: Manuscripts, Models, and Methodologies in the Composition of Ælfric's Catholic Homilies." *Bulletin of the John Rylands University Library of Manchester* 79 (1997): 43–65.

Hoen, Michel, and Peter Ford Dominey. "ERP Analysis of Cognitive Sequencing: A Left Anterior Negativity Related to Structural Transformation Processing." *NeuroReport* 11, no. 14 (2000): 3187–91.

Hofstetter, Walter. *Winchester und der spätaltenglische Sprachgebrauch: Untersuchungen zur geographischen und zeitlichen Verbreitung altenglischer Synonyme*. Munich: W. Fink, 1987.

Holcomb, Phillip J. "Semantic Priming and Stimulus Degradation: Implications for the Role of the N400 in Language Processing." *Psychophysiology* 30 (1993): 47–61.

Holle, Henning, Thomas C. Gunter, and Dirk Koester. "The Time Course of Lexical Access in Morphologically Complex Words." *Neuroreport* 21, no. 5 (2010): 319–23.

Hollowell, Ida Masters. "Linguistic Factors Underlying Style Levels in Four Homilies of Wulfstan." *Neophilologus* 61 (1977): 287–96.

– "On the Two-Stress Theory of Wulfstan's Rhythm." *Philological Quarterly* 61 (1982): 1–11.

– "Unferð the *þyle* in *Beowulf*." *Studies in Philology* 73 (1976): 239–65.

Holquist, Michael. *Dialogism: Bakhtin and His World*. 2nd ed. London: Routledge, 2002.

Holton, Frederick. "Old English Sea Imagery and the Interpretation of *The Seafarer*." *Yearbook of English Studies* 12 (1982): 208–17.

Hoover, David L. "Evidence for Primacy of Alliteration in Old English Metre." *ASE* 14 (1985): 75–96.
– *New Theory of Old English Meter*. New York: Peter Lang, 1985.
Horner, Shari. *The Discourse of Enclosure: Representing Women in Old English Literature*. Albany: State University of New York Press, 2001.
– "Spiritual Truth and Sexual Violence: The Old English *Juliana*, Anglo-Saxon Nuns, and the Discourse of Female Monastic Enclosure." *Signs* 19, no. 3 (1994): 658–75.
– "The Violence of Exegesis: Reading the Bodies of Ælfric's Female Saints." In *Violence against Women in Medieval Texts*, edited by Anna Roberts, 22–43. Gainesville: University Press of Florida, 1998.
Howe, Nicholas. *Migration and Mythmaking in Anglo-Saxon England*. 1989; reprinted Notre Dame, IN: University of Notre Dame Press, 2001.
– *The Old English Catalogue Poems*. Anglistica 23. Copenhagen: Rosenkilde and Bagger, 1985.
Hulbert, J.R. "A Note on Compounds in *Beowulf*." *JEGP* 31 (1932): 504–8.
Hutchison, Keith A. "Is Semantic Priming Due to Association Strength or Feature Overlap? A *Micro*analytic Review." *Psychonomic Bulletin & Review* 10, no. 4 (2003): 785–813.
Hymes, Dell. "Ways of Speaking." In *Explorations in the Ethnography of Speaking*, edited by Richard Bauman and Joel Sherzer, 433–51. Cambridge: Cambridge University Press, 1989.
Hyönä, Jukka, and Alexander Pollatsek. "Reading Finnish Compound Words: Eye Fixations Are Affected by Component Morphemes." *Journal of Experimental Psychology: Human Perception and Performance* 24, no. 6 (1998): 1612–27.
Inhoff, Albrecht Werner, Ralph Radach, and Dieter Heller. "Complex Compounds in German: Interword Spaces Facilitate Segmentation but Hinder Assignment of Meaning." *Journal of Memory and Language* 42 (2000): 23–50.
Innocenti, Beth. "A Normative Pragmatic Model of Making Fear Appeals." *Philosophy and Rhetoric* 44, no. 3 (2011): 273–90.
Innocenti Manolescu, Beth. "Norms of Presentational Force." *Argumentation and Advocacy* 41 (2005): 139–51.
Irvine, Martin. *The Making of Textual Culture: "Grammatica" and Literary Theory 350–1100*. Cambridge: Cambridge University Press, 1994.
Irvine, Susan. "The Authorship of the Alfredian Versions and the Relationship of Prose and Verse." Paper, Third Annual Symposium of The Alfredian Boethius Project, Oxford, 4 July 2005.
Isel, Frédéric, Thomas C. Gunter, and Angela D. Friederici. "Prosody-Assisted Head-Driven Access to Spoken German Compounds." *Journal of*

Experimental Psychology: Learning, Memory, and Cognition 29, no. 2 (2003): 277–88.

Jackendoff, Ray. "Compounding in the Parallel Architecture and Conceptual Semantics." In *The Oxford Handbook of Compounding*, edited by Rochelle Lieber and Pavol Štekauer, 105–28. Oxford: Oxford University Press, 2011.

Jackson, Elizabeth. "'Not Simply Lists': An Eddic Perspective on Short-Item Lists in Old English Poems." *Speculum* 73 (1998): 338–71.

Jager, Eric. "The Word in the 'Breost': Interiority and the Fall in *Genesis B*." *Neophilologus* 75 (1991): 279–99.

Jakobson, Roman. *Language in Literature*. Edited by Krystyna Pomorska and Stephen Rudy. Cambridge, MA: Belknap, 1987.

Jarema, Gonia. "Compound Representation and Processing: A Cross-Language Perspective." In *Representation and Processing of Compound Words*, edited by Gary Libben and Gonia Jarema, 45–70. Oxford: Oxford University Press, 2006.

Ji, Hongbo, Christina L. Gagné, and Thomas L. Spalding. "Benefits and Costs of Lexical Decomposition and Semantic Integration during the Processing of Transparent and Opaque English Compounds." *Journal of Memory and Language* 65 (2011): 406–30.

Jia, Xiaeofei, Suiping Wang, Bao Zhang, and John. X. Zhang. "Electrophysiological Evidence for Relation Information Activation in Chinese Compound Word Comprehension." *Neuropsychologia* 51, no. 7 (2013): 1296–1301.

Johnson, David F. "Hagiographical Demon or Liturgical Devil? Demonology and Baptismal Imagery in Cynewulf's *Elene*." *Leeds Studies in English* 37 (2006): 9–29.

Jones, Christopher A. "Ælfric and the Limits of the 'Benedictine Reform.'" In *A Companion to Ælfric*, edited by Hugh Magennis and Mary Swan, 67–108. Leiden: Brill, 2009.

– "*Meatim sed et rustica*: Ælfric of Eynsham as a Medieval Latin Author." *Journal of Medieval Latin* 8 (1998): 1–57.

Jorgensen, Alice. "The Trumpet and the Wolf: Noises of Battle in Old English Poetry." *Oral Tradition* 24 (2009): 319–36.

Jost, Karl, ed. *Die "Institutes of Polity, Civil and Ecclesiastical": Ein Werk Erzbischof Wulfstans von York*. Schweizer anglistische Arbeiten 47. Bern: Francke Verlag, 1959.

Juhasz, Barbara J. "Effects of Word Length and Sentence Context on Compound Word Recognition: An Eye Movement Investigation." PhD diss., University of Massachusetts – Amherst, 2006.

– "Sentence Context Modifies Compound Word Recognition: Evidence from Eye Movements." *Journal of Cognitive Psychology* 24 (2012): 855–70.

Juhasz, Barbara J., Albrecht W. Inhoff, and Keith Rayner. "The Role of Interword Spaces in the Processing of English Compound Words." *Language and Cognitive Processes* 20 (2005): 291–316.

Juhasz, Barbara J., Matthew S. Starr, Albrecht W. Inhoff, and Lars Placke. "The Effects of Morphology on the Processing of Compound Words: Evidence from Naming, Lexical Decisions and Eye Fixations." *British Journal of Psychology* 94 (2003): 223–44.

Jung, Berenike. *Narrating Violence in Post-9/11 Action Cinema: Terrorist Narratives, Cinematic Narration, and Referentiality*. Wiesbaden: VS Verlag für Sozialwissenschaften, 2010.

Kastovsky, Dieter. "Semantics and Vocabulary." In *The Cambridge History of The English Language*. Volume 1, *The Beginnings to 1066*, edited by Richard M. Hogg, 290–408. Cambridge: Cambridge University Press, 1992.

Kendall, Calvin B., ed. *Bedae Venerabilis Opera, Pars I: Opera Didascalica*. CCSL 123A. Turnhout: Brepols, 1975.

– ed. *De arte metrica*. In *Bedae Venerabilis Opera, Pars I: Opera Didascalica*, 82–141. CCSL 123A. Turnhout: Brepols, 1975.

– ed. *De schematibus et tropis*. In *Bedae Venerabilis Opera, Pars I: Opera Didascalica*, 142–71. CCSL 123A. Turnhout: Brepols, 1975.

– ed. and trans. *Libri II De arte metrica et De schematibus et tropis: The Art of Poetry and Rhetoric*. Saarbrücken: AQ-Verlag, 1991.

– *The Metrical Grammar of "Beowulf."* CSASE 5. Cambridge: Cambridge University Press, 1991.

– "The Prefix *un-* and the Metrical Grammar of *Beowulf*." *ASE* 10 (1982): 39–52.

Kennison, Shelia M. "Different Time Courses of Integrative Semantic Processing for Plural and Singular Nouns: Implications for Theories of Sentence Processing." *Cognition* 97 (2005): 269–94.

Ker, N.R. *Catalogue of Manuscripts Containing Anglo-Saxon*. 1957; reissued Oxford: Clarendon Press, 1990.

– "The Handwriting of Archbishop Wulfstan." In *England before the Conquest: Studies in Primary Sources Presented to Dorothy Whitelock*, edited by Peter Clemoes and Kathleen Hughes, 315–31. Cambridge: Cambridge University Press, 1971.

Keynes, Simon. "Appendix: Rulers of the English, c. 450–1066." In *The Blackwell Encyclopaedia of Anglo-Saxon England*, edited by Michael Lapidge, John Blair, Simon Keynes, and Donald Scragg, 500–20. Malden, MA: Blackwell, 1999.

– *The Diplomas of King Æthelred "The Unready," 978–1016*. Cambridge Studies in Medieval Life and Thought, 3rd ser., 13. Cambridge: Cambridge University Press, 1980.

– "The Power of the Written Word: Alfredian England 871–899." In *Alfred the Great: Papers from the Eleventh-Centenary Conferences*, edited by Timothy Reuter, 175–97. Aldershot, UK: Ashgate, 2003.

Kiernan, Kevin. "Alfred the Great's Burnt *Boethius*." In *The Iconic Page in Manuscript, Print, and Digital Culture*, edited by George Bornstein and Theresa Tinkle, 7–32. Ann Arbor: University of Michigan Press, 1998.

– *"Beowulf" and the Beowulf Manuscript*. Ann Arbor: University of Michigan Press, 1996.

Killingsworth, M. Jimmie. *Appeals in Modern Rhetoric: An Ordinary-Language Approach*. Carbondale: Southern Illinois University Press, 2005.

Kintgen, Eugene R. "Echoic Repetition in Old English Poetry, Especially *The Dream of the Rood*." *NM* 75 (1974): 202–23.

Kiparsky, Paul. "Dvandvas, Blocking, and the Associative: The Bumpy Ride from Phrase to Word." *Language* 86 (2010): 302–31.

Knappe, Gabriele. "Classical Rhetoric in Anglo-Saxon England." *ASE* 27 (1998): 5–29.

– "The Rhetorical Aspect of Grammar Teaching in Anglo-Saxon England." *Rhetorica: A Journal of the History of Rhetoric* 17, no. 1 (1999): 1–34.

– *Traditionen der klassischen Rhetorik im angelsächsischen England*. Anglistische Forschungen 236. Heidelberg: C. Winter, 1996.

Koban, Charles. "Substantive Compounds in *Beowulf*." PhD diss., University of Illinois, 1963.

Kock, Ernst A. "Old West Germanic and Old Norse." In *Studies in English Philology: A Miscellany in Honor of Frederick Klaeber*, edited by Kemp Malone and Martin R. Ruud, 14–20. Minneapolis: University of Minnesota Press, 1929.

Koester, Dirk, Henning Holle, and Thomas C. Gunter. "Electrophysiological Evidence for Incremental Lexical-Semantic Integration in Auditory Compound Comprehension." *Neuropsychologia* 47 (2009): 1854–64.

Koester, Dirk, Thomas C. Gunter, and Susanne Wagner. "The Morphosyntactic Decomposition and Semantic Composition of German Compound Words Investigated by ERPs." *Brain and Language* 102 (2007): 64–79.

Koester, Dirk, Th. C. Gunter, S. Wagner, and A.D. Friederici. "Morphosyntax, Prosody, and Linking Elements: The Auditory Processing of German Nominal Compounds." *Journal of Cognitive Neuroscience* 16, no. 9 (2004): 1647–68.

Kornexl, Lucia, ed. *Die "Regularis concordia" und ihre altenglische Interlinearversion*. Texte und Untersuchungen zur Englischen Philologie 17. Munich: Wilhelm Fink, 1993.

Krackow, Otto. *Die Nominalcomposita als Kunstmittel im altenglischen Epos*. Berlin: Mayer & Müller, 1903.

Krapp, George Philip, ed. *The Vercelli Book*. ASPR 2. New York: Columbia University Press, 1932.

Krapp, George Philip, and Elliot Van Kirk Dobbie, eds. *The Exeter Book*. ASPR 3. New York: Columbia University Press, 1936.

Kretzschmar, William A. "Adaptation and *Anweald*." *ASE* 16 (1987): 127–45.

Kunter, Gero. *Compound Stress in English: The Phonetics and Phonology of Prosodic Prominence*. Berlin: Walter de Gruyter & Co., 2011.

Kutas, Marta, and Kara D. Federmeier. "Electrophysiology Reveals Semantic Memory Use in Language Comprehension." *Trends in Cognitive Sciences* 4, no. 12 (2000): 463–70.

– "N400." *Scholarpedia* 4, no. 10 (2009): 7790.

– "Thirty Years and Counting: Finding Meaning in the N400 Component of the Event-Related Brain Potential (ERP)." *Annual Review of Psychology* 62 (2011): 621–47.

Lapidge, Michael. "Anglo-Latin Literature." In *Anglo-Latin Literature: 600–899*, 1–36. London: Hambledon Press, 1996.

– "The Archetype of *Beowulf*." *ASE* 29 (2000): 5–41.

– "*Beowulf* and Perception." *Proceedings of the British Academy* 111 (2001): 61–97.

– *The Cult of St Swithun*. Winchester Studies 4.ii. Oxford: Clarendon Press, 2003.

– "Cynewulf and the *Passio S. Iulianae*." In *Unlocking the Wordhord: Anglo-Saxon Studies in Memory of Edward B. Irving, Jr*, edited by Mark C. Amodio and Katherine O'Brien O'Keeffe, 147–71. Toronto: University of Toronto Press, 2003.

– "The Hermeneutic Style in Tenth-Century Anglo-Latin Literature." In *Anglo-Latin Literature, 900–1066*, 105–49. London: Hambledon Press, 1993. First printed in *ASE* 4 (1975): 67–111.

– "Old English Poetic Compounds: A Latin Perspective." In *Intertexts: Studies in Anglo-Saxon Culture Presented to Paul E. Szarmach*, edited by Virginia Blanton and Helene Scheck, 17–32. Arizona Studies in the Middle Ages and Renaissance 24. Tempe: Arizona Center for Medieval and Renaissance Studies, 2008.

– "Poeticism in Pre-Conqust Anglo-Latin Prose." In *Aspects of the Language of Latin Prose*, edited by Tobias Reinhardt, Michael Lapidge, and J.N. Adams, 321–38. Proceedings of the British Academy 129. Oxford: Oxford University Press, 2005.

Lass, Roger. *Old English: A Historical Linguistic Companion*. Cambridge: Cambridge University Press, 1994.

Law, Vivien. "Anglo-Saxon England: Aelfric's 'Excerptiones de arte grammatica anglice.'" *Histoire Épistémologie Langage* 9, no. 1 (1987): 47–71.

– *Grammar and Grammarians in the Early Middle Ages*. London: Longman, 1997.

– *The Insular Latin Grammarians*. Woodbridge: The Boydell Press, 1982.

– "Irish Symptoms and the Provenance of Sixth- and Seventh-Century Latin Grammars." In *Matériaux pour une histoire des théories linguistiques*, edited by Sylvain Auroux, Michel Glatigny, André Joly, Anne Nicolas, and Irène Rosier, 77–85. Lille: Université de Lille III, 1984.

Lees, Clare A. *Tradition and Belief: Religious Writing in Late Anglo-Saxon England*. Minneapolis: University of Minnesota Press, 1999.

Lees, Robert B. *The Grammar of English Nominalizations*. Bloomington: Indiana University Press, 1963.

Lehmann, Winfred P. *The Development of Germanic Verse Form*. Austin: University of Texas Press and Linguistic Society of America, 1956.

Lehtonen, Minna, Toni Cunillera, Antoni Rodríguez-Fornells, Annika Hultén, Jyrki Tuomainen, and Matti Laine. "Recognition of Morphologically Complex Words in Finnish: Evidence from Event-Related Potentials." *Brain Research* 1148 (2007): 123–37.

Lendinara, Patrizia. *Anglo-Saxon Glosses and Glossaries*. Variorum Collected Studies. Aldershot, UK: Ashgate, 1999.

Letson, D.R. "The Poetic Content of the Revival Homily." In *The Old English Homily and Its Background*, edited by Paul E. Szarmach and Bernard F. Huppé, 139–56. Albany: State University of New York Press, 1978.

Levi, Judith. *The Syntax and Semantics of Complex Nominals*. New York: Academic Press, 1978.

Lewis, Charleton T., and Charles Short. *A Latin Dictionary*. 1879. Oxford: Clarendon Press, 1989.

Libben, Gary. "Semantic Transparency in the Processing of Compounds: Consequences for Representation, Processing, and Impairment." *Brain and Language* 61 (1998): 30–44.

– "Why Study Compound Processing? An Overview of the Issues." In *Representation and Processing of Compound Words*, edited by Gary Libben and Gonia Jarema, 1–22. Oxford: Oxford University Press, 2006.

Libben, Gary, and Gonia Jarema, eds. *Representation and Processing of Compound Words*. Oxford: Oxford University Press, 2006.

Lieber, Rochelle, and Pavol Štekauer. "Introduction: Status and Definition of Compounding." In *The Oxford Handbook of Compounding*, edited by Rochelle Lieber and Pavol Štekauer, 3–18. Oxford: Oxford University Press, 2011.

– eds. *The Oxford Handbook of Compounding*. Oxford: Oxford University Press, 2011.

Lindsay, W.M., ed. *The Corpus Glossary*. Cambridge: Cambridge University Press, 1921.

Lionarons, Joyce Tally. "Cultural Syncretism and the Construction of Gender in Cynewulf's *Elene*." *Exemplaria* 10, no. 1 (1998): 51– 68.

– *The Homiletic Writings of Archbishop Wulfstan: A Critical Study*. Woodbridge: D.S. Brewer, 2010.

Lipka, Leonhard. "Lexicalization and Institutionalization." In *The Encyclopedia of Language and Linguistics*, edited by Roland E. Asher, 2164–7. Oxford: Pergamon, 1994.

Lipka, Leonhard, Susanne Handl, and Wolfgang Falkner. "Lexicalization and Institutionalization: The State of the Art in 2004." *SKASE Journal of Theoretical Linguistics* 1, no. 1 (2004): 2–19.

Liuzza, Roy Michael. "On the Dating of *Beowulf*." In *The "Beowulf" Reader*, edited by Peter S. Baker, 281–302. 1995; New York: Garland, 2000.

Lockett, Leslie. *Anglo-Saxon Psychologies in the Vernacular and Latin Traditions*. Toronto: University of Toronto Press, 2011.

Low, Anthony. "Exile, *The Wanderer*, and the Long Wave of Alienation and Subjectivity." In *Satura: Studies in Medieval Literature in Honor of Robert R. Raymo*, edited by Nancy M. Reale and Ruth E. Sternglantz, 1–19. Donington, UK: Shaun Tyas, 2001.

Low, Soon Ai. "The Anglo-Saxon Mind: Metaphor and Common Sense Psychology in Old English Literature." PhD diss., University of Toronto, 1999.

De Lubac, Henri. *Exégèse medievale: Les quatre sens de l'Ecriture*. 2 vols. Paris: Aubier, 1959–60.

Lucas, Peter J. "The Language of the Loner: From Splendid Isolation to 'Individual' in Early English Poetry?" In *Text and Gloss: Studies in Insular Learning and Literature Presented to Joseph Donovan Pheifer*, edited by Helen Conrad-O'Briain, Anne Marie D'Arcy, and John Scattergood, 102–18. Dublin: Four Courts Press, 1999.

Luhtala, Anneli. "Linguistics and Theology in the Early Medieval West." In *History of the Language Sciences*, edited by Sylvain Auroux, E.F.K. Koerner, Hans-Josef Niederehe, and Kees Versteegh, 510–25. Berlin: Walter de Gruyter, 2000.

MacGregor, Lucy J., and Yury Shtyrov. "Multiple Routes for Compound Word Processing in the Brain: Evidence from EEG." *Brain & Language* 126 (2013): 217–29.

Magennis, Hugh, and Mary Swan, eds. *A Companion to Ælfric*. Leiden: Brill, 2009.

Magoun, F.P., Jr. "Recurring First Elements in Different Nominal Compounds in *Beowulf* and in the *Elder Edda*." In *Studies in English Philology: A Miscellany in Honor of Frederick Klaeber*, edited by Kemp Malone and Martin R. Ruud, 73–8. Minneapolis: University of Minnesota Press, 1929.

Malmkjær, Kirsten. *Linguistics and the Language of Translation*. Edinburgh Textbooks in Applied Linguistics. Edinburgh: Edinburgh University Press, 2005.

Marelli, Marco, and Claudio Luzzatti. "Frequency Effects in the Processing of Italian Nominal Compounds: Modulation of Headedness and Semantic Transparency." *Journal of Memory and Language* 66 (2012): 644–64.

Marelli, Marco, Silvia Aggujaro, Franco Molteni, and Claudio Luzzatti. "The Multiple-Lemma Representation of Italian Compound Nouns: A Single Case Study of Deep Dyslexia." *Neuropsychologia* 50 (2012): 842–61.

Martin, John. *The Modern Dance*. Princeton: Princeton Book Company, 1933.

Matto, Michael. "True Confessions: *The Seafarer* and Technologies of the *Sylf*." *JEGP* 103, no. 2 (2004): 156–79.

– "A War of Containment: The Heroic Image in *The Battle of Maldon*." *Studia Neophilologica* 74 (2002): 60–75.

Mauss, Marcel. *The Gift: The Form and Reason for Exchange in Archaic Societies*. Translated by W.D. Halls. London: Routledge, 1990.

Mazo, Jeffrey Alan. "Compound Diction and Traditional Style in *Beowulf* and *Genesis A*." *Oral Tradition* 6, no. 1 (1991): 79–92.

– "'A Good Saxon Compound.'" *Folklore* 107 (1996): 107–8.

McCormick, Samantha F., Marc Brysbaert, and Kathleen Rastle. "Is Morphological Decomposition Limited to Low-Frequency Words?" *The Quarterly Journal of Experimental Psychology* 62, no. 9 (2009): 1706–15.

McIntosh, Angus. "Wulfstan's Prose." *Proceedings of the British Academy* 35 (1949): 109–42.

Meens, Rob. "The Frequency and Nature of Early Medieval Penance." In *Handling Sin: Confession in the Middle Ages*, edited by Peter Biller and A.J. Minnis, 35–61. York: York Medieval Press, 1998.

Meissner, Rudolph. *Die Kenningar der Skalden: Ein Beitrag zur skaldischen Poetik*. Leipzig: Kurt Schroeder, 1921.

Menzer, Melinda J. "*Aglæcwif* (*Beowulf* 1259a): Implications for *–wif* Compounds, Grendel's Mother, and Other *aglæcan*." *English Language Notes* 34 (1996): 1–6.

– "Ælfric's English *Grammar*." *JEGP* 103, no. 1 (2004): 106–24.

– "Ælfric's *Grammar*: Solving the Problem of the English-Language Text." *Neophilologus* 83 (1999): 637–52.

Metcalf, Allan A. "On the Authorship and Originality of the *Meters of Boethius*." *NM* 71 (1970): 185–6.

– *Poetic Diction in the Old English Meters of Boethius*. De Proprietatibus Litterarum, Series Practica 50. The Hague: Mouton, 1973.

– "The Poetic Language of the Old English *Meters of Boethius*." PhD diss., University of California, Berkeley, 1967.

Micheli, Raphaël. "Arguing without Trying to Persuade? Elements for a *Non-Persuasive* Definition of Argumentation." *Argumentation* 26 (2012): 115–26.

Milfull, Inge B. *The Hymns of the Anglo-Saxon Church: A Study and Edition of the "Durham Hymnal."* CSASE 17. Cambridge: Cambridge University Press, 1996.

Miller, Thomas, ed. *The Old English Version of Bede's Ecclesiastical History of the English People*. EETS os 95, 96, 110, and 111. London: Oxford University Press, 1890–8.

Minkova, Donka. *Alliteration and Sound Change in Early English*. Cambridge: Cambridge University Press, 2003.

Mitchell, Bruce. "The Relation between Old English Alliterative Verse and Ælfric's Alliterative Prose." In *Latin Learning and English Lore: Studies in Anglo-Saxon Literature for Michael Lapidge*, edited by Andy Orchard and Katherine O'Brien O'Keeffe, 2:349–62. 2 vols. Toronto: University of Toronto Press, 2005.

Mitchell, Bruce, and Fred C. Robinson, eds. *Beowulf: An Edition*. Malden, MA: Blackwell, 1998.

Mize, Britt. "The Representation of the Mind as an Enclosure in Old English Poetry." *ASE* 35 (2006): 57–90.

– *Traditional Subjectivities: The Old English Poetics of Mentality*. Toronto: University of Toronto Press, 2013.

Mombrizio, Bonino, ed. *Sanctuarium seu vitae sanctorum*. 2nd ed. 2 vols. 1910; reprinted Hildesheim: Georg Olms Press, 1978.

Momma, Haruko. *The Composition of Old English Poetry*. CSASE 20. Cambridge: Cambridge University Press, 1997.

Monnin, Pierre Eric. "The Making of the Old English *Meters of Boethius*: Studies in Traditional Art and Aesthetics." PhD diss., University of Massachussetts, 1975.

– "Poetic Improvements in the Old English *Meters of Boethius*." *English Studies* 60 (1979): 346–60.

Morita, Aiko, and Katsuo Tamaoka. "Semantic Involvement in the Lexical and Sentence Processing of Japanese Kanji." *Brain and Language* 82 (2002): 54–64.

Morrish, Jennifer. "King Alfred's Letter as a Source on Learning in England in the Ninth Century." In *Studies in Earlier Old English Prose: Sixteen Original Contributions*, edited by Paul E. Szarmach, 87–108. Albany: State University of New York Press, 1986.

Muir, Bernard J. *The Exeter Anthology of Old English Poetry: An Edition of Exeter Dean and Chapter MS 3501*. 2 vols. Exeter: University of Exeter, 1994.

Myers, James. "Processing Chinese Compounds: A Survey of the Literature." In *Representation and Processing of Compound Words*, edited by Gary Libben and Gonia Jarema, 169–96. Oxford: Oxford University Press, 2006.

Napier, A.S., ed. *Wulfstan: Sammlung der ihm zugeschriebenen Homilien nebst Untersuchungen über ihre Echtheit*. Sammlung englischer Denkmäler in kritischen Ausgaben 4. 1883; reprinted Dublin: Weidmann, 1967.

Nelson, Janet L. "Power and Authority at the Court of Alfred." In *Essays on Anglo-Saxon and Related Themes in Memory of Lynne Grundy*, edited by Jane Roberts and Janet Nelson, 311–37. London: King's College London, Centre for Late Antique and Medieval Studies, 2000.

Nichols, Ann Eljenholm. "Ælfric and the Brief Style." *JEGP* 70 (1971): 1–12.

Niles, John D. *"Beowulf": The Poem and Its Tradition*. Cambridge, MA: Harvard University Press, 1983.

– "Compound Diction and the Style of *Beowulf*." *English Studies* 62 (1981): 489–503.

– "Formula and Formulaic System in *Beowulf*." In *Oral Traditional Literature: A Festschrift for Albert Bates Lord*, edited by John Miles Foley, 394–415. Columbus, OH: Slavica, 1980. Reprinted in *"Beowulf": The Poem and Its Tradition*, 121–37. Cambridge, MA: Harvard University Press, 1983.

– *Homo Narrans: The Poetics and Anthropology of Oral Literature*. Philadelphia: University of Pennsylvania Press, 1999.

– "The Myth of the Anglo-Saxon Oral Poet." *Western Folklore* 62 (2003): 7–61.

Nolan, Barbara, and Morton W. Bloomfield. "*Beotword*, *Gilpcwidas*, and the *Gilphlæden* Scop of *Beowulf*." *JEGP* 79, no. 4 (1980): 499–516.

Nonnon, Elizabeth. "Activités argumentatives et élaboration de connaissances nouvelles: le dialogue comme espace d'exploration." *Langue française* 112 (1996): 67–87.

Nordal, Gúðrún. *Tools of Literacy: The Role of Skaldic Verse in Icelandic Textual Culture of the Twelfth and Thirteenth Centuries*. Toronto: University of Toronto Press, 2001.

O'Brien O'Keeffe, Katherine. "Body and Law in Late Anglo-Saxon England." *ASE* 27 (1998): 209–32.

– "Diction, Variation, the Formula." In *A Beowulf Handbook*, edited by Robert E. Bjork and John D. Niles, 85–104. Lincoln: University of Nebraska Press, 1997.

– *Stealing Obedience: Narratives of Agency and Identity in Late Anglo-Saxon England*. Toronto: University of Toronto Press, 2012.

– "Values and Ethics in Heroic Literature." In *The Cambridge Companion to Old English Literature*, 2nd ed., edited by Malcolm Godden and Michael Lapidge, 101–19. Cambridge: Cambridge University Press, 2013.

– *Visible Song: Transitional Literacy in Old English Verse*. CSASE 4. Cambridge: Cambridge University Press, 1990.

Ogura, Michiko. "Camel or Elephant? How to Lexicalize Objects Foreign to the Anglo-Saxons." In *Japanische Beiträge zu Kultur und Sprache: Studia Iaponica Wolfgango Viereck emerito oblata*, edited by Guido Oebel, 228–45. Munich: Lincom Europa, 2006.

Olsen, Alexandra Hennessey. "Cynewulf's Autonomous Women: A Reconsideration of *Elene* and *Juliana*." In *New Readings on Women in Old English Literature*, edited by Helen Damico and Alexandra Hennessey Olsen, 222–32. Bloomington: Indiana University Press, 1990.

Ólsen, Björn Magnússon, ed. *Den Tredje og Fjærde Grammatiske Afhandling i Snorres Edda*. Samfund til udgivelse af gammel nordisk literatur 12. Copenhagen: Fr. G. Knudtzons Bogtrykkeri, 1884.

Opland, Jeff. *Anglo-Saxon Oral Poetry: A Study of the Traditions*. New Haven: Yale University Press, 1980.

– "*Beowulf* on the Poet." *Mediaeval Studies* 38 (1976): 442–67.

Orchard, Andy. *A Critical Companion to "Beowulf."* Toronto: Toronto University Press, 2005.

– "Crying Wolf: Oral Style and the *Sermones Lupi*." *ASE* 21 (1992): 239–64.

– "Old English and Latin Poetic Traditions." In *A Companion to Medieval Poetry*, edited by Corinne Saunders, 65–82. Malden, MA: Wiley-Blackwell, 2010.

– "Oral Tradition." In *Reading Old English Texts*, edited by Katherine O'Brien O'Keeffe, 101–23. Cambridge: Cambridge University Press, 1997.

– *The Poetic Art of Aldhelm*. CSASE 8. Cambridge: Cambridge University Press, 1994.

– "The Word Made Flesh: Christianity and Oral Culture in Anglo-Saxon Verse." *Oral Tradition* 24, no. 2 (2009): 293–318.

Overholser, Lee Charles. "A Comparative Study of the Compound Use of *Andreas* and *Beowulf*." PhD diss., University of Michigan, 1971.

Oxford Latin Dictionary. Edited by P.G.W. Glare. 2nd ed. Oxford: Oxford University Press, 2012.

Pálsson, Heimir, ed., and Anthony Faulkes, trans. *The Uppsala Edda: DG 11 4to*. London: Viking Society for Northern Research, 2012.

Parker, Roscoe E. "*Gyd*, *Leoð*, and *Sang* in Old English Poetry." *University of Tennessee Studies in the Humanities* 1 (1956): 59–63.

Pàroli, Teresa. "Indice della terminologia grammaticale de Aelfric." *Istituto Orientale di Napoli: Annali, Sezione Linguistica* 8 (1968): 113–38.

Parry, Milman. *The Making of Homeric Verse*. Edited by Adam Parry. Oxford: Clarendon Press, 1971.

Payne, F. Anne. *King Alfred and Boethius: An Analysis of the Old English Version of the Consolation of Philosophy*. Madison: University of Wisconsin Press, 1968.

Peters, Leonard J. "The Relationship of the Old English *Andreas* and *Beowulf*." *PMLA* 66 (1951): 844–63.

Pinto, Robert C. "Argumentation and the Force of Reasons." *Informal Logic* 29, no. 3 (2009): 268–95.

– "The Uses of Argument in Communicative Contexts." *Argumentation* 24 (2010): 227–52.

Plag, Ingo. "Compound Stress Assignment by Analogy: The Constituent Family Bias." *Zeitschrift für Sprachwissenschaft* 29, no. 2 (2010): 243–82.

– "The Variability of Compound Stress in English: Structural, Semantic and Analogical Factors." *English Language and Linguistics* 10, no. 1 (2006): 143–72.

Plag, Ingo, Gero Kunter, and Sabine Lappe. "Testing Hypotheses about Compound Stress Assignment in English: A Corpus-Based Investigation." *Corpus Linguistics and Linguistic Theory* 3, no. 2 (2007): 199–233.

Plag, Ingo, Gero Kunter, Sabine Lappe, and Maria Braun. "The Role of Semantics, Argument Structure, and Lexicalization in Compound Stress Assignment in English." *Language* 84, no. 4 (2008): 760–94.

Pollatsek, Alexander, and Jukka Hyönä. "The Role of Semantic Transparency in the Processing of Finnish Compound Words." *Language and Cognitive Processes* 20 (2005): 261–90.

Pollatsek, Alexander, Jukka Hyönä, and Raymond Bertram. "The Role of Morphological Constituents in Reading Finnish Compound Words." *Journal of Experimental Psychology: Human Perception and Performance* 26, no. 2 (2000): 820–33.

Pons Sanz, Sara María. *Analysis of the Scandinavian Loanwords in the Aldredian Glosses to the Lindisfarne Gospels*. Valencia: Lengua Inglesa, Universitat de València, 2000.

– *The Lexical Effects of Anglo-Scandinavian Linguistic Contact on Old English*. Studies in the Early Middle Ages 1. Turnhout: Brepols, 2013.

– *Norse-Derived Vocabulary in Late Old English Texts: Wulfstan's Works, A Case Study*. Odense: University Press of Southern Denmark, 2007.

Pope, John C., ed. *Homilies of Ælfric: A Supplementary Collection*. 2 vols. EETS os 259–60. London: Oxford University Press, 1967.

Pratt, David. "Problems of Authorship and Audience in the Writings of King Alfred the Great." In *Lay Intellectuals in the Carolingian World*, edited by Patrick Wormald and Janet L. Nelson, 162–91. Cambridge: Cambridge University Press, 2007.

Prince, Stephen. *Savage Cinema: Sam Peckinpah and the Rise of Ultraviolent Movies*. Austin: University of Texas Press, 1998.

Raffray, Claudine N., Martin J. Pickering, and Holly P. Branigan. "Priming the Interpretation of Noun-Noun Combinations." *Journal of Memory and Language* 57 (2007): 380–95.

Ramsey, Lee C. "The Sea Voyages in *Beowulf*." *NM* 72 (1971): 51–9.

– "The Theme of Battle in Old English Poetry." PhD diss., Indiana University, 1965.

Rankin, Susan, ed. *The Winchester Troper*. Early English Church Music 50. London: Stainer and Bell, 2007.

Reibel, David A. "A Grammatical Index to the Compound Nouns of Old English Verse." PhD diss., Indiana University, 1963.

Reichl, Karl. "Old English *giedd* and Middle English *yedding* as Genre Terms." In *Words, Texts, and Manuscripts: Studies in Anglo-Saxon Culture Presented to Helmut Gneuss on the Occasion of His Sixty-fifth Birthday*, edited by Michael Korhammer, Karl Reichl, and Hans Sauer, 349–70. Cambridge: D.S. Brewer, 1992.

Reuter, Timothy, ed. *Alfred the Great: Papers from the Eleventh-Centenary Conferences*. Aldershot, UK: Ashgate, 2003.

Rice, Robert C. "The Penitential Motif in Cynewulf's *Fates of the Apostles* and in His Epilogues." *ASE* 6 (1977): 105–19.

Riedinger, Anita. "The Old English Formula in Context." *Speculum* 60 (1985): 294–317.

Roach, Joseph. *Cities of the Dead: Circum-Atlantic Performance*. New York: Columbia University Press, 1996.

Robinson, Fred C. *"Beowulf" and the Appositive Style*. Knoxville: University of Tennessee Press, 1985.

– "A Sub-Sense of Old English *fyrn*(–)." *NM* 100 (1999): 471–5.

– "Two Aspects of Variation in Old English Poetry." In *Old English Poetry: Essays on Style*, edited by Daniel G. Calder, 125–44. Berkeley: University of California Press, 1979.

Rosier, James L. "Generative Composition in *Beowulf*." *English Studies* 58 (1977): 193–203.

– "The Literal-Figurative Identity of *The Wanderer*." *PMLA* 79 (1964): 366–9.

Rowley, Sharon M. *The Old English Version of Bede's "Historia Ecclesiastica."* Cambridge: D.S. Brewer, 2011.

Rudolf, Winfried. "The Spiritual Islescape of the Anglo-Saxons." In *The Sea and Englishness in the Middle Ages*, edited by Sebastian I. Sobecki, 31–58. Cambridge: D.S. Brewer, 2011.

Russo, Tommaso. "Iconicity and Productivity in Sign Language Discourse: An Analysis of Three LIS Discourse Registers." *Sign Language Studies* 4 (2004): 164–97.

Russom, Geoffrey. "Aesthetic Criteria in Old English Heroic Style." In *On the Aesthetics of "Beowulf" and Other Old English Poems*, edited by John M. Hill, 64–80. Toronto: University of Toronto Press, 2010.

– "Artful Avoidance of the Useful Phrase in *Beowulf*, *The Battle of Maldon*, and *The Fates of the Apostles*." *Studies in Philology* 75, no. 4 (1978): 371–90.

– *"Beowulf" and Old Germanic Metre*. CSASE 23. Cambridge: Cambridge University Press, 1998.

– *Old English Meter and Linguistic Theory*. Cambridge: Cambridge University Press, 1987.

Sauer, Hans. "Language and Culture: How Anglo-Saxon Glossators Adapted Latin Words and Their World." *The Journal of Medieval Latin* 18 (2008): 437–68.

– *Nominalkomposita im Frühmittelenglischen: Mit Ausblicken auf die Geschichte der englischen Nominalkomposition*. Anglia Book Series 30. Tübingen: Max Niemeyer, 1992.

de Saussure, Ferdinand. *Writings in General Linguistics*. Edited by Simon Bouquet and Rudolf Engler. Oxford: Oxford University Press, 2006.

Scalise, Sergio, and Irene Vogel. "Why Compounding?" In *Cross-Disciplinary Issues in Compounding*, edited by Sergio Scalise and Irene Vogel, 1–18. Amsterdam: John Benjamins, 2010.

Schreuder, Robert, and R. Harald Baayen. "Modeling Morphological Processing." In *Morphological Aspects of Language Processing*, edited by Laurie Beth Feldman, 131–54. Hillsdale, NJ: Lawrence Erlbaum, 1995.

Scragg, Donald G. "The Nature of Old English Verse." In *The Cambridge Companion to Old English Literature*, edited by Malcolm Godden and Michael Lapidge, 2nd ed., 50–65. Cambridge: Cambridge University Press, 2013.

– "Source Study." In *Reading Old English Texts*, edited by Katherine O'Brien O'Keeffe, 39–58. Cambridge: Cambridge University Press, 1997.

– ed. *The Vercelli Homilies and Related Texts*. EETS os 300. Oxford: Oxford University Press, 1992.

Semenza, Carlo, and Sara Mondini. "The Neuropsychology of Compound Words." In *The Representation and Processing of Compound Words*, edited by Gary Libben and Gonia Jarema, 71–95. Oxford: Oxford University Press, 2006.

Sheppard, Alice. "A Word to the Wise: Thinking, Knowledge, and Wisdom in *The Wanderer*." In *Source of Knowledge: Old English and Early Medieval Latin Studies in Honour of Thomas D. Hill*, edited by Charles D. Wright, Frederick M. Biggs, and Thomas N. Hall, 130–45. Toronto: University of Toronto Press, 2007.

Shook, Lawrence Kennedy. "Aelfric's *Latin Grammar*: A Study in Old English Grammatical Terminology." PhD diss., Harvard University, 1939.

Silk, Edmund Taite, ed. *Saeculi noni auctoris in Boetii Consolationem philosophiae commentarius*. Rome: American Academy in Rome, 1935.

Sisam, Kenneth. "Cynewulf and His Poetry." In *Studies in the History of Old English Literature*, 1–28. Oxford: Clarendon Press, 1953.

– "The Order of Ælfric's Early Books." In *Studies in the History of Old English Literature*, 298–301. Oxford: Clarendon Press, 1953.

– *Studies in the History of Old English Literature*. Oxford: Clarendon Press, 1953.

Smythe, Ross. "King Alfred's Translations: Authorial Integrity and the Integrity of Authority." *Quaestio Insularis* 4 (2003): 98–114.

Sobecki, Sebastian I. *The Sea and Medieval English Literature*. Cambridge: D.S. Brewer, 2008.

Sontag, Susan. "The Imagination of Disaster." *Commentary* 40 (1965): 42–8.

Southern, Mark R.V. "Formulaic Binomials, Morphosymbolism, and Behaghel's Law: The Grammatical Status of Expressive Iconicity." *American Journal of Germanic Linguistics & Literatures* 12 (2000): 256–7.

Spalding, Thomas L., and Christina L. Gagné. "Relation Priming in Established Compounds: Facilitation?" *Memory & Cognition* 39 (2011): 1472–86.

Spalding, Thomas L., Christina L. Gagné, Allison C. Mullaly, and Hongbo Ji. "Relation-Based Interpretation of Noun-Noun Phrases: A New Theoretical Approach." In *New Impulses in Word Formation*. Linguistische Berichte Sonderheft 17, edited by Susan Olsen, 283–315. Hamburg: Helmut Buske Verlag, 2010.

Spencer, Andrew. "What's in a Compound?" *Journal of Linguistics* 47, no. 2 (2011): 481–507.

Stanley, E.G. "Paleographical and Textual Deep Water: <a> for <u> and <u> for <a>, <d> for <ð> and <ð> for <d> in Old English." *ANQ* 15, no. 2 (2002): 64–72.

– "Studies in the Prosaic Vocabulary of Old English Verse." *NM* 72 (1971): 385–418.

Stanton, Robert. *The Culture of Translation in Anglo-Saxon England*. Cambridge: D.S. Brewer, 2002.

Steen, Janie. *Verse and Virtuosity: The Adaptation of Latin Rhetoric in Old English Poetry*. Toronto: University of Toronto Press, 2008.

Stenton, F.M. *Anglo-Saxon England*. 3rd ed. Oxford: Clarendon Press, 1971.

Stephenson, Rebecca. "Ælfric of Eynsham and Hermeneutic Latin: *Meatim sed et rustica* Reconsidered." *Journal of Medieval Latin* 16 (2006): 111–41.

– *The Politics of Language: Byrhtferth, Ælfric, and the Multilingual Identity of the Benedictine Reform*. Toronto: University of Toronto Press, 2015.

– "Scapegoating the Secular Clergy: The Hermeneutic Style as a Form of Monastic Self-Definition." *ASE* 38 (2009): 101–35.

Stévanovitch, Collette. "Envelope Patterns in Translation: The Old English *Metres of Boethius*." In *The Medieval Translator* 6, edited by Roger Ellis, René Tixier, and Bernd Weitemeier, 101–13. Turnhout: Brepols, 1998.

Stevens, John. *Words and Music in the Middle Ages: Song, Narrative, Dance and Drama, 1050–1350*. Cambridge: Cambridge University Press, 1986.

Stewart, Thomas W., Jr. "The Mind and Spirit of Old English *mōd* and *fer(h)ð*: The Interaction of Metrics and Compounding." *Ohio State University Working Papers in Linguistics* 52 (1999): 51–62.

Stock, Brian. *The Implications of Literacy: Written Language and Models of Interpretation in the Eleventh and Twelfth Centuries*. Princeton: Princeton University Press, 1983.

Stodnick, Jacqueline A. "The Interests of Compounding: *Angelcynn* to *Engla land* in the *Anglo-Saxon Chronicle*." In *The Power of Words: Anglo-Saxon Studies Presented to Donald Scragg on His Seventieth Birthday*, edited by Hugh Magennis and Jonathan Wilcox, 337–67. Medieval European Studies 8. Morgantown: West Virginia University Press, 2006.

– "'Old Names of Kings or Shadows': Reading Documentary Lists." In *Conversion and Colonization in Anglo-Saxon England*, edited by Catherine E. Karkov and Nicholas Howe, 109–31. Medieval and Renaissance Texts and Studies 318, ISAS Essays in Anglo-Saxon Studies 2. Tempe: Arizona Center for Medieval and Renaissance Studies, 2006.

Storch, Theodor. *Angelsächsische Nominalcomposita*. Strassburg: Trübner, 1886.

Strubel, Armand. "'Allegoria in factis' et 'allegoria in verbis.'" *Poétique: Revue de Theorie et d'Analyse Litteraires* 6 (1975): 342–7.

Sturluson, Snorri. *Edda*. Translated by Anthony Faulkes. London: Dent, 1987.

Sweet, Henry, ed. *King Alfred's West-Saxon Version of Gregory's Pastoral Care*. EETS os 45 and 50. London: Trübner, 1871.

Szarmach, Paul. "Boethius's Influence in Anglo-Saxon England: The Vernacular and the *De consolatione philosophiae*." In *A Companion to Boethius in the Middle Ages*, edited by Noel Harold Kaylor, Jr, and Philip Edward Phillips, 221–54. Leiden: Brill, 2012.

– "*Meter 20*: Context Bereft." *ANQ* 15, no. 2 (2002): 28–34.

– "The *Timaeus* in Old English." In *Lexis and Texts in Early English: Studies Presented to Jane Roberts*, edited by Christian J. Kay and Louise M. Sylvester, 255–68. Costerus ns 133. Amsterdam: Rodopi, 2001.

Taft, Marcus. "Interactive-Activation as a Framework for Understanding Morphological Processing." *Language and Cognitive Processes* 9 (1994): 271–94.

Taft, Marcus, and Kenneth I. Forster. "Lexical Storage and Retrieval of Prefixed Words." *Journal of Verbal Learning and Verbal Behavior* 14 (1975): 638–47.

Talentino, Arnold V. "Fitting *Guðgewæde*: Use of Compounds in *Beowulf*." *Neophilologus* 63 (1979): 592–6.

Terasawa, Jun. *Nominal Compounds in Old English: A Metrical Approach*. Anglistica 27. Copenhagen: Rosenkilde and Bagger, 1994.

– *Old English Metre: An Introduction*. Toronto: University of Toronto Press, 2011.

Thieme, Adelheid L.J. "The Gift in *Beowulf*: Forging the Continuity of Past and Present." *Michigan Germanic Studies* 22 (1996): 126–43.

Thijs, Christine B. "Early Old English Translation: Practice before Theory?" *Neophilologus* 91 (2007): 149–73.

Thomas, Kate. "The Meaning, Practice and Context of Private Prayer in Late Anglo-Saxon England." PhD diss., University of York, 2011.

Thornbury, Emily V. *Becoming a Poet in Anglo-Saxon England*. Cambridge: Cambridge University Press, 2014.

Timofeeva, Olga. "Anglo-Latin Bilingualism before 1066: Prospects and Limitations." In *Interfaces between Language and Culture in Medieval England: A Festschrift for Matti Kilpiö*, edited by Alaric Hall, Olga Timofeeva, Ágnes Kiricsi, and Bethany Fox, 1–36. Leiden: Brill, 2010.

Toury, Gideon. *Descriptive Translation Studies and Beyond*. Descriptive Translation Studies 4. Amsterdam: John Benjamins, 1995.

Townend, Matthew. "Contextualizing the *Knútsdrápur*: Skaldic Praise-Poetry at the Court of Cnut." *ASE* 30 (2001): 145–79.

– *Language and History in Viking Age England: Linguistic Relations between Speakers of Old Norse and Old English*. Turnhout: Brepols, 2002.

– "Norse Poets and English Kings: Skaldic Performance in Anglo-Saxon England." *Offa* 58 (2001): 269–75.

– "Pre-Cnut Praise-Poetry in Viking Age England." *The Review of English Studies* ns 51, no. 203 (2000): 349–70.

– "Viking Age England as a Bilingual Society." In *Cultures in Contact: Scandinavian Settlement in England in the Ninth and Tenth Centuries*, edited by Dawn M. Hadley and Julian D. Richards, 89–105. Turnhout: Brepols, 2000.

– ed. *Wulfstan, Archbishop of York: The Proceedings of the Second Alcuin Conference*. Turnhout: Brepols, 2004.

Tranter, Stephen Norman. *Clavis metrica: Háttatal, Háttalykill and the Irish Metrical Tracts*. Basel: Helbing and Lichtenhahn, 1997.

Treharne, Elaine. *Living through Conquest: The Politics of Early English, 1020–1220*. Oxford: Oxford University Press, 2012.

Trilling, Renée. *The Aesthetics of Nostalgia: Historical Representation in Old English Verse*. Toronto: University of Toronto Press, 2009.

Tyler, Elizabeth M. *Old English Poetics: The Aesthetics of the Familiar in Anglo-Saxon England*. Woodbridge: York Medieval Press, 2006.

VanderBilt, Deborah. "Translation and Orality in the Old English *Orosius*." *Oral Tradition* 13, no. 2 (1998): 377–97.

Vergara-Martínez, Marta, Jon Andoni Duñabeitia, Itziar Laka, and Manuel Carreiras. "ERP Correlates of Inhibitory and Facilitative Effects of Constituent Frequency in Compound Word Reading." *Brain Research* 1257 (2009): 53–64.

Vološinov, V.N. "Discourse in Life and Discourse in Art (Concerning Sociological Poetics)." In *Freudianism: A Marxist Critique*, translated by I.R. Titunik, edited by I.R. Titunik and Neal H. Bruss, 93–116. New York: Academic Press, 1976.

Warren, Beatrice. *Semantic Patterns of Noun-Noun Compounds*. Goteborg: Acta Universitatis Gothoburgensis, 1978.

Watkins, Calvert. *How to Kill a Dragon: Aspects of Indo-European Poetics*. Oxford: Oxford University Press, 1995.

Whallon, William. "Formulas for Heroes in the *Iliad* and in *Beowulf*." *Modern Philology* 63, no. 2 (1965): 95–104.

Whitney, William Dwight. *Sanskrit Grammar: Including Both the Classical Language, and the Older Dialects, of Veda and Brahmana*. 2nd ed. Cambridge, MA: Harvard University Press, 1889.

Wieland, Gernot. "*Geminus Stilus*: Studies in Anglo-Latin Hagiography." In *Insular Latin Studies: Papers on Latin Texts and Manuscripts of the British Isles*, edited by Michael Herren, 113–33. Toronto: Pontifical Institute of Mediaeval Studies, 1981.

Wilcox, Jonathan, ed. *Ælfric's Prefaces*. Durham Medieval Texts 9. Durham: Durham Medieval Texts, 1994.

– "The Dissemination of Wulfstan's Homilies: The Wulfstan Tradition in Eleventh-Century Vernacular Preaching." In *England in the Eleventh Century: Proceedings of the 1990 Harlaxton Symposium*, edited by Carola Hicks, 199–217. Harlaxton Medieval Studies 2. Stamford, UK: Paul Watkins, 1992.

– "Wulfstan's *Sermo Lupi ad Anglos* as Political Performance." In *Wulfstan, Archbishop of York: The Proceedings of the Second Alcuin Conference*, edited by Matthew Townend, 375–96. Turnhout: Brepols, 2004.

Wilcox, Miranda. "Vernacular Biblical Epics and the Production of Anglo-Saxon Cultural Exegesis." PhD diss., University of Notre Dame, 2006.

Williams, Edna Rees. "Ælfric's Grammatical Terminology." *PMLA* 73 (1958): 453–62.

Wine, Joseph D. *Figurative Language in Cynewulf: Defining Aspects of a Poetic Style*. New York: Peter Lang, 1993.

– "*Juliana* and the Figures of Rhetoric." *Papers on Language and Literature* 28, no. 1 (1992): 3–18.

Winterbottom, Michael. "The Style of Æthelweard." *Medium Ævum* 36 (1967): 109–18.

Woolf, Rosemary, ed. *Cynewulf's "Juliana."* Rev. ed. Exeter: University of Exeter Press, 1977; repr. 1981, 1993 with further revisions.

Wormald, Patrick. "Archbishop Wulfstan: Eleventh-Century State-Builder." In *Wulfstan, Archbishop of York: The Proceedings of the Second Alcuin Conference*, edited by Matthew Townend, 9–27. Turnhout: Brepols, 2004.

– *Legal Culture in the Early Medieval West*. London: Hambledon Press, 1999.

– *The Making of English Law: King Alfred to the Twelfth Century.* Volume 1, *Legislation and Its Limits*. Malden, MA: Blackwell, 1999.

El Yagoubi, Radouane, Valentina Chiarelli, Sara Mondini, Gelsomina Perrone, Morena Danieli, and Carlo Semenza. "Neural Correlates of Italian Nominal Compounds and Potential Impact of Headedness Effect: An ERP Study." *Cognitive Neuropsychology* 25, no. 4 (2008): 559–81.

Yoshino, Yoshihiro. "Poetic Syntax in the Old English *Meters of Boethius*: A Comparative Study of Verse and Prose." PhD diss., University of Pennsylvania, 1984.

Zacher, Samantha. *Preaching the Converted: The Style and Rhetoric of the Vercelli Homilies.* Toronto: University of Toronto Press, 2009.

Zbinden, Karine. Review of Bronckart and Bota, *Bakhtine démasqué*. *Slavic Review* 72, no. 2 (2013): 430–1.

Zupitza, Julius. *Ælfrics Grammatik und Glossar: Text und Varianten*. 4th ed., with an introduction by Helmut Gneuss. Hildesheim: Weidmann, 2003.

Index

Toronto Anglo-Saxon Series

1 *Preaching the Converted: The Style and Rhetoric of the Vercelli Book Homilies*, Samantha Zacher

2 *Say What I Am Called: The Old English Riddles of the Exeter Book and the Anglo-Latin Riddle Tradition*, Dieter Bitterli

3 *The Aesthetics of Nostalgia: Historical Representation in Anglo-Saxon Verse*, Renée Trilling

4 *New Readings in the Vercelli Book*, edited by Samantha Zacher and Andy Orchard

5 *Authors, Audiences, and Old English Verse*, Thomas A. Bredehoft

6 *On Aesthetics in* Beowulf *and Other Old English Poems*, edited by John M. Hill

7 *Old English Metre: An Introduction*, Jun Terasawa

8 *Anglo-Saxon Psychologies in the Vernacular and Latin Traditions*, Leslie Lockett

9 *The Body Legal in Barbarian Law*, Lisi Oliver

10 *Old English Literature and the Old Testament*, edited by Michael Fox and Manish Sharma

11 *Stealing Obedience: Narratives of Agency and Identity in Later Anglo-Saxon England*, Katherine O'Brien O'Keeffe

12 *Traditional Subjectivities: The Old English Poetics of Mentality*, Britt Mize

13 *Land and Book: Literature and Land Tenure in Anglo-Saxon England*, Scott T. Smith

14 *Writing Women Saints in Anglo-Saxon England*, edited by Paul E. Szarmach

15 *Anglo-Saxon Manuscripts: A Bibliographical Handlist of Manuscripts and Manuscript Fragments Written or Owned in England up to 1100*, Helmut Gneuss and Michael Lapidge

16 *The King's Body: Burial and Succession in Anglo-Saxon England*, Nicole Marafioti

17 *From Lawmen to Plowmen: Anglo-Saxon Legal Tradition and the School of Langland*, Stephen Yeager

18 *The Politics of Language: Byrhtferth, Ælfric, and the Multilingual Identity of the Benedictine Reform*, Rebecca Stephenson

19 *Weaving Words and Binding Bodies: The Poetics of Human Experience in Old English Literature*, Megan Cavell

20 *Joinings: Compound Words in Old English Literature*, Jonathan Davis-Secord